Stochastic Optimization for Large-scale Machine Learning

Stochastic Optimization for Large-scale Machine Learning

Vinod Kumar Chauhan, PhD

CRC Press
Taylor & Francis Group
Boca Raton London New York

CRC Press is an imprint of the
Taylor & Francis Group, an **informa** business

First edition published 2022
by CRC Press
6000 Broken Sound Parkway NW, Suite 300, Boca Raton, FL 33487-2742

and by CRC Press
2 Park Square, Milton Park, Abingdon, Oxon, OX14 4RN

Library of Congress Cataloging-in-Publication Data

Names: Chauhan, Vinod Kumar, author.
Title: Stochastic optimization for large-scale machine learning / Vinod Kumar Chauhan.
Description: First edition. | Boca Raton : CRC Press, 2022. | Includes bibliographical references and index.
Identifiers: LCCN 2021031740 | ISBN 9781032131757 (hardback) | ISBN 9781032146140 (paperback) | ISBN 9781003240167 (ebook)
Subjects: LCSH: Machine learning--Statistical methods. | Big data. | Mathematical optimization. | Stochastic processes.
Classification: LCC Q325.5 .C43 2022 | DDC 006.3/1--dc23 LC
record available at https://lccn.loc.gov/2021031740

ISBN: 978-1-032-13175-7 (hbk)
ISBN: 978-1-032-14614-0 (pbk)
ISBN: 978-1-003-24016-7 (ebk)

DOI: 10.1201/9781003240167

Access the Support Material: www.routledge.com/9781032131757

To my parents...

Contents

SECTION III SECOND ORDER METHODS

List of Figures

List of Tables

Preface

The advancements in the technology and the availability of data sources have led to the data explosion. The classical techniques are incapable to handle this large data so the term 'Big Data' is coined, which is mainly characterized by three 'V's: volume, velocity and variety. When we consider the volume aspect of big data in machine learning the problem is called large-scale learning problem or big data problem, which have large number of data points or large number of features or both. One side, this large data has potential to uncover more fine-grained patterns, take timely and accurate decisions, and on other side it creates a lot of challenges to make a sense of it, like, slow training and scalability of models etc. So, one of the major challenge in machine learning is to develop efficient and scalable learning algorithms to deal with the big data challenge, i.e., to solve large scale learning problems.

Stochastic approximation and coordinate descent approaches are very effective techniques to deal with the big data challenge. Stochastic approximation makes each iteration of a learning algorithm independent of number of data points by randomly selecting one or mini-batch of data points, on the other hand, coordinate decent approach makes each iteration independent of number of features by selecting one or block of features as variables and rest as constants. To tackle the big data challenge, we have utilized the best of stochastic approximation and coordinate descent approaches to develop batch block optimization framework (BBOF) and used the framework with first and second order methods. BBOF samples a mini-batch of data points and a block of features, and formulates a reduced subproblem which can be easily solved using appropriate methods.

We have proposed stochastic average adjusted gradient (SAAG-I and II) and mini-batch block-coordinate Newton (MBN) methods to work with BBOF. SAAG-I and II are variance reduction techniques, used for solving large-scale problems using first order methods. MBN also intends to solve large-scale problems by reducing the per-iteration complexity of Newton method. But this is noticed that stochastic approximation and coordinate descent approaches does not work well together. This is because the advantage of using them together under BBOF is over run by the overhead to implement them due to double sampling of data and features. We further extend SAAG-I and II to SAAG-III and IV, respectively, using stochastic approximation only as variance reduction techniques to deal with the large-scale learning problems. SAAG-III and IV are based on iterate averaging, unlike SAAG-I, starting point is set to average of previous epoch in SAAG-III, and unlike SAAG-II, the snap point and starting point are set to average and last iterate of previous epoch in SAAG-IV, respectively.

The training time of models depends on two factors: time to access data and time to learn from data. Before our work, a little attention was paid to data access part and the whole focus of research was on developing techniques to learn from data. We proposed systematic and sequential sampling techniques, to sample mini-batches of data, to reduce the training time of models by reducing the data access time. These techniques are based on contiguous access of memory, which is faster than dispersed data access in random sampling. We were able to get up to six times faster training of models. The idea is based on data access so it is independent of the problem under consideration and the method used to solve the problem.

Techniques based on first order methods are limited to linear convergence, far away from the quadratic rates offered by the second order methods, like Newton's method. So, we proposed stochastic trust region Newton method (STRON) which uses conjugate gradient to solve the trust region subproblem. It introduces subsampling to gradient and Hessian calculations and uses progressive batching to take benefit of both the stochastic and batch regimes. We also extend STRON to use preconditioned conjugate gradient to solve the trust region subproblem.

Thus, this book performs comprehensive literature review to characterize the big data challenge and lists the areas to tackle the challenge and the current research directions. Further, this offers solutions to solve big data challenge using first and second order methods, and proposes SAAGs (I, II, III and IV), MBN, STRON and simple sampling techniques.

I

BACKGROUND

CHAPTER 1

Introduction

A rtificial intelligence (AI), sometimes also called as machine intelligence, is a branch of computer science, which deals with the study and development of machines that are intelligent like human beings. AI is a buzzword and some popular lines about AI highlight its importance, such as, 'AI is the future' and 'AI is the new electricity' etc. AI has several components/sub-fields, like knowledge representation, reasoning/inferencing and pattern recognition etc., and machine learning is one of them and one of the important sub-field.

Machine learning is one of the very interesting fields where machine learn to perform some task from examples, i.e., from data. This is unlike traditional programming where we need to code the logic for the task we want the machine to perform. In machine learning, we need to program only the learning algorithms and not the logic to perform the task. So, machine learning is very important in certain cases, like performing complex task with millions of variables which could be difficult for human beings to code and performing tasks where the exact algorithm to solve the problem is not known. Technically, machine learning is an inter-disciplinary field which takes contributions form optimization, probability, algebra, statistics, neuroscience and psychology etc.

Machine learning is one of the hot research topic in academia and one of the most exploited term in the industry. It has been used across different fields for solving complex and challenging problems, right from medicine, physics, chemistry, engineering to cultural problems. Industry is investing heavily on machine learning and nowadays, knowingly or unknowingly everyone of us is using machine learning in our day to day life. Ham or spam classification in Gmail, Alexa from Amazon, Siri form Apple, Cortana from Microsoft, Google assistant, auto tagging of our and our friends' faces on Facebook and product recommendations in online shopping etc., all are based on machine learning. Recently, Gmail introduced a new feature of auto-completion while composing a mail, which is again based on machine learning.

Machine learning comes in different flavours: supervised learning, unsupervised learning, semi-supervised learning and reinforcement learning. In supervised learning, machine is provided with the input and output (target) value pairs, e.g., classification and regression problems. Unsupervised learning involves only input and machine groups the similar inputs, e.g., clustering. Semi-supervised learning is a combination

DOI: 10.1201/9781003240167-1

of supervised and unsupervised learning. In reinforcement learning, machine interacts with its environment and it is rewarded for its actions. Machine learning has several problems, like classification, regression, clustering and ranking etc.

Mathematically, machine learning problems are data intensive optimization problems and in this work, we have proposed several optimization techniques to solve large-scale linear classification problem.

Next, main technical terms used in the book are defined.

1.1 LARGE-SCALE MACHINE LEARNING

The emerging technologies and the availability of different data sources have lead to rapid expansion of data in all science and engineering domains. One side, this massive data has potential to uncover more fine-grained patterns, take timely and accurate decisions, and on other side it creates a lot of challenges to make sense of it, like, slow training and scalability of models, because of inability of traditional technologies to process this huge data. The term 'Big Data' was coined to highlight the data explosion and need of new technologies to process this massive data. Big data is a vast subject in itself. Big data can be characterized using three Vs: Volume, Velocity and Variety, but recently a lot of other Vs are also used. When one deal with 'volume' aspect of big data in machine learning, it is called the large-scale machine learning problem or big data problem. The large-scale learning problems have large number of data points or large number of features in each data point, or both, which lead to large per-iteration complexity of learning algorithms, and ultimately lead to slow training of machine learning models. Thus, one of the major challenges before machine learning is to develop efficient and scalable learning algorithms [23, 25].

1.2 OPTIMIZATION PROBLEMS

The problems where we try to find the optimum value, i.e., minimum or maximum, are called optimization problems and can be represented in general form as:

$$\min_{w} F(w) \quad \text{s.t.} \quad w \in \Omega, \tag{1.1}$$

where F is an objective function which is to be minimized, $w \in \mathbb{R}^n$ is the parameter vector to be found and Ω represent the constraint set of w.

Machine learning involves data intensive optimization problems, as it learns the model from the data and try to minimize the model error, i.e., difference in the value predicted by the model and the actual value. We consider unconstrained convex optimization problem of expected risk, as given below:

$$\min_{w} R(w) = \mathbb{E}\left[f\left(w; \xi\right)\right], \tag{1.2}$$

where $f\left(w; \xi\right) = f\left(w; x_i, y_i\right) = f\left(h\left(w; x_i\right), y_i\right)$ is a composition of linear prediction model h and loss function f over randomly selected data point (x_i, y_i) from the unknown distribution $P\left(x_i, y_i\right)$ and targets, parameterized by the model parameter $w \in \mathbb{R}^n$. Since it is not feasible to solve (7.1) as P is unknown so the model is approximated by taking a set $N = \{(x_1, y_1), ..., (x_l, y_l)\}$ of l data points from the unknown distribution P and then solving the empirical risk minimization (ERM) problem, as given below:

$$\min_w F(w) = \frac{1}{l} \sum_{i=1}^{l} f(w; x_i, y_i). \tag{1.3}$$

For simplicity, we take $f(w; x_i, y_i) = f_i(w)$. Finite sum optimization problems of type (7.2) exists across different fields, like signal processing, statistics, operations research, data science and machine learning.

In ERM, component function $f_i(w)$ denotes value of loss function at one data point, e.g., in binary classification, it can be logistic loss, i.e., $f_i(w) = \log(1 + \exp(-y_i w^T x_i))$ and hinge-loss, i.e., $f_i(w) = \max(0, 1 - y_i w^T x_i)$; for regression problem, it can be least squares, i.e., $f_i(w) = 1/2(w^T x_i - y_i)^2$. The regularizer can be $\lambda_1 \|w\|_1$ (l_1-regularizer), $\lambda_2/2\|w\|^2$ (l_2-regularizer) and $\lambda_1 \|w\|_1 + \lambda_2/2\|w\|^2$ (elastic net regularizer), where λ_1 and λ_2 are regularization coefficients. Thus, problems like logistic regression, SVM, ridge regression and lasso etc., fall under ERM.

1.3 LINEAR CLASSIFICATION

Classification is one of the machine learning problems which learns to assign labels, i.e., a value from a predefined set of values, e.g., label an incoming new mail as ham or spam is a classification problem. Classification can be classified into two categories: linear and non-linear, and accordingly, we can have linear and non-linear classifiers. Geometrically, linear classifier separates the data linearly, unlike non-linear classifier which separates the data non-linearly. Mathematically, linear classifiers use linear function for the prediction model, unlike non-linear classifiers. For high dimensional problems, like document classification, it is observed that linear classifiers have similar accuracy as non-linear classifiers but the training time of linear classifiers are much faster than non-linear classifiers.

1.3.1 Support Vector Machine (SVM)

Support Vector Machine (SVM, [12]) is a binary linear classification technique in machine learning, which separates the classes with largest gap (called margin) between the border line instances (called support vectors). That's why it is known as optimal margin classifier. Figure 1.1. represents the geometrical view of SVM. SVM has been extended to multi-class problems using techniques like One-versus-One [72], One-versus-Rest [132], Directed Acyclic Graph SVM [107] etc. For non-linearly separable data problems, SVM has been extended using Kernels. Kernels are mathematical functions that transform the data from given space (known as input space) to a new high dimensional space (known as feature space) where data can be separated with a linear surface (called hyperplane). Figure 1.2. represents the geometrical view of Kernels. Mathematically, a Kernel is a function that takes two arguments, apply a mapping on the arguments and then return the value of their dot product. Suppose

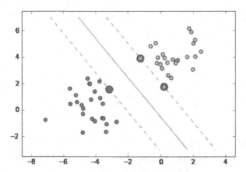

FIGURE 1.1 An infinite number of classifiers can be drawn for the given data but SVM finds the classifier with largest gap between support vectors. Circles represent the support vectors.

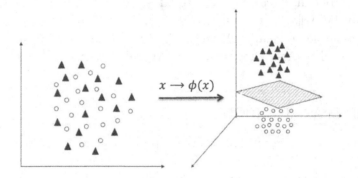

FIGURE 1.2 Left part represents data in input space and right part represents data in feature space. Data has been Transformed from input space to feature space using Kernels. Initially input space is two dimensional and data is inseparable. Kernels transformed the data to three dimensional space where data is separable by a hyperplane.

x_1 and x_2 are two data points, ϕ is a mapping and K denotes Kernel which is given by

$$K(x_1, x_2) = \phi(x_1)^T \phi(x_2) \tag{1.4}$$

In some applications, the input space is rich in features and it is sufficient to take the mapping ϕ as an identity mapping, i.e., $\phi(x) = x$. Kernel where mapping is identity mapping, that is, input space and feature space are equal, is called linear Kernel and SVM using linear Kernel is called linear SVM. Mathematically, linear Kernel is given by

$$K(x_1, x_2) = x_1^T x_2 \quad \Longrightarrow \quad \phi(x) = x$$

Linear SVM is very efficient in high dimensional data applications. While their accuracy on test set is close to the non-linear SVM, it is much faster to train for such applications. For example, document classification applications have high dimensional input space and there is no need to add more features to the input space because it does not make much difference in the performance. So, test accuracy of linear SVM is close to that of non-linear SVM (see, [46]) but at the same time, training of linear SVM is much faster than non-linear SVM due to the difference in their computational complexities.

L2-regularized soft margin SVM is the most commonly used SVM formulation and is given below. Different problem formulations of SVM are discussed in detail in the Section 2.3.

$$\min_{w} F(w) = \frac{1}{2}\|w\|^2 + C\sum_{i=1}^{l} \max(0, 1 - y_i w^T x_i)^2, \tag{1.5}$$

where C is the regularization coefficient.

1.3.2 Logistic Regression

This is a binary classification technique based on the logistic loss function (also called sigmoid function) which gives value between 0 and 1. This is a smooth and strongly convex (by adding l_2 regularization) problem which has nice theoretical properties. It can be represented as given below:

$$\min_{w} F(w) = \frac{1}{l}\sum_{i=1}^{l} \log\left(1 + \exp\left(-y_i w^T x_i\right)\right) + \frac{\lambda}{2}\|w\|^2. \tag{1.6}$$

1.3.3 First and Second Order Methods

An optimization problem can be solved using analytical methods and numerical methods. Analytical methods are suitable to solve the simple problems, have a direct formula to calculate the exact solution. On the other hand, numerical methods are used to solve complex problems, iteratively and approximately. Since machine learning problems are data intensive complex problems so numerical methods are used to solve them.

A general iterative method to solve problem (7.2), can be written as:

$$w_{k+1} = w_k - \alpha_k s_k, \tag{1.7}$$

where k is the iteration number, α_k is the learning rate (also known as step size) and s_k is the step direction.

1.3.3.1 First Order Methods

When $s_k = \nabla F(w_k)$ then the method is called gradient descent (GD). GD and its modifications which involve only first order derivatives are called first order methods. We have proposed SAAGs which are variance reduction techniques to deal with the noise introduced due to gradient approximations. These are first order methods which will be discussed in Part II.

1.3.3.2 Second Order Methods

When $s_k = \nabla^2 F(w_k)^{-1} \nabla F(w_k)$ then the method is called Newton method. Newton method and its modifications which involve second order derivatives are called second order methods. These methods use curvature information to guide the step direction towards the solution. We have proposed MBN and STRON methods which are based on second order information. These are subsampled Newton methods which will be discussed in Part III.

1.4 STOCHASTIC APPROXIMATION APPROACH

Stochastic approximation (SA) [113] is an iterative optimization approach to solve optimization problems which cannot be solved directly but using approximations. In machine learning problems, it is computationally very expensive, and might be infeasible in some cases, to use all data points in each iteration of learning algorithms. So, SA is used which makes each iteration independent of number of data points (l) by considering one data point or mini-batch of data points, i.e., instead of going through all data points, only one data point or mini-batch of data points are processed in each iteration which makes a large computational difference for large values of l. Similarly, remaining data points can be used in mini-batches during other iterations. Thus, SA is computationally very efficient optimization approach to deal with large-scale problems. No doubt that might affect the convergence of learning algorithm, which can be compensated by using larger mini-batches and other techniques like variance reduction, e.g., SAAGs [23, 28].

1.5 COORDINATE DESCENT APPROACH

Coordinate Descent (CD) [137] is a recursive approach to solve optimization problems by approximate minimization along coordinate directions or coordinate hyperplanes, i.e., it recursively solves small subproblems consisting of only one or few variables. As SA makes iteration complexity independent of l, similarly, CD makes iteration complexity independent of number of features (n) by considering one feature or block of features as variables, fixing the rest features and solving the reduced subproblem thus formed. Then, new one feature or block of features are selected as variables while fixing the rest and resulting subproblem is solved. This process is repeated until all subproblems covering all features are solved, then whole process is repeated until convergence. Thus, CD is a good approach to solve large-scale problems with large number of features.

1.6 DATASETS

Table 1.1 lists the datasets used in the book, which are available to download at LIBSVM website: https://www.csie.ntu.edu.tw/~cjlin/libsvmtools/datasets/.

TABLE 1.1 Datasets Used in the Book

Dataset	#classes	#features	#datapoints	Reference
HIGGS	2	28	11,000,000	[5]
SUSY	2	18	5,000,000	[5]
SensIT Vehicle (combined)	3	100	78,823	[36]
mnist	10	780	60,000	[75]
protein	3	357	17,766	[82]
rcv1.binary	2	47,236	20,242	[79]
webspam	2	254	350,000	[134]
covtype.binary	2	54	581,012	[82]
ijcnn1	2	22	49,990	[108]
news20.binary	2	1,355,191	19,996	[65]
real-sim	2	20,958	72,309	[82]
gisette	2	5000	6000	[82]

1.7 ORGANIZATION OF BOOK

Book consists of eight chapters, which are divided into four parts, as discussed below:

PART I BACKGROUND

This part has two chapters, including current chapter, which provide basic introduction about the work, provide literature review and motivations of the work, as given below:

Chapter 2: In this chapter, we have presented a review on evolution of linear Support Vector Machine classification, its solvers, strategies to improve solvers, experimental results, current challenges (big data challenge) and research directions [25].

PART II FIRST ORDER METHODS

This part has three chapters which provide techniques to solve large-scale learning problems using first order methods:

Chapter 3: In this chapter, Batch Block Optimization Framework has been developed to solve big data problems using the best of stochastic approximation as well as the best of coordinate descent approaches, independent of any solver. Two novel Stochastic Average Adjusted Gradient methods (SAAG) have been proposed to reduce variance in mini-batch and block-coordinate setting of the developed framework [23].

Chapter 4: In this chapter, we have proposed novel variants of SAAG-I and II, called SAAG-III and IV, respectively. We also extend SAAGs (I, II, III, IV), to solve non-smooth problems and design two update rules for smooth and non-smooth problems [28].

Chapter 5: In this chapter, we have proposed simple sampling techniques to handle the big data problems in machine learning. The idea is to reduce the training time through reducing data access time by proposing systematic sampling and cyclic/sequential sampling to select mini-batches from the dataset [26].

PART III SECOND ORDER METHODS

This part has two chapters which provide techniques to solve large-scale learning problems using second order methods:

Chapter 6: In this chapter, we have combined the best of stochastic approximation and coordinate descent approaches with second order methods to propose mini-bath block-coordinate Newton (MBN).

Chapter 7: In this chapter, we have proposed a novel stochastic **trust region** inexact **Newton** method, called as STRON, which uses conjugate gradient (CG) to solve trust region subproblem. The method uses progressive subsampling in the calculation of gradient and Hessian values to take the advantage of both stochastic approximation and full batch regimes [29].

PART IV CONCLUSION

This part has one chapter which provides the concluding remarks.

Chapter 8: This chapter concludes the research work and provides possible future extensions of the current work.

CHAPTER 2

Optimization Problem, Solvers, Challenges and Research Directions

B ehind the scenes, machine learning problems are actually optimization problems. So, optimization problem formulation and selection of appropriate solvers are very important for the final performance of machine learning models. We take the example of SVM to illustrate that how a problem can be formulated in multiple ways and how each formulation can be solved using multiple solvers. SVM is a binary linear classifier which has been extended to non-linear data using Kernels and multi-class data using various techniques like one-versus-one, one-versus-rest and Crammer Singer SVM, etc. SVM with a linear Kernel is called linear SVM and one with a non-linear Kernel is called non-linear SVM. Linear SVM is an efficient technique for high dimensional data applications like document classification, word-sense disambiguation, drug design, etc., because under such data applications, test accuracy of linear SVM is closer to non-linear SVM while its training is much faster than non-linear SVM. SVM is continuously evolving since its inception and researchers have proposed many problem formulations, solvers and strategies for solving SVM. Moreover, due to advancements in the technology, data has taken the form of 'Big Data' which have posed a challenge for machine learning to train a classifier on this large-scale data. In this chapter, we have presented a review on evolution of linear Support Vector Machine classification, its solvers, strategies to improve solvers, experimental results, current challenges and research directions.

2.1 INTRODUCTION

Please refer to Section 1.3.1 for basic introduction of SVM. Linear SVM involves problem formulations, solvers to solve the problem and optimization strategies to make the solvers efficient. Generally, SVM problem is formulated as a convex problem [33, 31] because there is no issue of local optimum in convex problems as every local optimum is a global optimum. In formulating the problem, commonly L1 ($\|w\|$) and

DOI: 10.1201/9781003240167-2

L2 regularization ($\|w\|^2$), L1 and L2 loss functions are used which are given below. So, considering L1 and L2 regularization, L1 and L2 loss functions and linear Kernel, there are eight different formulations for linear SVM as depicted in Fig. 2.1, which indicates the diverse range of possible problem formulations. L1 and L2 loss functions for parameter vector w and data point (x_i, y_i) are given below:

$$\text{L1-loss:} \quad \max(0, 1 - y_i w^T x_i), \quad \text{L2-loss:} \quad \left[\max(0, 1 - y_i w^T x_i)\right]^2 \qquad (2.1)$$

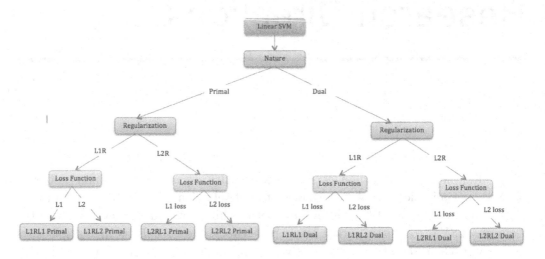

FIGURE 2.1 Eight different problem formulations for the Linear SVM with L1-regularized (L1R), L2-regularized (L2R), L1 loss and L2 loss functions.

For a particular SVM either primal or dual problems can be solved. Generally, when number of features (n) are much less than number of training points (l) then primal formulations of SVM [85] are solved otherwise dual formulations [53] are solved. This is because lesser the number of variables in the problem easier is the problem to solve.

Nowadays, major challenge in SVM (which is shared with machine learning) is to deal with 'Big Data' problems and to handle such problems researchers are trying to exploit the platform/framework structures (like parallel and distributed computing) and proposing new problem formulations, solvers, optimization strategies and algorithms etc. The current research directions for handling big data problems in machine learning are: First, stochastic approximation algorithms [63, 71, 35, 115] which makes the learning algorithm scalable by removing the dependency of algorithm over number of data points by using only one data point during each iteration of the algorithm. Several variations of stochastic approximation, like mini-batch approach [128, 119], have been proposed during last five years. Second, coordinate descent algorithms [130, 100, 6, 112, 137, 90, 122] which reduce large problem into a smaller subproblem by taking one feature as a variable and rest as constants. Extensive research has been done in this direction during last few years and researcher have proposed its several variations. Third, proximal algorithms [104] which are used with first and second order methods. These algorithms are applicable to non-smooth problems with separable components. Fourth, parallel and distributed computing [141] which exploits the computing resources. Nowadays, a lot of research is going in parallel and distributed computing since dataset sizes are going beyond the capacity of single computer and other approaches seem to be saturated. In addition to these research directions, their hybrid versions are also being studied very extensively, e.g., [140, 23].

Chapter Organization: Section 2.2 discusses literature, Section 2.3 discusses evolution of linear SVM problem formulations and Section 2.4 discusses problem solvers for SVM. Section 2.5 presents comparative study, Section 2.6 presents big data challenge, areas of improvement to tackle big data problems and research directions for linear SVM and Section 2.7 presents the concluding remarks.

Notations: $\langle \cdot, \cdot \rangle$ denotes dot product, $\forall$ means for all, $x_i \in \mathbb{R}^n$ denotes a training instance with n features and $i = 1, 2, ..., l$ where l denotes the number of training points. $y_i \in \{-1, +1\}$ denotes the labels of training instances. $m \in \mathbb{R}$ is used to denote the number of classes. $w \in \mathbb{R}^n$ and $b \in \mathbb{R}$ denote the parameters of the objective function. ξ denotes the slack variable, C denotes the penalty parameter, $\| \cdot \|$ denotes Euclidean norm, $\mathbf{1}$ denotes a unit vector of arbitrary dimension and α denotes vector of dual variables.

2.1.1 Contributions

The contributions of the chapter are listed below:

- We have discussed different problem formulations, i.e., optimization problems for SVM and some general solvers for solving the optimization problem.

- The big data challenge in machine learning has been characterized which highlights the need to develop efficient and scalable optimization techniques to tackle the challenge.

- Different areas have been discussed to solve the big data challeng and out of the different research areas, the current research directions have been discussed to tackle the challenge.

- A comparative study of related primal SVMs has been presented using mini-batch stochastic gradient descent method which has pointed out why soft margin SVM is the most widely used problem formulation for SVM.

2.2 LITERATURE

Support Vector Machines (SVMs, [12, 31]) is a classification technique in Machine Learning. The concepts used in SVMs, like hyperplane, optimal margin and Kernels etc., are several decades old but in the current form, SVM developments have started from [12], namely. 'A Training Algorithm for Optimal Margin Classifiers' in 1992 in COLT. This SVM formulation is also known as 'Hard Margin SVM'. [31] improved the hard margin SVM. They considered the outliers and noise, and relaxed the margin to mis-classify some data points by introducing slack variables. This led to the 'Soft

Margin SVM'. Till this time, SVM was used as a binary classifier, when [132] proposed a multi-class SVM using one-versus-rest (OVR) technique. [61] proposed Transductive SVM for text classification. [127] proposed least squared version of SVM. Later, [72] proposed another multi-class SVM using one-versus-one (OVO) technique but both, OVR and OVO, were based on binary classification problems. [135] proposed first multi-class SVM (WWSVM), which solves a single SVM problem and was not based on multiple binary classification problems. [107] proposed Directed Acyclic Graph SVM (DAGSVM) for multi-class classification problems, which was similar to OVO technique in solving SVM problem but it employs an efficient, rooted acyclic binary tree to find the label for the test data. [116] proposed a new ν-SVM, which removes parameter C and introduces parameter ν that roughly gives the fraction of support vectors. [45] proposed Proximal SVM (PSVM) which uses the proximity of data point to the proximal planes to classify the data point. PSVM replaces bounding planes of the standard SVM with the proximal planes and uses proximal planes for classification instead of the separating hyperplane. [77] introduced Smooth SVM which handles the non-differentiability issues of the standard SVM. [95] proposed Lagrangian SVM. [33] proposed another multi-class classification SVM that solves a single SVM problem unlike OVO and OVR techniques. Later [86] proposed a new formulation called Fuzzy SVM (FSVM) which was further extended by [2] and [1]. Fuzzy SVM introduces fuzzy membership of data points to each of the classes and contributions of these points are used to find the separating plane. Fuzzy SVM is very useful in reducing the effect of outliers and noise. [109] extended ν-SVM [116] to $E\nu$-SVM and helped to control margin, errors and consequently support vectors. [57] combined the idea of FSVM [86] and PSVM [45] and proposed Fuzzy Proximal SVM (FPSVM). Here fuzzy membership is assigned to data points and points are classified on the basis of proximity to two parallel planes which are kept as far from each other as possible. [131] proposed Structured SVM which generalizes the multi-class SVM, namely, WWSVM and CSSVM, to a new formulation that has structured outputs like sequences, strings, graphs, labeled trees or lattices etc. [37] extended the standard SVM, i.e., single task learning SVM and proposed a new binary SVM for multi-task learning. [49] proposed a parallel SVM known as Cascade SVM which deploys a divide and conquer strategy to solve the SVM problem. Cascade SVM divides the dataset into subsets and trains multiple SVMs in parallel on each subset. [96] proposed Generalized Eigenvalue Proximal SVM (GEPSVM) with two non-parallel hyperplanes and the data points are classified according to the proximity to one of the two non-parallel planes. [40] extended the idea of multi-view learning to SVM and proposed Multi-View SVM. [56], extended Proximal SVM to Twin SVM which solves two small sized SVM problems and gives two non-parallel hyperplanes. [126] proposed SloppySVM which can learn from the sloppily labeled data. [102] have proposed CappedSVM using capped l_p-norm based loss function, to tackle the challenge of data outliers.

Figure 2.2. depicts the year-wise evolution of different SVMs which are not necessarily improvements over previous ones. The mathematical formulations and other details of different SVM evolution and their solvers are discussed in the coming sections. The focus of this chapter is on supervised linear Support Vector Classification

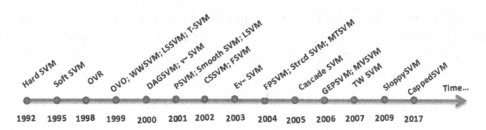

FIGURE 2.2 Time line of SVM: OVR – One versus Rest, T-SVM – Transductive SVM, OVO – One-versus-One, WWSVM – Weston and Watkins SVM, LSSVM – Least Squares SVM, DAGSVM – Directed Acyclic Graph SVM, LSVM – Lagrangian SVM, CSSVM – Crammer Singer SVM, FSVM – Fuzzy SVM, PSVM – Proximal SVM, FPSVM – Fuzzy Proximal SVM, Strcd SVM – Structured SVM, MTSVM – Multi-Task SVM, GEPSVM – Generalized Eigenvalue Proximal SVM, MVSVM – Multi-View SVM, TW SVM – Twin SVM.

(SVC), so only those SVM formulations are discussed which are used for classification and have major contributions. As far as linear and non-linear SVMs are concerned, they have same formulations except the space in which they perform classification. Linear SVMs perform in the input space and non-linear SVMs perform in the feature space. The chapter discusses only linear SVMs but the mathematical formulations for non-linear SVMs can be derived from the linear SVMs by using the following replacements:

$$x_1^T x_2 \mapsto K\left(x_1, x_2\right),$$

where x_1 and x_2 denote data points and K denotes the Kernel function.

2.3   PROBLEM FORMULATIONS

Problem formulation is the mathematical representation of the problem under study. SVM Classification problem is an optimization problem whose mathematical representation consists of an objective function and constraints (if any). Researchers have proposed a variety of ideas for SVM classification with different problem formulations. The evolution of the SVM is discussed in the following subsections[1]:

2.3.1   Hard Margin SVM (1992)

Although the concepts like hyperplane, optimal margin and Kernels are in use for several decades but [12] are the first to formulate SVM in its current form. This SVM is a binary classifier which can work with only linearly separable data applications and presence of any noise or outliers strongly affects the margin. It does not allow mis-classification errors, that's why it is known as hard margin SVM. Hard margin SVM is represented by the Fig. 1.1.

---

[1]There are several problem formulations for the SVM and here we have presented some of the representative SVMs. Few more formulations can be found in the paper [25]

Suppose the training set of instance-label pairs is denoted by (x_i, y_i), for $i = 1, 2, ..., l$ where $x_i \in \mathbb{R}^n$, $y_i \in \{+1, -1\}$, n is the number of features and l is the number of training data points. Then hard margin linear SVM solves the following optimization problem:

$$\min_{w,b} \quad \frac{1}{2}\|w\|^2 \tag{2.2}$$
$$\text{s.t.} \quad y_i(w^T x_i + b) \geq 1, \ \forall i,$$

where w, b are parameters. The decision function is:

$$h(x) = sign(w^T x + b).$$

Parameters w and b can be combined into a single parameter by adding a new feature to every instance for notational convenience as follow:

$$x_j^T \leftarrow [x_j^T, 1] \quad w^T \leftarrow [w^T, b]$$

So now eq. (2.2) and decision function can be rewritten as:

$$\min_{w} \quad \frac{1}{2}\|w\|^2 \tag{2.3}$$
$$\text{s.t.} \quad y_i w^T x_i \geq 1, \ \forall i$$
$$h(x) = sign(w^T x)$$

Equation (2.3) represents the primal form of the hard margin linear SVM. The dual form of the hard margin linear SVM, obtained using the Lagrangian Multipliers technique is:

$$\min_{\alpha} \quad \frac{1}{2}\alpha^T Q\alpha - \mathbf{1}^T \alpha \tag{2.4}$$
$$\text{s.t.} \quad \alpha_i \geq 0, \quad \alpha y = 0$$

where $Q_{ij} = y_i y_j x_i^T x_j$, α is vector of dual variables α_i, y is vector of output labels y_i and $\mathbf{1}$ is a unit vector. The decision function and relation between w and α are given as:

$$h(x) = sign\left(\sum_{i=1}^{l} y_i \alpha_i x_i^T x\right), \quad w = \sum_{i=1}^{l} y_i \alpha_i x_i.$$

2.3.2 Soft Margin SVM (1995)

The problem with hard margin SVM is that if the dataset is not linearly separable then it becomes impossible to classify the data (that is, no separating hyperplane is found) and the presence of noise or outliers greatly affect the margin. [31], introduced a slack variable into the hard margin SVM to allow some mis-classification errors. This new SVM is known as soft margin SVM. Figure 2.3. depicts an example of soft margin SVM. Soft margin SVM solves the following optimization problem:

$$\min_{w} \quad \frac{1}{2}\|w\|^2 + C\sum_{i=1}^{l} \xi_i \tag{2.5}$$
$$\text{s.t.} \quad y_i w^T x_i \geq 1 - \xi_i, \quad \xi_i \geq 0, \ \forall i,$$

where ξ_i is the slack variable to allow some mis-classification and C is a penalty parameter. ξ_i is replaced by loss functions in SVM. L1 and L2 loss are two common loss functions in literature, given by eq. (2.1). The decision function is given by

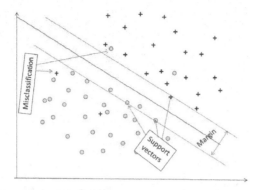

FIGURE 2.3 An example of two dimensional inseparable data. Since data is not completely separable so SVM allows some mis-classification errors to find the separating hyperplane.

$$h(x) = sign(w^T x).$$

Equation (2.5) represents the primal form, the dual form of soft margin SVM is given by

$$\min_{\alpha} \quad f(\alpha) = \frac{1}{2}\alpha^T \bar{Q}\alpha - 1^T \alpha$$
$$\text{s.t.} \quad 0 \le \alpha_i \le U, \forall i, \tag{2.6}$$

where $\bar{Q} = Q + D$, D is a diagonal matrix, $Q_{ij} = y_i y_j x_i^T x_j$,

$$U = \begin{cases} C & \text{for L1 loss SVM} \\ \infty & \text{for L2 loss SVM} \end{cases} \quad \text{and } D_{ii} = \begin{cases} 0 & \text{for L1 loss SVM} \\ \dfrac{1}{2C} & \text{for L2 loss SVM} \end{cases} \quad \forall i.$$

2.3.3 One-versus-Rest (1998)

One-versus-Rest (OVR, [132]) technique is also called as one-versus-all and one-against-all. This is probably the earliest multi-class SVM implementation and is one of the mostly used multi-class SVM. In this technique, we solve m binary SVM problems where m is the number of classes. Each SVM classifier separates one class from the rest of the classes. In this way, multi-class classification problem is reduced to binary classification problem. OVR technique is pictorially represented in the Fig. 2.4.

$$\min_{w^i, b^i, \xi^i} \quad \frac{1}{2}(w^i)^T w^i + C \sum_{j=1}^{l} \xi_j^i$$
$$\text{s.t.} \quad (w^i)^T x_j + b^i \ge 1 - \xi_j^i, \quad \text{if } y_j = i, \tag{2.7}$$
$$(w^i)^T x_j + b^i \le -1 + \xi_j^i, \quad \text{if } y_j \ne i,$$
$$\xi_j^i \ge 0, \quad j = 1, 2, ..., l, \ i = 1, 2, ..., m.$$

After solving, it needs m decision functions to predict the class of a test data point as given below:

$$(w^1)^T x + b^1, \quad (w^2)^T x + b^2, \quad ... \quad , \quad (w^m)^T x + b^m. \tag{2.8}$$

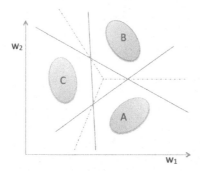

FIGURE 2.4 One versus Rest, multi-class classification technique: An example of three classes A, B and C in two dimensions.

A test data point is assigned a particular class only when the data point is accepted by that class and rejected by all other classes. But this leads to a problem when a data point is accepted by more than one class and that leads to a common region in the feature space. [132] suggested that data point should be assigned to the class with highest value of decision function, regardless of sign. The final output label is given to the class that has highest output value:

$$\text{class of x} \quad \equiv \underset{i=1,2,...,m}{argmax} \quad ((w^i)^T x + b^i). \tag{2.9}$$

The main disadvantage of this technique is that it used to solve m different optimization problems and need to evaluate m decision functions for each test data point. But it is a simple technique.

2.3.4   One-versus-One (1999)

One-versus-One technique (OVO, [72]) is also called as one-against-one (OAO, 1-a-1) or pair-wise classification . In this classification technique, a binary SVM is trained for each possible pair of classes. This idea of pair-wise classification was proposed by [68] and later [44], proposed 'Max Wins' algorithm which suggested that each one-vs-one classifier contributes one vote to its predicted class and final output is the class with the maximum number of votes. [72], applied this idea to SVM. Suppose there are m classes then OVO technique would lead to $m(m-1)/2$ binary SVM classification problems, each one is trained on data from two classes. Figure 2.5. depicts the OVO multi-class SVM. For training data from the ith and j^{th} classes, the problem is given by

$$\underset{w^{i,j},b^{i,j},\xi^{i,j}}{\min} \quad \frac{1}{2}(w^{i,j})^T w^{i,j} + C\sum_t \xi_t^{i,j} \tag{2.10}$$

$$\begin{aligned} \text{s.t.} \quad & ((w^{i,j})^T x + b^{i,j}) \geq 1 - \xi^{i,j}, \quad \text{for } y = i, \\ & ((w^{i,j})^T x + b^{i,j}) \leq -1 + \xi^{i,j}, \quad \text{for } y = j, \\ & \xi_{i,j} \geq 0, \end{aligned} \tag{2.11}$$

where $t \in X_{i,j}$ and $X_{i,j}$ is the set of data points with labels i and j.

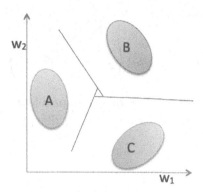

FIGURE 2.5 One versus One multi-class classification technique: An example of three classes A, B and C in two dimensions.

2.3.5 Least Squares SVM (1999)

Least Squares SVM (LSSVM, [127]) proposes a least squared version of SVM with equality constraints. Due to equality constraints, it solves a set of linear equations to find the solution, unlike standard SVM which solves quadratic programming. In LSSVM, number of support vectors is proportional to number of errors. LSSVM is given by

$$\min_{w,b,\xi} \quad \frac{1}{2}\|w\|^2 + \frac{C}{2}\sum_{i=1}^{l}\xi_i^2, \tag{2.12}$$

$$\text{s.t.} \quad y_i\left(w^T x_i + b\right) = 1 - \xi_i, \quad i = 1, 2, ..., l. \tag{2.13}$$

LSSVM has been extended by [80] which assigns a degree of importance to each training data point, this idea is similar to Fuzzy SVM [86].

2.3.6 ν-SVM (2000)

ν-SVM [116] proposes a new SVM formulation for classification and regression problems where a new parameter ν is introduced. ν roughly controls the fraction of support vectors. In addition to that, ν also helps to eliminate one of the other free parameters of the algorithm, ϵ (accuracy parameter) in regression and C (regularization coefficient) in the classification. Primal formulation for ν-SVM is:

$$\min_{w,b,\xi,\rho} \quad \tau(w,\xi,\rho) = \frac{1}{2}\|w\|^2 - \nu\rho + \frac{1}{l}\sum_i \xi_i$$
$$\text{s.t.} \quad y_i\left(x_i^T w + b\right) \geq \rho - \xi_i \tag{2.14}$$
$$\xi_i \geq 0, \quad \rho \geq 0, \quad \nu \in [0,1]$$

Dual problem for ν-SVM:

$$\max_{\alpha} \quad W(\alpha) = -\frac{1}{2}\sum_{ij} \alpha_i \alpha_j y_i y_j x_i^T x_j$$
$$\text{s.t.} \quad 0 \leq \alpha_i \leq \frac{1}{l}, \quad 0 = \sum_i \alpha_i y_i, \quad \sum_i \alpha \leq \nu \tag{2.15}$$

Decision function is:

$$h(x) = sign\left(\sum_i \alpha_i y_i x^T x_i + b\right) \tag{2.16}$$

On comparing with original soft margin dual problem, ν-SVM has two differences: Additional constraints and the linear term $\sum_i \alpha_i$ disappears from objective function in eq. (2.15).

2.3.7 Smooth SVM (2001)

Smooth SVM [77] proposes a new smooth formulation for SVM, to handle its non-differentiability issue. Smooth SVM is a strongly convex and infinitely differentiable. It enjoys globally, quadratically convergent solutions using a fast Newton-Armijo algorithm. It uses Newton's method for obtaining the step direction and Armijo rule for determining the step size.

Suppose there are l training points in n dimensional space represented by $l \times n$ matrix A with membership of each data A_i in classes $+1$ and -1 is represented by the diagonal $l \times l$ matrix D with values $+1$ or -1 on the diagonal. The standard SVM with some $\nu > 0$ and linear Kernel $A^T A$, is given by

$$\min_{(w,\gamma,y)\in\mathbb{R}^{n+1+l}} \nu \mathbf{1}^T y + \frac{1}{2}\|w\|^2 \tag{2.17}$$
$$\text{s.t.} \quad D(Aw - \mathbf{1}\gamma) + y \geq \mathbf{1}, \quad y \geq 0$$

where w, γ are parameters and y is the slack variable. The standard SVM is first modified to get the following SVM:

$$\min_{w,\gamma,y} \frac{\nu}{2} y^T y + \frac{1}{2}\left(\|w\|^2 + \gamma^2\right) \tag{2.18}$$
$$\text{s.t.} \quad D(Aw - \mathbf{1}\gamma) + y \geq \mathbf{1}, \quad y \geq 0.$$

From the constraints of problem (2.18), we get,

$$y = (\mathbf{1} - D(Aw - \mathbf{1}\gamma))_+, \tag{2.19}$$

where $(.)_+$ function replaces negative components of a vector with zeros. So, substituting the value of y in eq. (2.18), equivalent SVM is obtained as:

$$\min_{w,\gamma} \frac{\nu}{2}\|(\mathbf{1} - D(Aw - \mathbf{1}\gamma))_+\|^2 + \frac{1}{2}\left(\|w\|^2 + \gamma^2\right) \tag{2.20}$$

The objective function of this problem is not twice differentiable so x_+ is replaced with a smooth approximation, given by

$$p(x,\alpha) = x + \frac{1}{\alpha}log\left(1 + e^{-\alpha x}\right), \quad \alpha > 0, \tag{2.21}$$

where α is the smoothing parameter and e is the exponential constant. So, using eq. (2.21) in eq. (2.20), it gives the Smooth SVM as:

$$\min_{w,\gamma} \frac{\nu}{2}\|p\left(\mathbf{1} - D\left(Aw - \mathbf{1}\gamma\right),\alpha\right)\|^2 + \frac{1}{2}\left(\|w\|^2 + \gamma^2\right) \tag{2.22}$$

The decision function for Smooth SVM is given by $sign(w^T x - \gamma)$.

2.3.8 Proximal SVM (2001)

Proximal SVM (PSVM, [45]) classifies data points on the basis of proximity to the two parallel planes (called as proximal planes). Standard SVM classifies points using a separating hyperplane which assigns them to one of the half spaces generated by it (separating hyperplane). Figure 2.6. depicts the bounding planes in standard SVM and proximal planes of PSVM. The performance of PSVM on test dataset, is comparable to the standard SVM but its training speed on the training dataset, is considerably faster than the Standard SVM [45]. Primal form of PSVM is given by

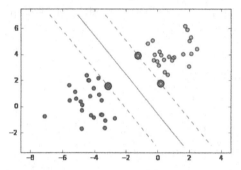 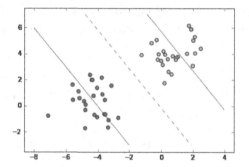

(a) Standard SVM: Separating plane with bounding planes. Circles represent support vectors

(b) Proximal SVM: Separating plane with planes which are no longer bounding planes but proximal planes. The data points are clustered around the proximal planes.

FIGURE 2.6 Standard SVM versus Proximal SVM.

$$\min_{(w,\gamma,y)} \quad \nu\frac{1}{2}\|y\|^2 + \frac{1}{2}\left(w^T w + \gamma^2\right) \tag{2.23}$$
$$\text{s.t.} \quad D\left(Aw - \mathbf{1}\gamma\right) + y = \mathbf{1}$$

where w, γ are parameters, A is $l \times n$ matrix representing l data points in n-dimensional real space $\mathbb{R}^n$, according to the membership of each point A_i in the class $A+$ or $A-$ as specified by a given $l \times l$ diagonal matrix D with $+1$ or -1 along its diagonal. $\nu > 0$, $\mathbf{1} =$ unit vector, y represents errors. The solution of this problem can be written directly in terms of problem data.

The planes $x^T w - \gamma = \pm 1$ are not boundary planes anymore but can be thought as proximal planes around which the points of each class are clustered and which are pushed as far apart as possible by the term $(w^T w + \gamma^2)$ in the objective function.

The decision function for Proximal SVM $sign(w^T x - \gamma)$. Lagrangian with coefficient u is given by

$$L(w, \gamma, y, u) = \frac{\nu}{2} \|y\|^2 + \frac{1}{2} \left\| \begin{bmatrix} w \\ \gamma \end{bmatrix} \right\|^2 - u^T (D(Aw - 1\gamma) + y - 1) \tag{2.24}$$

Solving using Karush–Kuhn–Tucker (KKT) conditions gives

$$w = A^T Du, \quad \gamma = -1^T Du, \quad y = \frac{u}{\nu}$$

$$u = \left(\frac{I}{\nu} + D(AA^T + 11^T)D \right)^{-1} 1 = \left(\frac{I}{\nu} + HH^T \right)^{-1} 1 \tag{2.25}$$

where $H = D[A \quad -1]$. Equation (2.25) gives the explicit solution to eq. (2.23).

2.3.9 Crammer Singer SVM (2002)

[33], proposed a multi-class SVM (CSSVM) which unlike OVR [132] and OVO [72] trains a single SVM classifier and evaluates m (number of classes) decision functions to classify a test data point. The problem formulations are:

$$\min_{w_k, \xi_i} \quad \frac{1}{2} \sum_{k=1}^{m} w_k^T w_k + C \sum_{i=1}^{l} \xi_i \tag{2.26}$$
$$\text{s.t.} \quad w_{y_i}^T x_i - w_k^T x_i \geq e_i^k - \xi_i, \quad i = 1, ..., l,$$

$$\text{where} \quad e_i^k \equiv 1 - \delta_{y_i,k} \text{ and } \delta_{y_i,k} = \begin{cases} 1 & \text{if } y_i = k \\ 0 & \text{if } y_i \neq k \end{cases}$$

Decision function is

$$\underset{k=1,2,...,m}{argmax} \quad w_k^T x. \tag{2.27}$$

The main difference between Crammer Singer SVM (CSSVM) and other problems is that CSSVM does not need to explicitly write down constraints $\xi_i \geq 0$ as when $y_i = k$, $e_i^k = 0$, so eq. (2.26) becomes $0 \geq 0 - \xi_i$ which is exactly $\xi_i \geq 0$. It contains only ξ_i, $i = 1, 2, ..., l$, l slack variables, instead of using ξ_i^k as the gap between each pair of decision planes. Dual problem of CSSVM is:

$$\min_{\alpha} \quad \frac{1}{2} \sum_{k=1}^{m} \|w_k\|^2 + \sum_{i=1}^{l} \sum_{k=1}^{m} e_i^k \alpha_i^k \tag{2.28}$$
$$\text{s.t.} \quad \sum_{k=1}^{m} \alpha_i^k = 0, \quad i = 1, ..., l,$$
$$\alpha_i^k \leq C_{y_i}^k, \quad i = 1, .., l, \; k = 1, ..., m,$$

where $w_k = \sum_{i=1}^{l} \alpha_i^k x_i, \forall k$ and $C_{y_i}^k = \begin{cases} C & \text{if } y_i = k \\ 0 & \text{if } y_i \neq k \end{cases}$.

2.3.10 $E\nu$-SVM (2003)

The ν-SVM [116] for classification (ν-SVC) has proposed a different formulation for solving SVM in which a new parameter ν has been introduced. ν gives an upper bound on the number of support vectors. ν also removes C which is a measure of trade-off between the margin size and training errors. This is difficult to choose C priori. The value of ν cannot always take all possible values between 0 and 1 which limits the range of possible solutions. Either because the training set is non-separable or because the classes are unbalanced. So, ν-SVM [116] is extended to $E\nu$-SVM [109], where a new problem is constructed using ν that helps to control the margin, errors and the support vectors. In $E\nu$-SVM, the value of ν cannot take full range of values from 0 to 1. For l training points, the value of ν can be defined as:

$$\nu_* = \lim_{C \to \infty} \frac{1}{lC} \sum_{i=1}^{l} \alpha_i^C, \quad \nu_* = \lim_{C \to 0} \frac{1}{lC} \sum_{i=1}^{l} \alpha_i^C \tag{2.29}$$

where $\nu_* > 0$ and $\nu_* \leq 1$. Primal problem is given below:

$$\min_{\rho,w,b,\xi_i} \quad -l\nu\rho + \sum_{i=1}^{l} \xi_i$$
$$\text{s.t.} \quad y_i \left(x_i^T w + b\right) \geq \rho - \xi_i, \quad \xi_i \geq 0, \forall i \tag{2.30}$$
$$\frac{1}{2}\|w\|^2 = 1$$

Dual problem is:

$$\max_{\alpha_i,\lambda} \quad L_D = -\frac{1}{2\lambda} \sum_{i=1}^{l} \sum_{j=1}^{l} y_i y_j \alpha_i \alpha_j x_i^T x_j - \lambda$$
$$\tag{2.31}$$
$$\text{s.t.} \quad \nu = -\frac{1}{l} \sum_{i=1}^{l} \alpha_i, \quad \sum_{i=1}^{l} \alpha_i y_i = 0, \quad 0 \leq \alpha_i \leq 1, \forall i$$

$$\lambda = +\sqrt{\frac{1}{2} \sum_{i=1}^{l} \sum_{j=1}^{l} y_i y_j \alpha_i \alpha_j x_i^T x_j}. \tag{2.32}$$

2.3.11 Twin SVM (2007)

Twin SVM (TWSVM, [56]) is an extension of PSVM [45] via generalized eigen values. As the name suggests, TWSVM is a binary classifier that solves two related small sized SVM problems and gives two non-parallel planes. A new test point is classified as per the closest plane. TWSVM is faster than standard SVM and gives good generalization results [56]. It helps in automatically discovering two-dimensional projections of the data. Each of the non-parallel planes is closer to one of class and is as far as possible from the other class. TWSVM is comprised of two quadratic programming problems in which the objective function of one problem is represented by the data points of one class and constraints are represented by the data points of other class. This leads to two smaller SVM problems given below.

$$
\text{(TWSVM 1)} \quad \min_{w^{(1)},b^{(1)},q} \frac{1}{2} \left(Aw^{(1)} + \mathbf{1}_1 b^{(1)} \right)^T \left(Aw^{(1)} + \mathbf{1}_1 b^{(1)} \right) + C_1 \mathbf{1}_2^T q
$$

$$
\text{s.t.} \qquad - \left(Bw^{(1)} + \mathbf{1}_2 b^{(1)} \right) + q \geq \mathbf{1}_2, \quad q \geq 0
$$

$$
\text{(TWSVM 2)} \quad \min_{w^{(2)},b^{(2)},q} \frac{1}{2} \left(Bw^{(2)} + \mathbf{1}_2 b^{(2)} \right)^T \left(Bw^{(2)} + \mathbf{1}_2 b^{(2)} \right) + C_2 \mathbf{1}_1^T q
$$

$$
\text{s.t.} \qquad \left(Aw^{(2)} + \mathbf{1}_1 b^{(2)} \right) + q \geq \mathbf{1}_1, \quad q \geq 0
$$

(2.33)

where C_1, C_2 are penalty parameters and $\mathbf{1}_1, \mathbf{1}_2$ are unit vectors. First term represents distance of data points form hyperplane and second term represents errors. Here data points belonging to classes $+1$ and -1 are represented with A and B. Let l_1 and l_2 denotes number of data points in A and B. So, size of A and B is $l_1 \times n$ and $l_2 \times n$. Dual form is:

$$
\text{(DTWSVM 1)} \quad \max_{\alpha} \quad \mathbf{1}_2^T \alpha - \frac{1}{2} \alpha^T G \left(H^T H \right)^{-1} G^T \alpha
$$

$$
\text{s.t.} \qquad 0 \leq \alpha \leq C_1
$$

$$
\text{(DTWSVM 2)} \quad \max_{\gamma} \quad \mathbf{1}_1^T \gamma - \frac{1}{2} \gamma^T P \left(Q^T Q \right)^{-1} P^T \gamma
$$

$$
\text{s.t.} \qquad 0 \leq \gamma \leq C_2
$$

(2.34)

where α and γ are dual variables.

$$
\text{where} \quad H = [A \quad \mathbf{1}_1], \quad G = [B \quad \mathbf{1}_2]
$$
$$
P = [A \quad \mathbf{1}_1], \quad Q = [B \quad \mathbf{1}_2]
$$

TWSVM has been further extended to ν-TWSVM [105] which introduces parameter ν into TWSVM for controlling the margin, errors and consequently support vectors. All extensions and applications of TWSVM can be found in [58].

2.3.12 Capped l_p-norm SVM (2017)

Capped l_p-norm SVM (CappedSVM, [102]) proposes a new SVM problem formulation using capped l_p-norm based loss function, to tackle the challenge of data outliers. Data outliers have large residue values so capped norm helps the CappedSVM to eliminate these outliers during the training process. CappedSVM is also extended to multi-class problems. Unlike one-vs-one, one-vs-rest which solve several binary problems, CappedSVM solves single optimization problem, like, CSSVM. Authors have proved the utility of primal formulation and its binary formulation is given below [102]:

$$
\min_{w,b} \sum_{i=1}^{l} \xi_{ch} \left(w, b \, | x_i \right) + \gamma \, \|w\|_2^2 \tag{2.35}
$$

Here γ is regularization parameter and $\xi_{ch} \left(w, b \, | x_i \right)$ is capped l_p-norm given by

$$
\xi_{ch} \left(w, b \, | x_i \right) = \min \left(\epsilon, \max \left(0, 1 - y_i w^T x_i \right)^p \right).
$$

where ϵ is capping value and p is any real value. Multi-class problem for c classes is given by

$$\min_{W,b,M\geq0} \sum_{i=1}^{l} \min\left(\|W^T x_i + b - y_i - y_i \circ m_i\|_2^p, \epsilon\right) + \gamma \|W\|_F^2 \qquad (2.36)$$

where m_i is a slack variable to encode the unilateral loss of x_i, $W \in \mathbb{R}^{n \times c}$, $b \in \mathbb{R}^{c \times 1}$, $m_i \in \mathbb{R}^{c \times 1}$, $M \in \mathbb{R}^{c \times n}$ with the i-th column as m_i and

$$\xi_{chm}\left(W, b | x_i\right) = \min\left(\min_{m_i\geq0}\|W^T x_i + b - y_i - y_i \circ m_i\|_2^p, \epsilon\right),$$

is capped l_p-norm loss function for multi-class problem.
A summary of some of important SVMs is given in Table 2.1.

TABLE 2.1 Summary of SVM Problem Formulations

Hard SVM [12]	This SVM separates the data points using a hyperplane without allowing any mis-classification errors and that's why know as hard margin SVM. Because of hard margin, this is not applicable (in primal formulation) to problems where data can't be separated completely by the hyperplane.	This is a standard SVM, used for general class of problems and is not suitable to specific requirements like noisy or outliers data applications.	-This was the first SVM. -This has been improved by Soft SVM so it is hardly used.
Soft SVM [31]	This is an extension of hard margin SVM which introduced a slack variable into the hard margin SVM to allow some misclassification errors. Thus, it can be applied to problems where data can't be separated completely by the hyperplane.	-Being extension of hard SVM, this is also a standard SVM, used for general class of problems and is not very good to specific requirements like noisy or outliers data applications. -This is used in large and sparse data applications and acts as a very good tool in image and document classification problems.	This is the most popular and widely used formulation of SVM.
One-versus-Rest (OVR) [132]	This is a multi-class SVM formulation which reduces the multi-class problem to binary problem by considering one class at a time and separating it from the rest of the classes. Thus, for m classes, it solves m binary SVM problems and evaluates same number of decision functions to find the class of a test point.	This is used for multi-class data applications.	This is a simple, one of the mostly used and probably the earliest multi-class SVM implementation but its disadvantage is that it needs to train and evaluate multiple SVMs and decision functions, respectively.
Transductive SVM [61]	Unlike, standard SVM, this considers both training and test data for training the model to reduce the test errors.	This is used for text classification problems.	This targets a particular dataset and try to have a minimum test error on that dataset. This is not suitable for other applications because of different goals.

TABLE 2.1 Summary of SVM Problem Formulations (*Continued*)

Name	Idea	Applications	Remarks
Weston Watkins SVM [135]	This is a multi-class SVM formulation which solves a single optimization problem and evaluates m (number of classes) decision functions.	This is used for multi-class data applications.	Unlike OVR, it solves a single optimization problem but, like OVR evaluates m (number of classes) decision functions to predict the class of a test data point.
One-versus-One (OVO) [72]	This is a multi-class SVM which trains a binary SVM for each possible pair of classes, leading to $\dfrac{m(m-1)}{2}$ binary SVM optimization problems.	This is used for multi-class data applications.	Unlike OVR, WWSVM it solves $\dfrac{m(m-1)}{2}$ optimization problems and evaluates same number of decision functions to predict the class of a test data point.
Least Squares SVM (LSSVM) [127]	This proposes an SVM which can be put in the least squares form, with equality constraints.	This is a standard SVM, used for general class of problems.	-Due to equality constraints, it solves a set of linear equations to find the solution, unlike, standard SVM which solves quadratic programming. Thus, faster to solve it. -In LSSVM, number of support vectors are proportional to number of errors. -LSSVM behaves like Hard SVM when data points are linearly independent [143]. -LSSVM has been extended by [80] which assigns a degree of importance to each training data point, this idea is similar to Fuzzy SVM [86].
ν-SVM [116]	This proposed a new SVM formulation for classification and regression problems where a new parameter ν replaces the existing C parameter in classification problem.	This is successfully used by researchers for image boundary detection and in personal email assistant.	-ν roughly controls the fraction of support vectors and thus its value is limited to $[0,1]$, unlike, C which can take any positive value. -This is difficult to optimize as compared with standard SVM and is not scalable for large problems.
Directed Acyclic Graph SVM (DAGSVM) [107]	It uses a rooted binary directed acyclic graph which has $\dfrac{m(m-1)}{2}$ internal nodes and m leaves where m is the number of classes. Each internal node represents a binary SVM classifier which tests two classes. The leaf nodes represent the output class labels. For m classes, it needs only $m-1$ evaluations of decision functions.	This is used for multi-class classification problems.	This is similar to OVO technique and like OVO, it solves $\dfrac{m(m-1)}{2}$ binary SVM classifier but to classify a test data point, it uses a different strategy and needs only $m-1$ evaluations of decision functions.

TABLE 2.1 Summary of SVM Problem Formulations (*Continued*)

Name	Idea	Applications	Remarks
Smooth SVM [77]	This proposes a smooth variant of the standard SVM to handle the non-differentiability issue.	This is a binary SVM which can use faster optimization methods available for smooth and strongly convex problems.	Smooth SVM is strongly convex and infinitely differentiable so it enjoys globally, quadratically convergent solutions using a fast Newton-Armijo algorithm.
Lagrangian SVM (LSVM) [95]	This is obtained by reformulating the standard primal linear SVM and taking an implicit Lagrangian of its dual form.	This is a binary SVM.	This gives an unconstrained differentiable convex function and thus easier to solve.
Proximal SVM (PSVM) [45]	This SVM finds two parallel hyperplane (called proximal hyperplanes), unlike, standard SVM which finds single. This classifies data points on the basis of proximity to the two parallel planes, unlike, standard SVM which assigns them to one of the half spaces generated by separating hyperplane.	This is a binary SVM.	Proximal hyperplanes are pushed much apart from each other because these are no longer bounding planes (refer to Fig. 2.6).
Crammer Singer SVM (CSSVM) [33]	This is a multi-class SVM formulation which trains a single SVM classifier and evaluates m (number of classes) decision functions to classify a test data point	This is used for multi-class classification problems.	-The main difference between CSSVM and other problems is that CSSVM does not need to explicitly write down constraints. -Unlike OVO, OVR, DAGSVM (which solve multiple problems) and like WWSVM, it solves a single optimization problem but unlike DAGSVM, OVO and like WWSVM, it evaluates m (number of classes) decision functions to classify a test data point.
Fuzzy SVM (FSVM) [86]	This assigns each data point a fuzzy membership to the labeled class and reformulates the SVM problem where contributions of points are used to find the separating hyperplane.	It is suitable for fault diagnosis and applications where data points have modeled characteristics.	-FSVM is useful in reducing the effect of outliers and noise. -FSVM has been further extended to multi-class problems (refer to, [2, 1])
Eν-SVM [109]	This extends ν-SVM by using the idea that ν can't take all values from 0 to 1, either because the training set is non-separable or because the classes are unbalanced.	This is successfully used by researchers for image boundary detection and in personal email assistant.	ν helps to control the margin, errors and the support vectors.
Structured SVM [131]	This problem formulation handles the structured outputs like sequences, strings, graphs, labeled trees or lattices.	It has applications in a number of areas like multi-label classification, supervised grammar learning and to label sequence learning etc.	-This is different from all other SVMs because its outputs are structured. -This is a generalization of CSSVM and WWSVM.

TABLE 2.1 Summary of SVM Problem Formulations (*Continued*)

Name	Idea	Applications	Remarks
Multi-Task SVM (MTSVM) [37]	MTSVM extends the standard SVM, i.e., single task learning SVM to multi-task learning.	This is useful when multiple learning tasks, having some commonalities, need to be solved at the same time.	MTSVM has been further extended to multi-class problems in [59, 60].
Fuzzy Proximal SVM (FPSVM) [57]	This uses the concept of FSVM and PSVM to propose a new SVM where fuzzy membership is assigned to data points in the labeled class and data points are classified on the basis of proximity to two parallel planes	It is suitable for fault diagnosis and applications where data points have modeled characteristics.	This is useful in reducing the effect of outliers and noise.
Cascade SVM [49]	The dataset is broken into multiple subsets and an SVM is trained on each subset. The partial results (support vectors) from the different SVMs are combined together by taking two SVM at a time in multiple layers until a single set of support vectors is obtained.	This is a binary SVM.	-This is based on divide and conquer strategy of solving the SVM problem. -[54], has further extended the Cascade SVM to DC-SVM (Divide-and-Conquer SVM) which uses clustering of data in the division step so most of the support vectors of subproblems are also the support vectors of the combined problem.
GEPSVM [96]	This proposes a new formulation with two non-parallel hyperplanes and data points are classified according to the proximity to one of the two non-parallel planes. The non-parallel planes are the eigen vectors corresponding to the smallest eigen values of two related generalized eigen value problems.	This is a binary SVM.	Unlike PSVM which have parallel proximal planes, it has non-parallel proximal planes.
Multi-View SVM (MVSVM) [40]	MVSVM extends the idea of Multi-view learning to SVM.	This is helpful in problems where data is obtained from different sources or obtained using different feature extractors and show heterogeneous properties.	-It aims to improve the generalization performance of the classifier through multiple views of the problem. -MVSVM has been further extended to Twin SVM by [139].
Twin SVM (TWSVM) [56]	This is an extension of PSVM via generalized eigen values which solves two related small sized SVM problems and give two non-parallel planes.	This is a binary SVM.	-PSVM finds two parallel proximal planes but TWSVM, like, GEPSVM finds two non-parallel planes. -TWSVM has been extended to ν-TWSVM [105], and been studied extensively. All extensions and applications can be found in the book [58].

TABLE 2.1 Summary of SVM Problem Formulations (*Continued*)

Name	Idea	Applications	Remarks
SloppySVM [126]	SloppySVM formulation proposes a new non-convex objective functional which is a uniform estimate of noise free objective function of standard C-SVM.	This can be efficiently used only for sloppily labeled data, i.e., labeling of data can be wrong.	This is a non-convex formulation so difficult to solve than standard SVM and thus this is rarely used.
Capped SVM [102]	CappedSVM has proposed a new problem formulation using capped l_p-norm based loss function, to tackle the challenge of data outliers.	It is useful for tackling the data outliers challenge, like in fault detection, and multi-class problems.	It is available as binary and multi-class formulations.
C-SVM [38]	This is a name given to standard SVM, which uses penalty parameter C, to distinguish it from the ν-SVM.	This is a class of problems and have same applications as standard SVM like soft SVM.	This is only a terminology and not a specific SVM formulation.
Kernel SVM [21]	This is a name given to a class of dual SVM problem formulations which uses non-linear Kernels.	-This is used for non-linearly separable data applications where it is not possible to find a separable hyperplane in the Input Space. -This is further very helpful when primal problem have issues, like, non-differentiability, and can't be solved efficiently.	Any convex SVM problem can be converted into corresponding Kernel SVM.

2.4 PROBLEM SOLVERS

Once the SVM problem is formulated, the next task is to solve the problem using certain methods called SVM solvers. The method/solver to solve a particular SVM formulation depends upon a number of factors and some of them are:

(i) Problem formulation properties: Convex and non-convex nature, strong convexity, smooth and non-smooth nature, primal or dual nature, constrained and unconstrained nature, etc.

(ii) Dataset properties: #data_points >> #features or #features >> #data_points, sparsity, binary or multi-class data etc.

(iii) What do we expect: Low or high accuracy solution, accuracy is important or time etc.

Different types of optimization problems, depending upon the nature of objective function and constraints, are depicted in Fig. 2.7. SVM problem is an optimization problem, which may be convex problem [33] or non-convex problem [126]. It depends upon the problem formulation. It is easy to solve the convex optimization problem than non-convex problems because every local optimum is a global optimum in a convex optimization problem. Therefore, SVM problem is generally formulated as a convex optimization problem. Generally, our problem lies in the category of Constrained Convex Optimization problem as per the Fig. 2.7. Convex Optimization

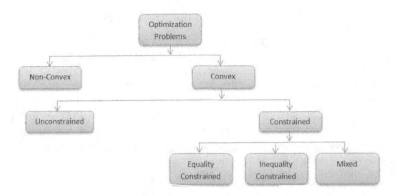

FIGURE 2.7 Different types of Optimization problems.

Problem (COP) can be divided into two types: Unconstrained Convex Optimization Problem (UCOP) and Constrained Convex Optimization Problem (CCOP). CCOP can be further into three types: Equality Constrained (EC), Inequality Constrained (IC) and Hybrid Constrained (HC).

Gradient-based methods are generally used for solving the UCOP problems. CCOP can be converted to UCOP and then gradient-based methods can be applied to them. In literature, generally gradient-based methods [30] are used for solving the SVM problem with occasional use of other methods like Interior Point Methods [41]. All these methods are taken from the Mathematics, highlighting the inter-disciplinary nature of Machine Learning, so it is beyond the scope of this chapter to discuss all methods for solving the optimization problems. This section gives an idea about SVM solvers and discusses some methods for solving SVM problems. Review of SVM solvers can be found in [13], [121] and for general discussion of optimization methods for large-scale machine learning, refer to [16].

Large-scale problems (SVMs) are solved using iterative methods and there is a trade-off between the computational complexity of each iteration and number of iterations required by the method to solve problem up to the desired accuracy. Generally, smaller the complexity of each iteration, slower is the convergence and larger is the number of iterations taken by the method to solve the problem [85]. For example, first order methods (like Gradient Descent method) have low iteration complexity (like in Gradient Descent, only gradient is calculated) but they converge very slowly and take large number of iterations to reach the desired accuracy [118]. On the other hand, second order methods have high computational complexity (like in Newton method, it requires computing and inverting the Hessian matrix) of each iteration but they converge very fast and take lesser number of iterations [85] to reach the same level of accuracy.

For an iterative method, solution in the $(k+1)^{th}$ iteration is given by

$$w_{k+1} = w_k + d_k s_k, \quad d_k > 0 \tag{2.37}$$

where s_k is the step direction and d_k is the step size along that direction. The process of finding d_k is also called as line search because of finding the value of step size along the step direction. The descent method is a method in which the value of a function

---

Algorithm 1 General Descent Method for Optimization

1: Initialization: Take initial solution w_0 and tolerance ϵ_0
2: **for** k=1,2,... **do**
3:     Find descent direction s_k.
4:     Line Search: Choose a step size $d_k > 0$.
5:     Update solution using eq. (2.37).
6:     **if** $\|\nabla f(w_{k+1})\|_2 \leq \epsilon_0$ **then**
7:         Exit.
8:     **end if**
9: **end for**

---

decreases with every iteration, i.e., suppose function f is to be minimized then for $(k+1)^{th}$ iteration

$$f(w_{k+1}) < f(w_k)$$

except when w_k is optimal. s_k in a descent method must satisfy the following equation:

$$\nabla f(w_k)^T s_k < 0 \tag{2.38}$$

This means that the search direction should make an acute angle with the negative of gradient of function. Such a direction is known as a descent direction. A general algorithm for a descent optimization method is given by Algorithm 1. The step size and step direction can be found by separate methods or by a single method, and other exit criteria can be tried.

Some methods for finding the step size are given below:

2.4.1 Exact Line Search Method

In this method [102] of finding the step size (d), an exact optimization problem is solved to minimize f along the ray $\{w + ds | d > 0\}$:

$$d = \underset{v \geq 0}{argmin} \quad f(w + vs) \tag{2.39}$$

The limitation of exact line search method is that it takes a lot of overhead for large problems. So, generally this method is not used for large problems.

2.4.2 Backtracking Line Search

Backtracking Line Search [22] is an inexact line search method where instead of solving the exact optimization problem, a set of values for step size, are tried along the ray $\{w+ds | d > 0\}$. The backtracking line search algorithm is given in Algorithm 2.

This method is called as backtracking line search method because it starts with unit size for step size and then decreases its value by a factor of β. Small value of β (0.1) corresponds to very crude search and large value (0.9) to less crude. The typical values of α are between 0.01 and 0.3, i.e., 1% to 30% decrease of prediction in f is accepted based on linear exploration.

Algorithm 2 Backtracking Line Search Method

1: Initialization: Let step direction be s_k and take $d = 1$, $\alpha \in (0, 1)$ and $\beta \in (0, 1)$.
2: **while** $f(w_k + ds_k) \leq f(w_k) + \alpha d \nabla f(w_k)^T s_k$ **do**
3:    $d = \beta d$
4: **end while**
5: Set $d_k = d$.

2.4.3 Constant Step Size

This is the simplest method of finding the step length. In order to get the value of step size no optimization problem is solved rather a constant value (generally $d = 1$) is used as a step size. For larger value, the convergence is uncertain. For smaller value, the convergence is slower but certain in convex functions.

2.4.4 Lipschitz and Strong Convexity Constants

Lipschitz (L) and strong convexity (μ) constants can also be used for calculating step sizes. These constants helps in easy calculation of step sizes but depends on correct estimation of L and μ. The main disadvantage of this method is that sometimes, these constants are not available. Using these constants, step size can be calculated as [115]:

$$d = \frac{1}{L} \quad \text{and} \quad d = \frac{2}{L + \mu}, \tag{2.40}$$

These expressions for d, can change depending upon the implementation.

2.4.5 Trust Region Method

In Trust Region (TR) method [24], a step direction and a step size is selected, then if the step is successful in some sense then the step is accepted else rejected and another step direction and step size is found. Here an approximate model (m_k) of a function (f) to be minimized is taken and solved to get the solution. The region around the current iterate in which the model has good approximation of function is called as trust-region. A basic Trust Region algorithm is given by Algorithm 3. Typically used values are $\eta_v = 0.75$, $\eta_s = 0.25$, $\sigma_i = 2$ and $\sigma_d = 0.5$.

Some optimization methods for finding the step direction are given below:

2.4.6 Gradient Descent Method

Gradient Descent method [20] is also known as Steepest Descent (SD) method, is a first order optimization method. SD method is based on the observation that a function decreases fastest on moving along the direction of negative gradient of the function. In this method, the step direction is taken as negative of gradient, i.e.,

$$s_k^{GD} = -\nabla f(w_k) \tag{2.43}$$

Algorithm 3 Basic Trust-Region Method

1: Given: Trust-region radius $\triangle_0 > 0$ and initial solution w_0.
2: Set $k = 0$, $\eta_v \in (0, 1)$, $\eta_s \in (0, \eta_v)$, $\sigma_i \geq 1$ and $\sigma_d \in (0, 1)$.
3: **repeat**
4:     Build a quadratic model $m_k(w_k + p)$ for $f(w_k + p)$ as

$$m_k(w_k + p_k) = f(w_k) + g^T p_k + \frac{1}{2} p_k^T H p_k \tag{2.41}$$

    where g and H are gradient and Hessian, respectively.
5:     Solve Trust-Region problem approximately for p_k,

$$\min_{\|p\| \leq \triangle_k} m_k(w_k + p)$$

6:     Find the ratio,

$$\rho_k = \frac{f(w_k) - f(w_k + p_k)}{f(w_k) - m_k(w_k + p_k)} \tag{2.42}$$

7:     **if** $\rho_k \geq \eta_v$ ("very successful" step), **then**
8:         set $w_{k+1} = w_k + p_k$ and $\triangle_{k+1} = \sigma_i \triangle_k$.
9:     **else if** $\rho_k \geq \eta_s$ ("successful" step), **then**
10:       set $w_{k+1} = w_k + p_k$ and $\triangle_{k+1} = \triangle_k$.
11:     **else if** $\rho_k < \eta_s$ ("unsuccessful" step), **then**
12:       set $w_{k+1} = w_k$ and $\triangle_{k+1} = \sigma_d \triangle_k$.
13:     **end if**
14:     k++
15: **until** convergence

---

and step size can be determined by either exact or backtracking line search. So, substituting the values of step size and step direction into the Algorithm 1., it gives Gradient Descent Algorithm. SD method generally exhibits approximately linear convergence. On using backtracking line search, the parameters α and β have noticeable effect over the convergence rate but it does not have dramatic effect. Advantage of this method is its simplicity, it does not require second order derivative and every iteration is inexpensive. Disadvantages are: it is often slow, depends upon scaling and can't handle non-differentiable problems.

2.4.7 Newton Method

For Newton's method [29], the step direction is given by

$$s_k^N = -\left(\nabla^2 f(w_k)\right)^{-1} \nabla f(w_k) \tag{2.44}$$

is called as Newton step which is a descent direction. When step size is taken as $d = 1$, then it is called as pure Newton method, else called as damped Newton or guarded Newton method. On replacing the step direction and method to find step size, in Algorithm 1, it gives algorithm for the Newton method. In general, Newton method has quadratic rate of convergence when $d = 1$. Advantages of Newton method are

(1) it is affine invariant to the choice of coordinates or condition number, (2) scales with problem size, (3) has fast convergence and (4) it is independent of algorithm parameters. Disadvantages of Newton method are (1) it need second order derivative, (2) high cost of computing and (3) storing the Hessian and calculating step direction.

2.4.8 Gauss-Newton Method

Gauss-Newton method [47] is an iterative optimization method for least squares problems which are of the form:

$$\min_{w} \quad f(w) = \frac{1}{2} \sum_{j=1}^{m} r_j^2(w) \tag{2.45}$$

where $w \in \mathbb{R}^n$ and $r_j : \mathbb{R}^n \to \mathbb{R}$ are residual functions.

Suppose $r : \mathbb{R}^n \to \mathbb{R}^m$ is a residual vector defined by

$$r(w) = (r_1(w), r_2(w), ..., r_m(w))$$

So eq. (2.45) becomes:

$$\min_{w} \quad f(w) = \frac{1}{2} \| r(w) \|^2 \tag{2.46}$$

From eq. (2.46), the gradient and Hessian can be expressed as:

$$\begin{aligned} \nabla f(w) &= \sum_{j=1}^{m} r_j(w) \nabla r_j(w) \\ &= J(w)^T r(w) \end{aligned} \tag{2.47}$$

$$\nabla^2 f(w) = J(w)^T J(w) + \sum_{j=1}^{m} r_j(w) \nabla^2 r_j(w) \tag{2.48}$$

For small value of $\nabla^2 r_j(w)$ or residuals ($r_j(w)$), eq. (2.48) simplifies to,

$$\nabla^2 f(w) = J(w)^T J(w) \tag{2.49}$$

Now using gradient and Hessian, for least squares problem, eq. (2.44) gives Gauss-Newton step direction for the $(k+1)^{th}$ iteration as:

$$s_k^G = - \left(J(w_k)^T J(w_k) \right)^{-1} J(w_k)^T r(w_k) \tag{2.50}$$

For small residual problem, the convergence rate is close to quadratic, otherwise not even linear is guaranteed.

2.4.9 Levenberg-Marquardt Method

[78] introduced a parameter λ into the Hessian and step direction given by eq. (2.50) changed to

$$s_k^L = - \left(J(w_k)^T J(w_k) + \lambda I \right)^{-1} J(w_k)^T r(w_k) \tag{2.51}$$

where I is the identity matrix. Later [97] replaced the identity matrix with diagonal matrix of Hessian matrix. So, eq. (2.51) gives Levenberg-Marquardt step direction as:

$$s_k^{LM} = - (H + \lambda \, diag(H))^{-1} g \tag{2.52}$$

where $H = J(w_k)^T J(w_k)$ and $g = J(w_k)^T r(w_k)$. λ is called the Levenberg-Marquardt parameter and is used to make the approximate Hessian $(H + \lambda \, diag(H))$ positive definite. This method is robust with respect to larger residual problems and poor initial solution. For $\lambda = 0$, Levenberg-Marquardt method behaves as Gauss-Newton method, and for large value of λ, it behaves as Steepest Descent method.

Levenberg-Marquardt (LM) method can be extended as Levenberg-Marquardt Trust Region (LMTR, [24]) method. In LM method λ is arbitrarily changed but in LMTR instead of changing the λ, trust region radius is changed. Trust Region method or line search methods are used to ensure sufficient decrease in the function. Trust Region method can be used with any method that uses quadratic model of the function for finding the solution.

2.4.10 Quasi-Newton Method

Quasi-Newton method [126] is an alternative to Newton method. In this method, instead of calculating the true Hessian $(\nabla^2 f_k)$ an approximation of Hessian (B_k) is used and updated at each step. So, the Quasi-Newton search direction is given by

$$s_k^Q = -B_k^{-1} g \tag{2.53}$$

Advantage of Quasi-Newton method is that it avoids calculation of second order derivatives. It has super-linear rate of convergence. There are many methods to update the Hessian value at each step. Two of the most famous formula for updating B_k are:

Symmetric Rank (SR1, [103]):

$$B_{k+1} = B_k + \frac{(y_k - B_k p_k)(y_k - B_k p_k)^T}{(y_k - B_k p_k)^T p_k} \tag{2.54}$$

where $y_k = \nabla f_{k+1} - \nabla f_k$ and $p_k = w_{k+1} - w_k$.

And BFGS [126] is named after its inventors, Broyden, Fletcher, Goldfarb and Shanno:

$$B_{k+1} = B_k - \frac{B_k p_k p_k^T B_k}{p_k^T B_k p_k} + \frac{y_k y_k^T}{y_k^T p_k} \tag{2.55}$$

2.4.11 Subgradient Method

Subgradient, subderivative and subdifferential refer to the derivative of a non-differentiable convex function. Subgradient methods [92, 118, 145] are optimization methods for solving the non-differentiable convex functions. The update rule for Subgradient method is given by

$$w_{k+1} = w_k - d_k g_k \tag{2.56}$$

where g_k is the subgradient of function f at w_k and for step size d_k.

Step size rule: (1) Fixed step: d_k is taken constant, (2) Fixed length: $d_k \| g_k \|_2$ is taken constant and (3) Diminishing: $d_k \to 0$, $\sum_{k=1}^{\infty} d_k = \infty$.

Advantage of Subgradient method is that it leads to a very simple algorithm. Disadvantage of Subgradient method are that the convergence can be very slow and there is no good stopping criterion for it.

2.4.12 Conjugate Gradient Method

Conjugate Gradient (CG) methods [85] are the optimization methods which are less reliable than Newton method but can be used to solve very large problems. It is proposed by [50] for linear systems in 1950s but has been extended to non-linear systems by [43] in the 1960s. Advantage of Conjugate method is that it does not need any matrix storage, it needs to calculate only objective function and its derivative which makes it suitable for very large problems. It is faster than Steepest Descent method. Inexact and Truncated Newton methods use it to approximate the Newton step. Conjugate Gradient method can be accelerated using preconditioning.

According to [43], step size is determined by any of the existing methods and step direction is found using the following formula and algorithm is given by Algorithm 4:

$$s_{k+1} = -\nabla f_{k+1} + \beta_{k+1} s_k \tag{2.57}$$

$$\text{where} \quad \beta_{k+1} = \frac{\nabla f_{k+1}^T \nabla f_{k+1}}{\nabla f_k^T \nabla f_k} \tag{2.58}$$

Algorithm 4 Fletcher and Reeves CG Method

1: Given: Initial solution w_0.
2: Calculate $f_0 = f(w_0)$, $\nabla f_0 = \nabla f(w_0)$. Let $s_0 = -\nabla f_0$ and k =0.
3: **while** $\nabla f_k \neq 0$ **do**
4:     Compute the step size d_k (using some method) and find $w_{k+1} = w_k + d_k s_k$
5:     Evaluate ∇f_{k+1}
6:     Evaluate β_{k+1} using eq. (2.58).
7:     Evaluate p_{k+1} using eq. (2.57).
8:     k++
9: **end while**

FR method has many variations and Polak-Ribiere (PR) method [123] is one of the them. It varies only in updating value of β_{k+1}. So, according to PR method the update formula is:

$$\beta_{k+1} = \frac{\nabla f_{k+1}^T (\nabla f_{k+1} - \nabla f_k)}{\nabla f_k^T \nabla f_k} \tag{2.59}$$

2.4.13 Truncated Newton Method

Truncated Newton (TN) methods are an alternative to Newton method where Newton system is approximately solved leading to early termination. TN methods are less reliable than Newton method but these can handle very large problems. TN methods do not calculate Hessian so also known as Hessian-free optimization. Conjugate Gradient method and Preconditioned Conjugate Gradient [85] methods are examples of Truncated Newton methods.

2.4.14 Proximal Gradient Method

Proximal Gradient (PG) method [140] is an optimization method for unconstrained problem where objective function can be split in two convex components. The proximity of a convex function $h(w)$ is given as:

$$prox_h(w) = \underset{u}{argmin} \quad \left(h(u) + \frac{1}{2}\|u - w\|_2^2 \right) \tag{2.60}$$

Suppose problem is given by

$$\min_{w} \quad f(w) = g(w) + h(w) \tag{2.61}$$

where g is convex, differentiable and $dom\ g = \mathbb{R}^n$. h is convex with inexpensive proximity. According to PG method the solution in the $(k+1)^{th}$ iteration is given by

$$w_{k+1} = prox_{d_k h} \left(w_k - d_k \nabla g \left(w_k \right) \right) \tag{2.62}$$

where $d_k > 0$ is step size, constant or determined by line search. Fast Proximal Gradient and Dual Proximal Gradient methods are the variations of PG method.

2.4.15 Recent Algorithms

Generally, a learning algorithm is a combination of various methods (like, step size methods and step direction methods) and optimization strategies. Some examples of recently used algorithms are: TRON (Trust RegiOn Newton method) [85], SVM-ALM algorithms [101], SAG (Stochastic Average Gradient) method [115], CappedSVM [102] etc. It is not possible to discuss all the latest algorithms so only three of them are discussed below:

TRON: In TRON, L2-regularized and L2-loss SVM problem is solved which is given below:

$$\min_{w} \quad f(w) = \frac{1}{2}\|w\|^2 + C\sum_{i=1}^{l}[\max(0, 1 - y_i w^T x_i)]^2 \tag{2.63}$$

Let quadratic model of $f(w)$ is:

$$m(s) = \nabla f(w)^T s + \frac{1}{2}s^T \nabla^2 f(w)s \tag{2.64}$$

TRON approximates $m(s)$ with trust region radius $\triangle$:

$$\min_{\|s\|\leq\triangle} \quad m(s) \tag{2.65}$$

It uses the following ratio for updating the trust region radius:

$$\mu = \frac{f(w + s) - f(w)}{m(s)} \tag{2.66}$$

TRON uses modified Newton method with Conjugate Gradient and Trust Region method for each iteration. The algorithm for TRON is given in Algorithm 5.

Algorithm 5 TRON for L2RL2 SVC [85]

1: Given: Initial solution w_0, trust-region radius $\triangle_0$ and η.

2: **for** $k = 0, 1, 2, \ldots$ **do**

3:    **if** Exit Criteria **then**

4:       Stop.

5:    **end if**

6:    Solve the subproblem (2.65) to get solution s using Conjugate Gradient method.

7:    Find the ratio μ, using eq. (2.66).

8:    **if** $\mu > \eta$ **then**

9:       Update solution: $w = w + s$

10:    **end if**

11:    Adjust $\triangle$, according to μ.

12: **end for**

2.5 COMPARATIVE STUDY

In this section, we have discussed the comparative study of different SVMs. The results are discussed from the literature and from our experimental study.

2.5.1 Results from Literature

According to literature, LIBLINEAR [38], Pegasos [118] and SVM^{perf} [62] are the state of the art solvers with LIBLINEAR being the most efficient [38], popular and widely used. LIBLINEAR uses TRON (Trust Region Newton method, [85]) to solve L2 regularized L2 loss primal SVM, PCD (Primal Coordinate Descent, [22]) to solve L1 regularized L2 loss primal SVM and DCD (Dual Coordinate Descent, [53]) algorithm to solve L2-regularized L1- and L2-loss dual SVM. SVM^{perf} uses cutting plane technique to solve L2-regularized L1-loss primal SVM, and Pegasos uses an algorithm which alternates between gradient descent steps and projection steps to solve L2-regularized L1-loss primal SVM. The comparisons of these state of the art solvers have been presented in the Fig. 1 of Section 4 in [38] (refer to latest version), which compares training time against testing accuracy for different linear solvers. Recently, [101] have proposed an SVM-ALM (Augmented Lagrange Multipliers) algorithm to solve L2-regularized L1-, L2- and Lp norm loss primal problem with linear computational cost, to tackle the big data challenge. SVM-ALM is faster than LIBLINEAR, and experimental results are reported in Table 1 and 2 of Section 4 in [101]. SVM-ALM uses gradient descent method for finding step direction and exact line search for finding the step size. The beauty of SVM-ALM algorithm is in transforming the Lp loss primal SVM problem using Augmented Lagrange Multipliers into a form which is very easy to solve. This highlights the point that it is not only a method but many other factors (refer to beginning of Section 2.4 for such factors) which make an algorithm efficient.

2.5.2 Results from Experimental Study

2.5.2.1 Experimental Setup and Implementation Details

The experiments have been performed on two datasets, namely, mushroom and rcv1, on single node MacBook Air (8 GB 1600 MHz DDR3, 1.6 GHz Intel Core i5, 256 SSD). Each dataset has been divided randomly into 80% and 20% for training data and test data, respectively. The experiments compare seven prominent variants of SVM, named, Soft SVM, Smooth SVM, Least Squares SVM, Twin SVM, Eν-SVM, Proximal SVM and Capped SVM, using two criteria of test accuracy versus epochs (one epoch refers to one pass through the dataset) and test accuracy versus training time (in seconds). For fair comparison, primal formulation of SVMs have been solved using same algorithmic structure/framework with differences only in the problem formulations and corresponding gradient values. The training algorithm uses mini-batch SGD (Stochastic Gradient Descent) method [148] to determine the step direction with decreasing step size, determined by $d_0/(1 + d_0 C k)$, for the kth epoch with initial step size d_0 and regularization parameter C. The training algorithm uses mini-batch size of five randomly selected data points. The problem formulations for each SVM uses squared slack variable, i.e., squared error for fair comparison, e.g., using L2-loss in Soft SVM instead of L1-loss. Further, regularization parameter (C) has been set to 0.1 for all the C-SVMs, including both subproblems of Twin SVM and parameter ν has been set to 0.06 (mushroom) and 0.006 (rcv1.binary) for ν-SVM. For Smooth SVM, the smoothing parameter (α) has been set to five and for Capped lp norm SVM, p is set to two and capping value ϵ is set to one. Since Twin SVM has two subproblems so the training time and epochs for Twin SVM has been taken as the sum of time and sum of epochs taken by subproblems, respectively.

2.5.2.2 Results and Discussions

First, this is to be noted that there are several challenges in comparative study of different SVMs and they are: (a) different scope and applications areas of different SVMs, e.g., SloppySVM is useful for applications where data is sloppily labeled; Transductive SVM is specifically proposed for text classification problems; Fuzzy SVM and CappedSVM are suitable for applications where data contains noise and data outliers; Structured SVM is useful for applications where the output labels are structured like strings; MVSVM and MTSVM are used for multi-view learning and multi-task learning, respectively, etc.; (b) Direct improvements of one over other, e.g., Soft SVM is an improvement over Hard SVM, Eν-SVM is an improvement over ν-SVM etc.; (c) Binary and multi-class data, e.g., Soft SVM, Least Square SVM and Smooth SVM are mainly binary classifiers which have been extended to multi-class data using one-vs-one, one-vs-all etc.; and (d) every problem can't be solved using every solver. One interesting point about solving a specific SVM problem formulation is that being an optimization problem, each problem can be solved using a number of methods. Different factors play role in the selection of a solver for a specific SVM, as discussed at the beginning of Section 2.4. Thus, only prominent variants of binary primal SVMs have been studied experimentally using mini-batch SGD method. For the comparative study of multi-class SVMs, refer to Tables V.2 to V.4 of Section V in [55]. One another interesting point is that from the experimental results, we can't generalize that a particular SVM is the best. This is as per the 'no free lunch' theorem, and the point that there are several trade-offs and factors (see, Section 2.4) that we have to be considered while solving SVMs.

The experimental results[2] are represented by Fig. 2.8, which plot test accuracy versus time (in seconds) and test accuracy versus epochs. For mushroom dataset, Soft SVM, CappedSVM, Smooth SVM and Least Square SVM follow each other closely and give the best result on accuracy versus epoch. But for accuracy versus time, Soft SVM outperforms other SVMs, then followed by CappedSVM. For rcv1.binary dataset, Soft SVM outperforms other SVMs, followed by Least Square SVM and then remaining SVMs. Thus, it is clear from the experiments that Soft SVM gives the best generalization results with respect to both training time and number of epochs, and perhaps that's why Soft SVM is the most popular and widely used SVM problem formulation. Further, it is clear from the results that Twin SVM and Eν-SVM does not perform well on given datasets, and Twin SVM lags far behind on mushroom dataset.

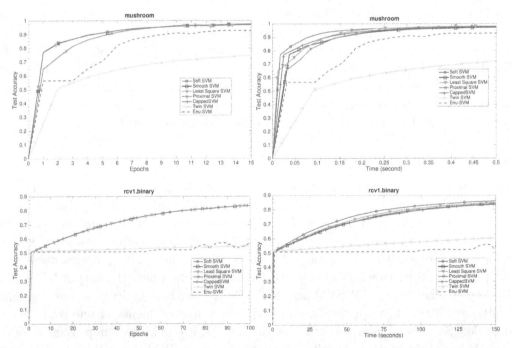

FIGURE 2.8 First row: mushroom (*#instances: 8124, #features: 112*), second row: rcv1, (*#instances: 20,242, #features: 47,236.*)

---

[2]for detailed experiments please check the paper [25]

2.6 CURRENT CHALLENGES AND RESEARCH DIRECTIONS

2.6.1 Big Data Challenge

With the advancements in the technology, data has taken the form of 'Big Data' and the meaning of 'big' in big data is continuously changing and will continue to change. Earlier, few hundred instances were considered to be a large dataset because of the limited computing resources and limited data available at that time. Later, meaning of large dataset changed to thousands of instances. Now, large dataset refers to millions of instances. In order to make use of this huge data, efficient machine learning algorithms are needed to handle these large datasets. Moreover, these algorithms are also needed to be scalable to deal with increasing sizes of datasets. *Thus, nowadays, the biggest challenge before SVC (which are shared with machine learning) is to develop efficient and scalable learning algorithms to deal with big data.*

To solve the big data challenge, we have identified different areas in SVC, most of which are also common with other areas in machine learning and these are discussed in the next subsection.

2.6.2 Areas of Improvement

Classification is one technique in Machine Learning which is used to assign labels to test data points from a set of predefined values with the help of a model which is trained on labeled data. Mathematically, classification problem is an optimization problem where margin between different classes is maximized while keeping the classification errors minimum. While solving the classification problem, there are two objectives: first, training speed of SVM models on the training data set and second, accuracy of prediction of labels on test data set. So, speed and accuracy are two goals while solving the classification problems but there is a trade-off between the speed and accuracy of algorithms. If simple algorithms are used to increase the speed then it does not give good accuracy of classification. On the other hand when complex algorithms are used for training the model, it increases the accuracy but training speed decreases, e.g., Steepest Descent method is fast but its convergence rate is slow as compared with Newton method. It depends upon the application, whether to sacrifice speed or accuracy. Both training speed and test accuracy of an algorithm depends upon these factors: Problem Formulations, Problem Solvers, framework/platform utilization and optimization strategies, as depicted in Fig. 2.9. So to make Linear SVM classification efficient and scalable, the challenge is to handle these factors effectively.

2.6.2.1 Problem Formulations

Problem formulation is very important in SVM, the solvers to be used in an SVM problem also depends on problem formulation to some extent. SVM can be formulated as convex [77] as well as non-convex optimization problem [126]. Generally SVM is formulated as a convex optimization problem because there is no problem of local minimum as every local minimum is a global minimum. SVC optimization problem has two components: margin and loss functions/errors. The trade-off between margin and errors is controlled by parameter C.

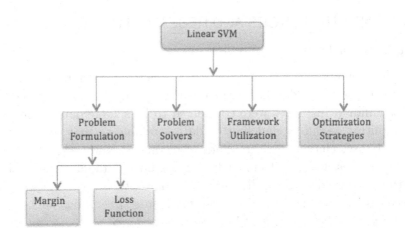

FIGURE 2.9 Improvement areas for Linear SVM Classification.

(a) Margin:
This component is used to control the distance between separating hyperplanes. Larger the margin, better is the generalization of classifier. Currently, L1R ($\|w\|$, [153]) and L2R ($\|w\|^2$, [29]) are widely used in the literature for representing margin in the SVM problem.

(b) Loss Functions:
This component introduced in soft margin SVM as a slack variable. It helps to minimize the mis-classification errors of classifier. Commonly, L1 loss [118] and L2 loss [76] functions (refer to, eq. 2.1) are widely used in literature. Other loss functions (e.g., [88]) can be used, it depends upon the problem formulation (refer to [129], for complete list of loss functions).

These two components combined together form the SVM problem (see, Section 2.3 for different problem formulations). So, the current challenge is to make appropriate choices for margin and errors or propose new ones to have an effective SVM problem. Inappropriate formulations can lead to local minimum problems, differentiability issues, slower and less accurate methods.

2.6.2.2 Problem Solvers

Problem Solvers, again play an important role to get faster and accurate results. There are many methods available for solving the optimization problems as discussed in Section 2.4. It depends upon problem formulation (to some extent) as which method is to be used for solving it. From literature, it is observed that different researchers have solved same problem with different solvers, has lead to different results ([85, 65] solve the same problem). Today challenge is to find efficient solvers which could produce accurate and faster results.

2.6.2.3 Problem Solving Strategies/Approaches

Approaches play a critical role in solving an SVM problem using an SVM solver. The problem formulation may be very good and problem solver may be very efficient too but still our algorithm may not perform well, due to lack of suitable optimization strategies e.g., suppose there is large sparse data problem, if sparsity of problem is not utilized then the training of this optimization technique could be very slow. Similarly using decomposition methods, stochastic approximation and problem shrinking etc., can make the problem solving process faster. Some of the strategies for machine learning (SVM) problems are:

(a) Exploit Problem Structures:
   The problem structures like sparsity [125] of the problem can be exploited to make learning more efficient. There are many problems like document classification where most of the features are zero. So, the problem solver should utilize this characteristic, while training the model which can help in faster training of the problem. Similarly, handling the data in memory also affects the SVM solvers like storing data feature wise [38] or instance wise.

(b) Decomposition Approaches:
   According to this approach, the problem is decomposed into smaller problems and then subproblems are solved using some solver to get the solution of original problem [64], e.g., suppose there are 10,000 parameters in a problem, then it could be solved by first taking first 100 parameters, fixing the remaining and solving this subproblem, then next 100 parameters can be solved and repeating this process until all the parameters are solved. This constitutes one iteration, the process can be repeated until convergence. One extreme case of decomposition approach is Coordinate Descent approach [137], according to this approach, problem is solved for one variable, keeping all other variables fixed. This approach of optimization helps in overcoming implementation issues of memory and CPU. No doubt this approach takes more iterations and slower convergence but it makes the problem feasible to implement because with large number of features (variables), it might not be possible to process the algorithm due to large memory and CPU requirements.
   Coordinate descent [38, 137], SMO [106] and Block Optimization [23] are three examples of decomposition approaches. This approach helps in solving the large problems. The general algorithm for Coordinate Descent approach is given in Algorithm 6.

   Advantages of Coordinate Descent approach: Parallel versions are available; No extra storage vector needed; No other pesky parameters are required here; It works well for very large problems and it's easy to implement. Disadvantages of Coordinate Descent approaches: Tricky if single variable optimization is hard; Convergence theory could be very complex; It can be slower near optimum.

Algorithm 6 Coordinate Descent Approach

1: Given: Initial solution $w_0 = \left(w_0^1, w_0^2, ..., w_0^n\right)$.
2: **while** Exit Criteria **do**
3:     Choose index $i \in \{1, 2, ..., n\}$, for the w_k^i to be optimized.
4:     Take w_k^i as a variable and rest variables as constants in objective function f.
5:     Solve the subproblem for w_k^i using some solver:
      $\min_{w_k^i} \; f(w_k)$
6:     Update w_k for the selected coordinate and keep other coordinates fixed.
7: **end while**

(c) Stochastic Approximation Approach:

Generally the parameters are optimized over all the data instances in each iteration but in stochastic approximation [113], the parameters are optimized over one instance at a time. Stochastic Approximation approach makes each iteration independent of data points and reduces the iteration complexity. Thus, this approach is very helpful in solving large-scale problems. This is because instead of going through all instances in the dataset, it takes only one instance during each iteration. There are other variations of this approach as 'mini-batch' approach [29] where instead of taking one instance during each iteration, it takes a subset of training instances.

(d) Problem Shrinking Strategy:

While optimizing different variables (parameters), it is observed that some of the variables does not change or remain zero. Such variables can be left from the optimization process until rest of the variables reach their approximate optimum values. This is called shrinking strategy [38, 66]. In this way, the number of variables to be minimized during intermediate iterations is reduced. This makes the training faster.

So the challenge is to devise new approaches and use existing ones in the problem solvers to make the learning faster and more accurate.

2.6.2.4 Platforms/Frameworks

Platform/Framework represents the environment that supports the execution of the SVM problem. By utilizing this environment, SVM problems can be further improved. From Fig. 2.9., it is clear that for large problems, speed and accuracy depends upon computing framework/platform also. Some examples of using the platform/framework are given below [84]:

(a) Parallel and Distributed Computing:

With the help of parallel computing [136], some tasks can be done in parallel on either multiple cores of a system or on clusters of computers. This makes the training process faster, but obviously inter-communication between different processing units is a bottleneck here.

(b) In Place Memory Calculations:
Reading and writing data takes more time than the processing of data. So, problems which need multi-stage processing, instead of reading and writing the data to disk after every stage, if the consecutive calculations are carried out in the memory then that could make the process faster while dealing with very large data problems. Apache Spark [84] uses the concept of in place memory calculations which makes it approximately 100 times faster than the Hadoop.

So nowadays challenge is to exploit the existing frameworks to make algorithms more efficient.

2.6.3 Research Directions

As per the Fig. 2.9, there are four areas of improvement which can help us in tackling big data problems. Our of these areas, the current research directions in linear SVM classification (which are shared with machine learning) are:

2.6.3.1 Stochastic Approximation Algorithms

For last five years, there have been extensive research in this area (refer to Subsection 2.6.2.3 for Stochastic Approximation Approach). Researchers have come up with a large number of algorithms using stochastic approximations (SA), especially with first order methods like gradient descent (GD) method [120, 115] as a solver. In addition, SA has also been used with second order methods like quasi-Newton [19]. SA with GD forms stochastic gradient descent (SGD) method and leads to variance problem in the gradient values. So, the research around SGD has been focused around reducing variance (e.g., [23]). On the other hand, research around SA with second order methods has been focused on incorporating curvature information in method for faster convergence. This approach is suitable to solve problems with large number of data points.

2.6.3.2 Coordinate Descent Algorithms

This is one of the decompositional approach (refer to Subsection 2.6.2.3) for dealing with big data problems. For last few years, there has been good work in this area also. Coordinate Descent (CD) approach formulates a subproblem by taking one parameter as a variable and rest as constants, which is much smaller and thus much easier to solve. A lot of algorithms have been proposed using CD approach [137] and its variations like block coordinate descent [90], with first order and seconder methods. This is generally applied to high dimensional primal or dual problems.

2.6.3.3 Proximal Algorithms

Proximal algorithms (PA) [104] are suitable for non-smooth, constrained, large-scale, or distributed convex problems and recently, they produced good results with high dimensional optimization problems. With PA, the main operation is to calculate the proximity operator (refer to Subsection 2.4.14) where we solve a small optimization problem. Current research has been involved in using PA for first order methods (like proximal gradient method [28]), second order methods (like quasi-Newton methods [7]) and their accelerated versions [147].

2.6.3.4 Parallel/Distributed Algorithms

Parallel and distributed algorithms [84] utilize the computing resources to handle the big data problems (like CPU cores of a system and clusters of computers) and can work with problems where datasets are extremely large and can't fit onto a single machine. The major bottleneck in these algorithms is the communication overhead. Researchers have been working on it for a long but still there is lot of scope in this area. This seems to be the hottest area in machine learning to handle the big data problems and in the coming time, research will probably focus in this direction because of increasing dataset sizes which eventually can go beyond the capability of single machine.

2.6.3.5 Hybrid Algorithms

Hybrid algorithms combine two or more of the above approaches. It is obvious that if we want to develop efficient and scalable algorithms to tackle big data problems, all these approaches have to be combined together. A lot of research is already going in this direction also, like, combination of stochastic approximation and coordinate descent approaches have been studied in [23].

2.7 CONCLUSION

Linear SVM is a very good tool in machine learning because this is much faster than non-linear Kernel SVM and at the same time, provides similar accuracy for high dimensional problems like document classification. Researchers have proposed a variety of SVM problem formulations, along with solvers and optimization strategies to solve them. Some of them are improvements over the other, like, 'Soft SVM' is an improvement over the 'Hard SVM'. Some of the SVMs have different contexts of application, like, SloppySVM is useful for applications where data is sloppily labeled; Transductive SVM is specifically proposed for text classification problems; Fuzzy SVM and CappedSVM are suitable for applications where data contains noise and data outliers; Structured SVM is useful for applications where the output labels are structured like strings; MVSVM and MTSVM are used for multi-view learning and multi-task learning, respectively, etc. Some of the SVMs are binary classifiers and need techniques like one-versus-one and one-versus-rest etc., to handle the multi-class problems, e.g., Soft SVM, Fuzzy SVM and Twin SVM etc. Some SVMs can handle the multi-class data using direct formulations like Crammer Singer SVM and Weston Watkins SVM. Amongst all the SVMs, Soft margin SVM or Soft SVM is the most popular and widely used SVM formulation due to faster training and better generalization results. That's why when one refers to SVM that means the Soft SVM.

According to literature, SVM-ALM is the fastest primal solver and LIBLINEAR is the most popular and widely used tool which provides primal and dual, both solvers and uses TRON, PCD (Primal Coordinate Descent) and DCD (Dual Coordinate Descent) methods.

Nowadays, the biggest challenge before machine learning is to develop efficient and scalable learning algorithms to deal with 'Big Data'. To solve this challenge, extensive research is going in four directions: stochastic approximation algorithms, coordinate descent algorithms, proximal algorithms and parallel and distributed algorithms. First two, stochastic approximation and coordinate descent algorithms, try to reduce the problem size and computations by considering fewer parameters or fewer instances during each iteration of learning algorithm. Proximal algorithms are used for solving large non-smooth convex problems with separable components and parallel and distributed algorithms try to exploit the computing resources to handle big data problems. Amongst these, parallel and distributed computing looks to have a great future scope.

II

FIRST ORDER METHODS

CHAPTER 3

Mini-batch and Block-coordinate Approach

B ig Data problems in Machine Learning have large number of data points or large number of features, or both, which make training of models difficult because of high computational complexities of single iteration of learning algorithms. To solve such learning problems, Stochastic Approximation offers an optimization approach to make complexity of each iteration independent of number of data points by taking only one data point or mini-batch of data points during each iteration and thereby helping to solve problems with large number of data points. Similarly, Coordinate Descent offers another optimization approach to make iteration complexity independent of the number of features/coordinates/variables by taking only one feature or block of features, instead of all, during an iteration and thereby helping to solve problems with large number of features. In this chapter, an optimization framework, namely, Batch Block Optimization Framework has been developed to solve big data problems using the best of Stochastic Approximation as well as the best of Coordinate Descent approaches, independent of any solver. This framework is used to solve strongly convex and smooth empirical risk minimization problem with gradient descent (as a solver) and two novel Stochastic Average Adjusted Gradient methods have been proposed to reduce variance in mini-batch and block-coordinate setting of the developed framework. Theoretical analysis prove linear convergence of the proposed methods and empirical results with bench marked datasets prove the superiority of proposed methods against existing methods.

3.1 INTRODUCTION

Big data problems have multiple aspects and one of them is the size/volume of data, i.e., big data problems have large number of data points or large number of features for each data point, or both, which pose a major challenge to machine learning to train models on the large datasets because of high computational cost of each iteration of the learning algorithms. This high iteration complexity is because of solving for all the variables (features) over all data points during each iteration of the learning algorithms. Since every computer has limited capability, each iteration might be very expensive or even infeasible to process. One another interesting point about big data is that its meaning, i.e., what is big in 'big data' is not fixed since dataset sizes are continuously growing. So, to solve big data problems, we need not only efficient learning algorithms to deal with high iteration complexity but also scalable learning algorithms to tackle growing size of datasets.

This chapter solves Empirical Risk Minimization (ERM) problem which consists of average of losses over all data points. For training data $\{(x_1, y_1), (x_2, y_2), ..., (x_l, y_l)\}$, where $x_i \in \mathbb{R}^p$, $y_i \in \{-1, +1\}$, $\forall i$, l is the number of data points, p is the number of features in each data point, and l or p, or both are assumed to be large. ERM problem is given below:

$$\min_{w} f(w), \quad f(w) = \frac{1}{l} \sum_{i=1}^{l} L_i(w, x_i, y_i) \tag{3.1}$$

where $w \in \mathbb{R}^p$ is parameter vector and L_i are loss functions for $i = 1, 2, ..., l$. We assume strong convexity and smoothness of ERM problem so L2 regularization can be used as given below:

$$f(w) = \frac{1}{l} \sum_{i=1}^{l} L_i(w, x_i, y_i) + \frac{C}{2} \|w\|^2, \tag{3.2}$$

where C is a regularization constant. For example, for logistic regression eq.(3.2) can be written as:

$$\min_{w} f(w), \quad f(w) = \frac{1}{l} \sum_{i=1}^{l} log(1 + exp(-y_i w^T x_i)) + \frac{C}{2} \|w\|^2, \tag{3.3}$$

where for the sake of simplicity, regularization can be hidden inside loss function, as $L_i(w, x_i, y_i) = log(1 + exp(-y_i w^T x_i)) + \frac{C}{2} \|w\|^2, \forall i$.

3.1.1 Motivation

In big data problems, high iteration complexity is due to dependency on all data points (l) and on all features (p), during each iteration of the learning algorithms. To reduce high iteration complexity, one approach is to use Stochastic approximation (SA, [113, 67]) which is an iterative optimization approach to solve optimization problems which cannot be solved directly but using approximations. In machine learning problems, it is computationally very expensive, and might be infeasible in some cases, to use all data points in each iteration of learning algorithms. So, SA is used which makes each iteration independent of l by considering one data point or mini-batch of data points, i.e., instead of going through all data points, only one data point or mini-batch of data points are processed in each iteration which makes a large computational difference for large values of l. Similarly, remaining data points can be used in mini-batches during other iterations. Thus, SA is computationally very efficient optimization approach to deal with large-scale problems with large number of data points because of using one data point or mini-batch of data points instead of using all data, during each iteration of approximation method. No doubt that might affect the accuracy of solution, which can be compensated by using larger mini-batches and other techniques like SAG [74] and SAGA [35] etc. But, SA might not be suitable for problems with large number of features (in each data point), because each iteration, in spite of being independent of l, is still dependent over p. Coordinate Descent (CD, [137]) offers another optimization approach to solve large-scale problems with large number of features. CD is a recursive approach to solve optimization problems by approximate minimization along coordinate directions or coordinate hyperplanes, i.e., it recursively solves small subproblems consisting of only one or few variables. As SA makes iteration complexity independent of l, similarly, CD makes iteration complexity independent of p by considering one feature or block of features as variables, fixing the rest features and solving the reduced subproblem thus formed. Then, new one feature or block of features are selected as variables while fixing the rest and resulting subproblem is solved. This process is repeated until all subproblems covering all features are solved, then whole process is repeated until convergence. Thus, CD is a good approach to solve large-scale problems with large number of features but again might not be sufficient to solve problems with large number of data points. So, it is observed that SA makes each iteration independent of l, but still, each iteration depends on p so SA is suitable for problems with large l but might not be suitable for problems with large values of p. On the other hand, CD makes each iteration independent of p, but still, each iteration depends on l so CD is suitable for problems with large values of p but might not be suitable for problems with large values of l. Thus, an optimization framework (see, Subsection 3.1.2) can be developed to solve big data problems, which makes use of best of SA as well as best of CD. In this framework, each iteration is independent of both l and p by considering only one data point or mini-batch of data points with one feature or block of features, i.e., each iteration solves a reduced subproblem of one feature or block of features over one data point or mini-batch of data points. Thus, whatever is the size of the problem, the iteration complexity is very low, making this framework efficient and scalable for solving big data problems. By considering suitable mini-batch of data points and a block of coordinates during each iteration, the framework can be further improved.

Let's apply the above stated ideas of SA and CD approaches to Gradient Descent (GD) method to understand how computational complexity of a single iteration is reduced to make each iteration simple and feasible. For solving problem given in eq.(3.1), the parameter update rule for $(k+1)^{th}$ iteration using GD method is given by

$$w^{k+1} = w^k - \alpha f'(w^k) = w^k - \frac{\alpha}{l} \sum_{i=1}^{l} L_i'(w^k, x_i, y_i) \qquad (3.4)$$

where α is the step size and L_i' is gradient of loss function. The computational complexity of this iteration is $O(lp)$ which is dependent on l and p both thus it would be very expensive and might be even infeasible for large values of l or p, or both. GD exhibits linear convergence rate but at the expense of high iteration complexity. Using SA approach with GD method, i.e., Stochastic Gradient Descent (SGD) method

[148], taking only one data point during each iteration, the subproblem and update rule are given by

$$
\begin{aligned}
\min_{w} & \ L_{i_k}(w, x_{i_k}, y_{i_k}), \quad i_k \in \{1, 2, ..., l\}, \\
w^{k+1} &= w^k - \alpha L'_{i_k}(w^k, x_{i_k}, y_{i_k}), \quad i_k \in \{1, 2, ..., l\}
\end{aligned}
\tag{3.5}
$$

where i_k is randomly selected data point. In SGD, computational complexity of iteration is $O(p)$ which is much smaller than GD method as it considers only one data point and it exhibits linear convergence rate [114] but solution is less accurate as compared to GD due to variance in the gradient values of SGD and GD which can be reduced either by using mini-batches of data points [81] in each iteration or using variance reduction methods, like SAG [74], SAGA [35], S2GD [71] and SVRG [63] etc.

For CD approach with GD method, i.e., for Coordinate Gradient Descent (CGD) method taking only one coordinate while keeping others fixed following subproblem and update rule are obtained:

$$
\begin{aligned}
\min_{w_j} & \ f(w_j, w_{/j}), \quad j = 1, 2, ..., p, \\
w_j^{k+1} &= w_j^k - \alpha \left[f'(w_{<j}^{k+1}, w_{\geq j}^k) \right]_j, \quad j = 1, 2, ..., p,
\end{aligned}
\tag{3.6}
$$

where w_j^k means j^{th} coordinate/variable of w^k, $w_{/j}^k$ means coordinates of w^k excluding j^{th}, $\left[f'(.) \right]_j$ denotes partial derivative w.r.t. j^{th} variable, $w_{<j}^{k+1}$ denotes variables of w^{k+1} which are already computed and $w_{\geq j}^k$ denotes variables of w^k that have not yet to be advanced to iteration $(k + 1)$ along with j^{th} variable being updated, i.e., eq.(3.6) updates coordinates in Gauss-Seidel-like manner. CGD is dependent on only one variable and still exhibits linear convergence rate [100, 137]. For CGD method computational complexity of iteration is $O(l)$ which is much smaller than GD method. Now, by combining SA and CD for GD method, i.e., eqs.(3.5) and (3.6), following subproblem and update rule are obtained:

$$
\begin{aligned}
\min_{w_j} & \ L_{i_k}(w_j, w_{/j}, x_{i_k}, y_{i_k}), \quad j = 1, 2, ..., p, \ i_k \in \{1, 2, ..., l\}, \\
w_j^{k+1} &= w_j^k - \alpha \left[L'_{i_k}(w_{<j}^{k+1}, w_{\geq j}^k) \right]_j, \quad j = 1, 2, ..., p, \ i_k \in \{1, 2, ..., l\},
\end{aligned}
\tag{3.7}
$$

which solves subproblem with one variable over one data point and thus have constant computational complexity of iteration as $O(1)$. Thus, combination of SA and CD provide an efficient and scalable solution to solve big data problems of any size.

3.1.2 Batch Block Optimization Framework (BBOF)

SA approach is used to solve the optimization problem by considering one or some of data points during each iteration which helps to reduce the iteration complexity but affects the accuracy of solution. But by considering suitable mini-batches of data points [81] in each iteration or using variance reduction techniques, like, SAG [74], SAGA [35], S2GD [71] and SVRG [63] etc., solutions can be improved. On the other hand, CD is used to solve the optimization problem by considering one or some of the features/variables to formulate a reduced subproblem, which helps to reduce the iteration complexity. By considering, a suitable block of coordinates/variables in CD, during each iteration of learning algorithm, performance can be improved. Now, combining mini-batch SA approach with block CD approach, an optimization framework is formed, which is used to solve a subproblem of block of variables over a mini-batch of data points, during each iteration of learning algorithm. This framework which can be called Batch Block Optimization Framework (BBOF), is an efficient and scalable framework and can be used to solve big data problems because of its low iteration complexity. BBOF is presented by Algorithm 7. Suppose $\{(x_1, y_1), (x_2, y_2), ..., (x_l, y_l)\}$ is the training set with l data points where $x_i \in \mathbb{R}^p$, $y_i \in \{-1, +1\} \ \forall \ i$, $X = (x_1, x_2, ..., x_l)$ and $Y = (y_1, y_2, ..., y_l)$. Suppose $w \in \mathbb{R}^p$ is partitioned into $(v_1, v_2, ..., v_s)$, s blocks, $v_j \in \mathbb{R}^{p_j}$, s.t. $\sum_{j=1}^{s} p_j = p$ and X is partitioned into m mini-batches $(B_1, B_2, ..., B_m)$ of size $|B_i|$ each, s.t. $\sum_{i=1}^{m} |B_i| = l$.

Algorithm 7 Batch Block Optimization Framework (BBOF)

1: **Inputs:** $m = $ #mini-batches, $s = $ #blocks, $n = $ #epochs and $\alpha = $ step size.
2: **Initialize:** w^0
3: **for** $k = 1, 2, ..., n$ **do**
4:     **for** $i = 1, 2, ..., m$ **do**
5:         Randomly select one mini-batch B_i without replacement.
6:         **for** $j = 1, 2, ..., s$ **do**
7:             Cyclically select one block of coordinates v_j.
8:             Formulate a subproblem using block v_j over mini-batch B_i as given in eq.(3.8).
9:             Solve eq.(3.8) and update the solution for block v_j and keep the rest blocks fixed.
10:         **end for**
11:     **end for**
12: **end for**

BBOF divides the given training set into m mini-batches, divides the features into s blocks of features and runs for n epochs, each of which goes through all data points, i.e., it runs over all batches and covers all blocks of features for each mini-batch to avoid the overhead of reading data again and again. It randomly selects one mini-batch of data points B_i without replacement and cyclically selects one block of features v_j. Other sampling schemes can be tried for sampling mini-batches and blocks of features in this framework. But cyclic sampling (CS) is used for blocks of features since it would be difficult otherwise to use sparse implementations. Moreover, as pointed out in [152], methods like, SAG, SAGA, SAAG-I, which use stochastic averaging scheme, i.e., maintain full gradient from previous iterations, can't be used with random sampling of blocks and mini-batches. A subproblem is formulated by taking selected block of coordinates as variables and fixing the values of rest coordinates, over the selected mini-batch of data points as given below:

$$\min_{w_{v_j}} \frac{1}{|B_i|} \sum_{h \in B_i} L_h(w_{v_j}, w_{/v_j}), \quad j = 1, 2, ..., s, \quad i = 1, 2, ..., m, \quad (3.8)$$

where w_{v_j} denotes block of coordinates v_j and $w_{/v_j}$ denotes coordinates excluding v_j. The size of mini-batches and blocks is selected in such a way to allow iteration complexity that can be handled efficiently by computers on which experiments are performed. On solving the subproblem, the selected block of coordinates are updated but other coordinates remains unchanged. This runs for predetermined number of epochs n but other exit criteria can be tried depending up on the method used to solve the subproblem and as per requirements. Before this, the idea of mini-batches and block coordinates is studied by few researchers like [133, 152] and [140] with Gradient/Proximal Gradient methods, but we project mini-batch and block coordinates setting as an optimization framework (BBOF) independent of any method, as an efficient and scalable framework for solving big data problems. BBOF is a tunable framework and can be tuned to eight different settings by changing the values of m (number of mini-batches) and s (number of blocks), e.g., using Gradient Descent method as a solver in BBOF, following different methods can be tuned:

i) $m = 1$, i.e., one batch contains all data points, $s = 1$, i.e., one block contains all coordinates, then method is GD.

ii) $m = l$, i.e., one batch contains only one data point, $s = 1$, then method is SGD.

iii) $m = 1$, $s = p$, i.e., one block contains only one coordinate, then method is CGD.

iv) $m = B$, $1 < B < l$, $s = 1$, then method is mini-batch SGD.

v) $m = B$, $1 < B < l$, $s = p$, then method is mini-batch CGD.

vi) $m = 1$, $s = v$, $1 < v < p$, then method is BCD (Block Coordinate Gradient Descent).

vii) $m = l$, $s = v$, $1 < v < p$, then method is stochastic BCD.

viii) $m = B$, $1 < B < l$, $s = v$, $1 < v < p$, then method is mini-batch block-coordinate GD (MBGD).

3.1.3 Brief Literature Review

Stochastic Approximation (SA) approach [113, 67] used with GD method gives SGD method [148], which introduces variance in the gradient values because of noisy approximations of gradient. This variance can be reduced by using suitable mini-batches [81] instead of using one data point, or by using some variance reduction techniques, like, SAG [74], SAGA [35], SVRG [63] and S2GD [71] etc., which have same convergence as GD but have iteration complexity nearly equal to SGD method. CD approach along with Block Coordinate Descent (BCD) approach have been studied extensively in literature e.g., [100, 137, 122] etc. The combination of BCD and mini-batch SA approach with GD/Proximal GD (PGD) method is studied recently in MRBCD [152], ORBCD [133] and BSG [140], which are specific cases of BBOF with GD/PGD method, used to solve different problems. MRBCD and ORBCD have similar idea and theoretical results. BSG solves for convex and non-convex problems and MRBCD solves only convex problems. Both the methods use variance reduction techniques. MRBCD and BSG use extension of SVRG for variance reduction in mini-batch and block coordinate setting. This chapter uses BBOF with GD method, i.e., mini-batch and block coordinate setting with GD as a solver, and proposes two new variance reduction methods (refer to Section 3.2), in addition to extending SAG, SAGA and S2GD to this setting.

3.1.4   Contributions

The contributions of the chapter are summarized below:

- Mini-batch and block-coordinate setting, i.e., a combination of Stochastic Approximation (SA) and Coordinate Descent (CD) approaches, have been projected as an efficient and scalable optimization framework, namely, Batch Block Optimization Framework (BBOF), independent of any solver, for solving big data problems. BBOF is a tunable framework and can generate eight different methods by changing m (number of mini-batches) and s (number of blocks) values (see, Sub-section 3.1.2).

- Two novel methods, namely, SAAG-I and SAAG-II (see, Section 3.2) have been proposed as a variance reduction methods, under mini-batch and block coordinate setting with GD method and used to solve strongly convex and smooth problem. SAAGs can be used in mini-batched stochastic gradient setting also. Theoretical analysis proves linear convergence for SAAG-II method.

- Variance reduction methods SAG, SAGA, SVRG and S2GD have been extended to mini-batch and block coordinate setting, and compared with the proposed methods.

3.2   STOCHASTIC AVERAGE ADJUSTED GRADIENT (SAAG) METHODS

SAG, SAGA, SVRG, S2GD and proposed SAAG methods are variance reduction techniques for stochastic gradient. It is very interesting to note that they have very small differences in their update rules, as it is clear from their equations given in this section. All these methods calculate one partial gradient over selected mini-batch at latest iterate which gives the latest gradient values, i.e., step direction to move, calculate one partial gradient over selected mini-batch at old iterate and one partial gradient over whole dataset calculated at old iterates which might not give correct step direction to move. Old gradient values help in reducing the variance in expectation but might lead in wrong direction. Our intuition behind proposing SAAGs is to give more weightage to latest gradient values to get better step direction. So, we have divided the latest value of gradient using mini-batch size but old values using number of data points. SAAGs are useful for sufficiently large mini-batches. Our intuitions are followed by the empirical results which clearly show the out-performance of SAAGs over other methods.

In this section, two methods are proposed with two training algorithms, namely, SAAG-I and SAAG-II, both of which use the mini-batch and block-coordinate setting, i.e., BBOF framework. First method is SAAG-I, given by eq.(3.10) and presented by Algorithm 8, which takes m, s and n as input and sets initial solution (w^0) and total gradient $(\mathbb{G})$ to zero vectors. It randomly selects one mini-batch of data points without replacement and cyclically selects one block of coordinates as in BBOF and formulates a reduced subproblem given by eq.(3.8) which is solved using eq.(3.9). The iteration complexity is very low since it calculates two partial gradients w.r.t. selected block of variables over the selected mini-batch of data points and reduces variance by using averaged gradient values calculated using the previous iterations. The parameters are updated for only selected block of coordinates and keeping the rest coordinates unchanged.

SAAG-II method is given by eq.(3.11) and presented by Algorithm 9. SAAG-II

Algorithm 8 SAAG-I

1: **Inputs**: $m = \#$mini-batches, $s = \#$blocks, $n = \#$epochs and $\alpha =$ step size.
2: **Initialize**: solution $w^0 \in \mathbb{R}^p$ and total gradient $\mathbb{G} \in \mathbb{R}^p$ to zero vector.
3: **for** $k = 1, 2, ..., n$ **do**
4:    Set $u^{k,0} = w^{k-1}$.
5:    **for** $i = 1, 2, ..., m$ **do**
6:        Randomly select one mini-batch B_i without replacement.
7:        **for** $j = 1, 2, ..., s$ **do**
8:            Cyclically select one block of coordinates v_j.
9:            Formulate a subproblem using block v_j over mini-batch B_i as given in eq.(3.8).
10:           Calculate: $g_{B_i, v_j} = \sum\limits_{h \in B_i} \left[L'_h \left(u^{k,i}_{<v_j}, u^{k,i-1}_{\geq v_j} \right) \right]_{v_j}$ and $\bar{g}_{B_i, v_j} = \sum\limits_{h \in B_i} \left[L'_h \left(u^{k,0} \right) \right]_{v_j}$.
11:           Update solution as:
12:
$$u^{k,i}_{v_j} = u^{k,i-1}_{v_j} - \alpha \left[\frac{1}{|B_i|} g_{B_i, v_j} - \frac{1}{l} \bar{g}_{B_i, v_j} + [\mathbb{G}]_{v_j} \right], \qquad (3.9)$$
$$u^{k,i}_{/v_j} = u^{k,i-1}_{/v_j}.$$

13:           Update total gradient vector, $[\mathbb{G}]_{v_j} += \frac{1}{l} \left(g_{B_i, v_j} - \bar{g}_{B_i, v_j} \right)$.
14:       **end for**
15:   **end for**
16:   $w^k = u^{k,m}$.
17: **end for**

---

algorithm is similar to SAAG-I and uses BBOF framework to provide an efficient and scalable solution to solve the big data problems. Similar to later, it calculates two partial gradients over the mini-batch of data points and uses one gradient over all data points which is calculated at the start of each epoch for variance reduction. Thus, the difference between SAAG-I and SAAG-II algorithms is only in the value of average gradient calculation, former maintains the value from previous iterations

---

Algorithm 9 SAAG-II

1: **Inputs:** $m = $ #mini-batches, $s = $ #blocks, $n = $ #epochs and $\alpha = $ step size.

2: **Initialize:** solution $w^0 \in \mathbb{R}^p$

3: **for** $k = 1, 2, ..., n$ **do**

4:     Set $u^{k,0} = w^{k-1}$.

5:     Calculate full gradient, $\mathbb{G}$.

6:     **for** $i = 1, 2, ..., m$ **do**

7:         Randomly select one mini-batch B_i without replacement.

8:         **for** $j = 1, 2, ..., s$ **do**

9:             Cyclically select one block of coordinates v_j.

10:            Formulate a subproblem using block v_j over mini-batch B_i as given in eq.(3.8).

11:            Calculate: $g_{B_i,v_j} = \sum_{h \in B_i} \left[L_h' \left(u_{<v_j}^{k,i}, u_{\geq v_j}^{k,i-1} \right) \right]_{v_j}$ and $\bar{g}_{B_i,v_j} = \sum_{h \in B_i} \left[L_h' \left(u^{k,0} \right) \right]_{v_j}$.

12:            Update solution using eq.(3.9).

13:         **end for**

14:     **end for**

15:     $w^k = u^{k,m}$.

16: **end for**

---

starting with zero vector unlike the later which calculates the full gradient at the start of each epoch.

SAG, SAGA, SVRG and S2GD are well known variance reduction methods for SGD setting. SVRG has been extended to mini-batch and block-coordinate setting, for variance reduction, in MRBCD [152] and BSG [140]. In this chapter, SAG, SAGA and S2GD are also extended to this setting for comparing against SAAG methods. To closely study, all these methods in the mini-batch and block-coordinate setting, the parameter update rules are given by eqs. (3.10–3.15), where $u_{v_j}^{k,i}$ denotes the kth parameter update rule for v_j block of coordinates over the ith mini-batch B_i, $u_{<v_j}^{k,i}$ denotes variables of $u^{k,i}$ which are already computed and $u_{\geq v_j}^{k,i-1}$ denotes variables of $u^{k,i-1}$ that have not yet to be advanced to iteration (k, i) along with v_j block of variables being updated. As it is clear from following equations, SAAG-I, like, SAG and SAGA, maintains the full gradient from previous iterations by saving the partial gradients over the mini-batches but SAAG-II, like S2GD and SVRG, calculates the full gradient at the start of the epochs and uses inside the inner loops to reduce the variance in gradient value. S2GD and SVRG have similar parameter update rules, although different learning algorithms, so only SVRG is given.

SAAG-I:

$$u_{v_j}^{k,i} = u_{v_j}^{k,i-1} - \alpha \left[\frac{1}{|B_i|} \sum_{h \in B_i} \left[L_h' \left(u_{<v_j}^{k,i}, u_{\geq v_j}^{k,i-1} \right) \right]_{v_j} - \frac{1}{l} \sum_{h \in B_i} \left[L_h' \left(u^{k,0} \right) \right]_{v_j} \right.$$
$$\left. + \frac{1}{l} \sum_{h=1}^{l} \left[L_h' \left(u_{<v_j}^{k,i}, u_{\geq v_j}^{k,i-1} \right) \right]_{v_j} \right] \tag{3.10}$$

SAAG-II:

$$u_{v_j}^{k,i} = u_{v_j}^{k,i-1} - \alpha \left[\frac{1}{|B_i|} \sum_{h \in B_i} \left[L_h' \left(u_{<v_j}^{k,i}, u_{\geq v_j}^{k,i-1} \right) \right]_{v_j} - \frac{1}{l} \sum_{h \in B_i} \left[L_h' \left(u^{k,0} \right) \right]_{v_j} + \frac{1}{l} \sum_{h=1}^{l} \left[L_h' \left(u^{k,0} \right) \right]_{v_j} \right]$$

(3.11)

SAGA:

$$u_{v_j}^{k,i} = u_{v_j}^{k,i-1} - \alpha \left[\frac{1}{|B_i|} \sum_{h \in B_i} \left[L_h' \left(u_{<v_j}^{k,i}, u_{\geq v_j}^{k,i-1} \right) \right]_{v_j} - \frac{1}{|B_i|} \sum_{h \in B_i} \left[L_h' \left(u^{k,0} \right) \right]_{v_j} \right.$$
$$\left. + \frac{1}{l} \sum_{h=1}^{l} \left[L_h' \left(u_{<v_j}^{k,i}, u_{\geq v_j}^{k,i-1} \right) \right]_{v_j} \right]$$

(3.12)

SAG:

$$u_{v_j}^{k,i} = u_{v_j}^{k,i-1} - \alpha \left[\frac{1}{l} \sum_{h \in B_i} \left[L_h' \left(u_{<v_j}^{k,i}, u_{\geq v_j}^{k,i-1} \right) \right]_{v_j} - \frac{1}{l} \sum_{h \in B_i} \left[L_h' \left(u^{k,0} \right) \right]_{v_j} \right.$$
$$\left. + \frac{1}{l} \sum_{h=1}^{l} \left[L_h' \left(u_{<v_j}^{k,i}, u_{\geq v_j}^{k,i-1} \right) \right]_{v_j} \right]$$

(3.13)

SVRG:

$$u_{v_j}^{k,i} = u_{v_j}^{k,i-1} - \alpha \left[\frac{1}{|B_i|} \sum_{h \in B_i} \left[L_h' \left(u_{<v_j}^{k,i}, u_{\geq v_j}^{k,i-1} \right) \right]_{v_j} - \frac{1}{|B_i|} \sum_{h \in B_i} \left[L_h' \left(u^{k,0} \right) \right]_{v_j} \right.$$
$$\left. + \frac{1}{l} \sum_{h=1}^{l} \left[L_h' \left(u^{k,0} \right) \right]_{v_j} \right]$$

(3.14)

MBGD:

$$u_{v_j}^{k,i} = u_{v_j}^{k,i-1} - \frac{\alpha}{|B_i|} \sum_{h \in B_i} \left[L_h' \left(u_{<v_j}^{k,i}, u_{\geq v_j}^{k,i-1} \right) \right]_{v_j}$$

(3.15)

Complexity Analysis The per-iteration complexity for all the methods is $O(Bv)$ (assuming constant mini-batch size B and block size v), which is controllable as per the machine capability, unlike, complexity $O(lp)$ of GD method which might be infeasible to process. Using same algorithm structure, as given in Algorithm 7, per epoch component gradient evaluations for S2GD, SVRG and SAAG-II are l (calculation of full gradient at start of epoch) + $2l$ ($2Bm$, as $Bm = l$), but for SAG, SAGA and SAAG-I are $2l$ since they maintain full gradient from previous iterations and don't calculate at start of epoch. Technically, later case take only l gradient evaluations per epoch at the expense of saving gradients which need $O(lp)$ extra memory in general but only $O(l)$ memory to solve problem given by eq. (3.3).

3.3 ANALYSIS

Theorem 1 *Suppose for objective function given by eq. (3.1), under the assumptions of μ-strong convexity, component-wise Lipschitz continuity of gradient, constant step size α random sampling without replacement for blocks and random sampling with* *replacement for mini-batches SAAG-II, converges linearly to optimal value p^*, for constant mini-batch size B, constant block size v, as given below,*

$$\mathbb{E}\left[f\left(w^k\right) - p^*\right] \leq \left(1 - \frac{2v\alpha\mu}{p}\right)^k \left(f\left(w^0\right) - p^*\right) + \frac{pR_0^2}{2v\mu}\left(L\alpha\left(3 + \frac{2B^2}{l^2}\right) - 1 + \frac{B}{l}\right)$$

(3.16)

where $\left\|\frac{1}{|B_i|}\sum_{h \in B_i}\left[L_h'(w)\right]_{v_j} e_j\right\| \leq R_0, \forall w, i, j, B_i, v_j$ *and* $e_j(i) = \begin{cases} 1 \; if \; i \in v_j \\ 0 \; else \end{cases}$.

Proof 3.1 *By definition of SAAG method,*

$$f\left(w^{k+1}\right) = f\left(w^k - \alpha G_{B_i,v_j}\right),$$

where $G_{B_i,v_j} = \left[\frac{1}{B}\sum_{h \in B_i}\left[L_h'\left(w^k\right)\right]_{v_j} e_j - \frac{1}{l}\sum_{h \in B_i}\left[L_h'(\tilde{w})\right]_{v_j} e_j + \left[f'(\tilde{w})\right]_{v_j} e_j\right]$ *and*

$e_j(i) = \begin{cases} 1 \; if \; i \in v_j \\ 0 \; else \end{cases}$.

Using Lipschitz continuity of gradient, we have,

$$f\left(w^{k+1}\right) \leq f\left(w^k\right) - \alpha G_{B_i,v_j}^T \left[f'\left(w^k\right)\right]_{v_j} e_j + \frac{L_{i,j}\alpha^2}{2}\left\|G_{B_i,v_j}\right\|^2$$

Subtracting optimal objective value p^* and taking expectation on both sides over mini-batches B_i, we have,

$$\mathbb{E}_i\left[f\left(w^{k+1}\right) - p^*\right] \leq f\left(w^k\right) - p^* - \alpha\mathbb{E}_i\left[G_{B_i,v_j}\right]^T \left[f'\left(w^k\right)\right]_{v_j} e_j$$
$$+ \frac{L_{i,j}\alpha^2}{2}\mathbb{E}_i\left[\left\|G_{B_i,v_j}\right\|^2\right]$$

(3.17)

Now, $\mathbb{E}_i\left[G_{B_i,v_j}\right] = \frac{1}{B}\mathbb{E}_i\left[\sum_{h \in B_i}\left[L_h'\left(w^k\right)\right]_{v_j} e_j\right] - \frac{1}{l}\mathbb{E}_i\left[\sum_{h \in B_i}\left[L_h'(\tilde{w})\right]_{v_j} e_j\right]$

$$+ \left[f'(\tilde{w})\right]_{v_j} e_j$$

$$= \frac{1}{B} \cdot \frac{1}{m}\sum_{i=1}^m \sum_{h \in B_i}\left[L_h'\left(w^k\right)\right]_{v_j} e_j - \frac{1}{l} \cdot \frac{1}{m}\sum_{i=1}^m \sum_{h \in B_i}\left[L_h'(\tilde{w})\right]_{v_j} e_j$$

$$+ \left[f'(\tilde{w})\right]_{v_j} e_j$$

$$= \frac{1}{l}\sum_{h=1}^l \left[L_h'\left(w^k\right)\right]_{v_j} e_j - \frac{1}{ml}\sum_{h=1}^l \left[L_h'(\tilde{w})\right]_{v_j} e_j + \left[f'(\tilde{w})\right]_{v_j} e_j$$

$$= \left[f'\left(w^k\right)\right]_{v_j} e_j - \frac{1}{m}\left[f'(\tilde{w})\right]_{v_j} e_j + \left[f'(\tilde{w})\right]_{v_j} e_j,$$

because of $mB = l$, *and*

$$\mathbb{E}_i \left[G_{B_i, v_j} \right]^T \left[f'(w^k) \right]_{v_j} e_j = \left(\left[f'(w^k) \right]_{v_j} e_j + \left(1 - \frac{1}{m} \right) \left[f'(\tilde{w}) \right]_{v_j} e_j \right)^T \left[f'(w^k) \right]_{v_j} e_j$$

$$\leq \left\| \left[f'(w^k) \right]_{v_j} e_j \right\|^2 + \left(1 - \frac{1}{m} \right) \left\| \left[f'(w^k) \right]_{v_j} e_j \right\|$$

$$\times \left\| \left[f'(\tilde{w}) \right]_{v_j} e_j \right\|,$$

because of using $\|ab\| \leq \|a\| \|b\|$.

$$\implies \mathbb{E}_i \left[G_{B_i, v_j} \right]^T \left[f'(w^k) \right]_{v_j} e_j = \left\| \left[f'(w^k) \right]_{v_j} e_j \right\|^2 + \left(1 - \frac{1}{m} \right) R_0^2, \qquad (3.18)$$

[because of taking $\left\| \frac{1}{|B_i|} \sum_{h \in B_i} \left[L'_h(w) \right]_{v_j} e_j \right\| \leq R_0 \quad \forall \, w, i, j, B_i, v_j$*].*

$$\mathbb{E}_i \left[\left\| G_{B_i, v_j} \right\|^2 \right] = \mathbb{E}_i \left[\left\| \left[\frac{1}{B} \sum_{h \in B_i} \left[L'_h(w^k) \right]_{v_j} e_j - \frac{1}{l} \sum_{h \in B_i} \left[L'_h(\tilde{w}) \right]_{v_j} e_j + \left[f'(\tilde{w}) \right]_{v_j} e_j \right] \right\|^2 \right]$$

$$\leq 2 \mathbb{E}_i \left[\left\| \left[\frac{1}{B} \sum_{h \in B_i} \left[L'_h(w^k) \right]_{v_j} e_j - \frac{1}{l} \sum_{h \in B_i} \left[L'_h(\tilde{w}) \right]_{v_j} e_j \right] \right\|^2 \right]$$

$$+ 2 \mathbb{E}_i \left[\left\| \left[f'(\tilde{w}) \right]_{v_j} e_j \right\|^2 \right],$$

because of using $\|a + b\|^2 \leq 2\|a\|^2 + \|b\|^2$.

$$\mathbb{E}_i \left[\left\| G_{B_i, v_j} \right\|^2 \right] \leq 4 \mathbb{E}_i \left[\left\| \left[\frac{1}{B} \sum_{h \in B_i} \left[L'_h(w^k) \right]_{v_j} e_j \right] \right\|^2 \right]$$

$$+ 4 \mathbb{E}_i \left[\left\| \left[\frac{B}{l} \cdot \frac{1}{B} \sum_{h \in B_i} \left[L'_h(\tilde{w}) \right]_{v_j} e_j \right] \right\|^2 \right] + 2 \mathbb{E}_i \left[\left\| \left[f'(\tilde{w}) \right]_{v_j} e_j \right\|^2 \right],$$

$$\implies \mathbb{E}_i \left[\left\| G_{B_i, v_j} \right\|^2 \right] = 4 R_0^2 + \frac{4B^2}{l^2} R_0^2 + 2 R_0^2 = 6 R_0^2 + \frac{4}{m^2} R_0^2 \qquad (3.19)$$

Substituting the values of eqs. (3.18) and (3.19) in eq. (3.17) and taking $\max_{i,j} L_{i,j} = L$, *we have,*

$$\mathbb{E}_i \left[f(w^{k+1}) - p^* \right]$$

$$\leq f(w^k) - p^* - \alpha \left\| \left[f'(w^k) \right]_{v_j} e_j \right\|^2 - \alpha \left(1 - \frac{1}{m} \right) R_0^2 + \frac{L\alpha^2}{2} \left(6 R_0^2 + \frac{4}{m^2} R_0^2 \right)$$

$$\leq f(w^k) - p^* - \alpha \left\| \left[f'(w^k) \right]_{v_j} e_j \right\|^2 + \alpha R_0^2 \left(L\alpha \left(3 + \frac{2}{m^2} \right) - 1 + \frac{1}{m} \right)$$

Taking expectation over the blocks v_j, *we have,*

$$\mathbb{E}_{i,j} \left[f(w^{k+1}) - p^* \right]$$

$$\leq f(w^k) - p^* - \alpha \mathbb{E}_j \left[\left\| \left[f'(w^k) \right]_{v_j} e_j \right\|^2 \right] + \alpha R_0^2 \left(L\alpha \left(3 + \frac{2}{m^2} \right) - 1 + \frac{1}{m} \right)$$

Since $\mathbb{E}_j \left[\left\| \left[f'(w^k) \right]_{v_j} e_j \right\|^2 \right] = \dfrac{1}{s} \sum_{j=1}^{s} \left\| \left[f'(w^k) \right]_{v_j} e_j \right\|^2 = \dfrac{1}{s} \left\| f'(w^k) \right\|^2$ *and because of*

strong convexity $f(w^k) - p^* \leq \dfrac{1}{2\mu} \left\| f'(w^k) \right\|^2.$

$$\implies \mathbb{E}_{i,j} \left[f(w^{k+1}) - p^* \right]$$

$$\leq f(w^k) - p^* - \frac{2\alpha\mu}{s} \left(f(w^k) - p^* \right) + \alpha R_0^2 \left(L\alpha \left(3 + \frac{2}{m^2} \right) - 1 + \frac{1}{m} \right)$$

$$\leq \left(1 - \frac{2\alpha\mu}{s} \right) \left(f(w^k) - p^* \right) + \alpha R_0^2 \left(L\alpha \left(3 + \frac{2}{m^2} \right) - 1 + \frac{1}{m} \right)$$

Applying this inequality recursively and taking expectation, after simplifying we have,

$$\mathbb{E}_{i,j} \left[f(w^{k+1}) - p^* \right]$$

$$\leq \left(1 - \frac{2\alpha\mu}{s} \right)^{k+1} \left(f(w^0) - p^* \right) + \alpha R_0^2 \left(L\alpha \left(3 + \frac{2}{m^2} \right) - 1 + \frac{1}{m} \right) \sum_{t=0}^{k} \left(1 - \frac{2\alpha\mu}{s} \right)^t$$

Since $\sum_{t=0}^{k} r^t \leq \sum_{t=0}^{\infty} r^t = \dfrac{1}{1-r}, \quad 1 > r > 0,$

$$\implies \mathbb{E}_{i,j} \left[f(w^{k+1}) - p^* \right]$$

$$\leq \left(1 - \frac{2\alpha\mu}{s} \right)^{k+1} \left(f(w^0) - p^* \right) + \alpha R_0^2 \left(L\alpha \left(3 + \frac{2}{m^2} \right) - 1 + \frac{1}{m} \right) \cdot \frac{s}{2\alpha\mu}$$

$$\leq \left(1 - \frac{2\alpha\mu}{s} \right)^{k+1} \left(f(w^0) - p^* \right) + \frac{s R_0^2}{2\mu} \left(L\alpha \left(3 + \frac{2}{m^2} \right) - 1 + \frac{1}{m} \right)$$

$$\implies \mathbb{E}_{i,j} \left[f(w^k) - p^* \right]$$

$$\leq \left(1 - \frac{2v\alpha\mu}{p} \right)^{k} \left(f(w^0) - p^* \right) + \frac{p R_0^2}{2v\mu} \left(L\alpha \left(3 + \frac{2B^2}{l^2} \right) - 1 + \frac{B}{l} \right) \qquad (3.20)$$

[because of $p = vs$, $l = Bm$ and replacing $k+1$ with k]
Thus, algorithm converges linearly.

3.4 NUMERICAL EXPERIMENTS

In this section, experimental results[1] are provided and proposed methods, SAAG-I and SAAG-II, are compared against the variance reduction techniques, like, BSG [140], MRBCD [152] and extensions of SAG [74], SAGA [35], SVRG [63] and S2GD [71] to mini-batch and block-coordinate setting. MBGD (Mini-batch Block-coordinate Gradient Descent) which is a simple method without any variance reduction is also considered as presented in eq.(3.15).

3.4.1 Experimental Setup

In this experimentation, logistic regression problem, given in eq.(3.3) is solved. Since BSG and MRBCD use SVRG for variance reduction, thus under our experimental

---

[1] for detailed experiments, please refer to paper [23]

settings BSG, MRBCD and extension of SVRG to mini-batch and block-coordinate setting become same so only SVRG is mentioned in the experiments. All the methods use the same algorithmic structure as given in Algorithm (7) with changes only in update rule (variance reduction method) at Step 9. All the methods use averaged gradient value for variance reduction, calculated either at start of epochs or maintained from previous iterations. To store the full gradient only a vector of length l is used since it stores only constant value for each data point instead of storing the complete gradient vector which will take $l * p$ memory space. Step size is calculated using two different methods, namely, back tracking line search method and constant step size determined using Lipschitz constant. It is interesting to note that in backtracking line search using all data points for big data problems can be very expensive so backtracking line search is performed only on selected mini-batch with parameter values as $\beta = 0.5$ (to decrease the step size) and $\gamma = 0.1$ (i.e., allow 10% decrease of objective function) for all methods. With Lipschitz constant L, step size is taken as $1/L$ for all the methods. This is to be noted that all experiments have been conducted on *single node, MacBook Air (8 GB 1600 MHz DDR3, 1.6 GHz Intel Core i5, 256 SSD)*. For all methods, regularization parameter is set as $C = 1/l$.

3.4.2 Convergence against Epochs

Figure 3.1 presents the experimental results with bench marked datasets (details of datasets are given in the Table 1.1), with different mini-batch and block sizes. Figures plot the difference of objective function and optimum value against the number of epochs. Following observations can be made from the experimental results:

(i) In general, SAAG methods, i.e., SAAG-I and SAAG-II, converges faster than other solvers with SAAG-II outperforms all other methods.

(ii) In general, with increase in size of the mini-batch and block, SAAG methods perform better as compared with rest of the solvers, but for smaller sizes, e.g., with mini-batch of one data point they don't perform.

(iii) Results with line search method and using Lipschitz constant to determine the step size give similar results and prove the superiority of SAAG methods over others.

(iv) As expected from equations of different solvers, when block size is equal to #features and mini-batch size is equal to #data points, i.e., in GD method setting all methods converge exactly same (due to space constraints figure is not included).

(v) Plots of sub-optimality against time shows similar results as shown for sub-optimality against epochs (refer to Subsection 3.4.3 for results).

(vi) Line search results are smoother than constant step size. Moreover, line search results are better than constant step for SUSY but for other datasets, constant step size gives better results. Major reason for this is the larger step size obtained using Lipschitz constant which is sometimes even greater than one but for line search maximum size is one which keeps on decreasing and other possible reason is that the line search is performed on selected mini-batch and not on full dataset.

(vii) SUSY has only 18 features so block size has been taken equal to number of features, moreover for webspam all features has been taken. These experiments form

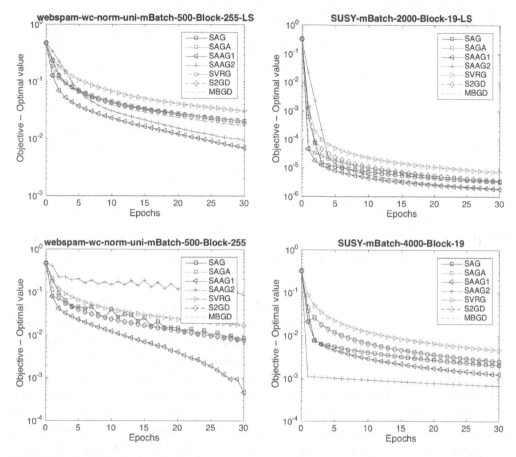

FIGURE 3.1 Results with line search method (on first row) and with constant step size (on second row).

mini-batched stochastic gradient setting and prove the effectiveness of SAAGs for this setting also, and algorithms and formulas can be obtained for this setting by setting $v = p$.

3.4.3 Convergence against Time

In the experiments depicted with Fig. 3.2, the difference of objective function and optimal value is plotted against the training time of different methods. As it is clear from the figure, SAAGs outperform other methods, similar to results against number of epochs. SAAG-I outperforms other methods using backtracking line search but SAAG-II outperforms other methods using constant step size.

3.5 CONCLUSION AND FUTURE SCOPE

In this chapter, Mini-batch and block-coordinate setting, i.e., a combination of stochastic approximation and coordinate descent approaches, has been proposed as

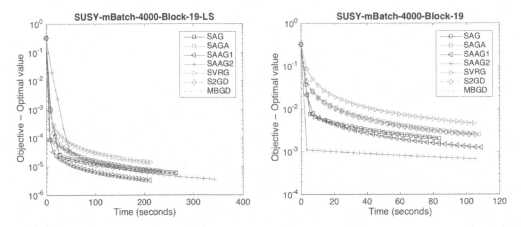

FIGURE 3.2 Sub-optimality against training time with line search method (on left) and constant step size using Lipschitz constant (on right) on SUSY dataset.

scalable optimization framework, namely, BBOF, independent of any solver, for solving big data problems. But it is observed that the stochastic approximation and coordinate descent, do not work well when combined together because the advantage is lost in extra overhead to implement batch block optimization framework. BBOF has been discussed with Gradient Descent as a solver and two novel variance reduction methods (SAAG-I and SAAG-II) have been proposed and used to solve strongly convex and smooth problems. Theoretical results prove linear convergence and empirical results with bench marked datasets prove faster convergence for the proposed methods than existing methods of variance reduction. BBOF and SAAG can be extended to parallel and distributed settings, and to non-convex problems. In addition, there is scope for improving the theoretical properties of proposed variance reduction methods.

CHAPTER 4

Variance Reduction Methods

S tochastic approximation is one of the effective approach to deal with the large-scale machine learning problems and the recent research has focused on reduction of variance, caused by the noisy approximations of the gradients. In this chapter, we have proposed novel variants of SAAG-I and II (Stochastic Average Adjusted Gradient) Chauhan et el. (2017) [23], called SAAG-III and IV, respectively. Unlike SAAG-I, starting point is set to average of previous epoch in SAAG-III, and unlike SAAG-II, the snap point and starting point are set to average and last iterate of previous epoch in SAAG-IV, respectively. To determine the step size, we use Stochastic Backtracking-Armijo line Search (SBAS) which performs line search only on selected mini-batch of data points. Since backtracking line search is not suitable for large-scale problems and the constants used to find the step size, like Lipschitz constant, are not always available so SBAS could be very effective in such cases. We extend SAAGs (I, II, III, IV), to solve non-smooth problems and design two update rules for smooth and non-smooth problems. Moreover, our theoretical results prove linear convergence of SAAG-IV for all the four combinations of smoothness and strong-convexity, in expectation. Finally, our experimental studies prove the efficacy of proposed methods against the state-of-art techniques.

4.1 INTRODUCTION

Please refer to Section 3.1 for discussion on the big data challenge and need of efficient and scalable algorithms for tackling the challenge.

Variance is defined as the difference between gradient calculated on the whole dataset and on randomly selected data point. This variance could cause divergence of the stochastic gradient methods or slow down the convergence of the method. There are different approaches for variance reduction like mini-batching, decreasing learning rates, importance sampling and variance reduction techniques. Here, we have proposed novel variance reduction methods by extending SAAG-I and II to solve large-scale learning problems.

DOI: 10.1201/9781003240167-4

4.1.1 Optimization Problem

In this chapter, we consider composite convex optimization problem, as given below:

$$\min_{w \in \mathbb{R}^d} \left\{ F(w) = f(w) + g(w) = \frac{1}{n} \sum_{i=1}^{n} f_i(w) + g(w), \right\} \qquad (4.1)$$

where $f(w)$ is a finite average of component functions $f_i(w) : \mathbb{R}^d \to \mathbb{R}$, $i = 1, 2, ..., n$, are convex and smooth, $g(w) : \mathbb{R}^d \to \mathbb{R}$ is a relatively simple convex but possibly non-differentiable function (also referred to as regularizer and sometimes as proximal function). This kind of optimization problems can be found in operation research, data science, signal processing, statistics and machine learning. For example, regularized Empirical Risk Minimization (ERM) problem is a common problem in machine learning, which is average of losses on the training dataset. In ERM, component function $f_i(w)$ denotes value of loss function at one data point, e.g., in binary classification, it can be logistic loss, i.e., $f_i(w) = \log\left(1 + \exp\left(-y_i w^T x_i\right)\right)$, where $\{(x_1, y_1), (x_2, y_2), ..., (x_n, y_n)\}$ is collection of training data points, and hinge-loss, i.e., $f_i(w) = \max\left(0, 1 - y_i w^T x_i\right)$; for regression problem, it can be least squares, i.e., $f_i(w) = 1/2(w^T x_i - y_i)^2$. The regularizer can be $\lambda_1 \|w\|_1$ (l_1-regularizer), $\lambda_2/2\|w\|^2$ (l_2-regularizer) and $\lambda_1 \|w\|_1 + \lambda_2/2\|w\|^2$ (elastic net regularizer), where λ_1 and λ_2 are regularization coefficients. Thus, problems like logistic regression, SVM, ridge regression and lasso etc., fall under ERM.

4.1.2 Solution Techniques for Optimization Problem

The simple first order method to solve problem (4.1) is given by Cauchy in his seminal work in 1847, known as Gradient Descent (GD) method [20], is given below for $(k+1)^{th}$ iteration as:

$$w_{k+1} = w_k - \eta_k \left[\frac{1}{n} \sum_{i=1}^{n} \nabla f_i(w_k) + \nabla g(w_k) \right], \qquad (4.2)$$

where η_k is the learning rate (also known as step size in optimization). For non-smooth regularizer, i.e., when $g(w)$ is non-smooth then typically, proximal step is calculated after the gradient step, and method is called Proximal Gradient Descent (PGD), as given below:

$$w_{k+1} = Prox_{\eta_k}^{g}(z_k) = \arg\min_{w \in \mathbb{R}^d} \left\{ \frac{1}{2\eta_k} \|w - z_k\|^2 + g(w) \right\}, \qquad (4.3)$$

where $z_k = w_k - \eta_k/n \sum_{i=1}^{n} \nabla f_i(w_k)$. GD converges linearly for strongly-convex and smooth problem, and (4.3) converges at a rate of $O(1/k^2)$ for non-strongly convex problems, where k is the number of iterations. The per-iteration complexity of GD and PGD methods is $O(nd)$. Since for large-scale learning problems, the values of n (number of data points) and/or d (number of features in each data point) is very large, so the per-iteration complexity of these methods is very large, each iteration becomes computationally expensive and might even be infeasible to process for a limited capacity machine, which leads to slow training of models in machine learning. Thus, the challenge is to develop efficient algorithms to deal with the large-scale learning problems [23].

To tackle the challenge, stochastic approximation is one of the popular approach, first introduced by Robbins and Monro, in their seminal work back in 1951, which makes each iteration independent of number of data points [113]. Based on this approach, we have Stochastic Gradient Descent (SGD) method [14], as given below, to solve problem (4.1) for the smooth case:

$$w_{k+1} = w_k - \eta_k \left[\nabla f_{i_k}(w_k) + \nabla g(w_k) \right], \tag{4.4}$$

where i_k is selected uniformly randomly from $\{1,2,...,n\}$ and $\eta_k \propto 1/\sqrt{k}$. The per-iteration complexity of SGD is $O(d)$ and it is very effective to deal with problems with large number of data points. Since $E\left[\nabla f_{i_k}(w_k)\right] = \nabla f(w_k)$, $\nabla f_{i_k}(w_k)$ is an unbiased estimator of $\nabla f(w_k)$, but the variance in these two values need decreasing learning rates. This leads to slow convergence of learning algorithms. Recently, a lot of research is going to reduce the variance between $\nabla f_{i_k}(w_k)$ and $\nabla f(w_k)$. First variance reduction method introduced by [74], called SAG (Stochastic Average Gradient), some other common and latest methods are SVRG (Stochastic Variance Reduced Gradient) [63], Prox-SVRG [138], S2GD (Semi-Stochastic Gradient Descent) [71, 142], SAGA [35], Katyusha [4], VR-SGD (Variance Reduced Gradient Descent) [39], SAAG-I, II [23] etc. Like, GD, these methods utilize full gradient and like, SGD, these methods calculate gradient for one (or few) data point during each iteration. Thus, just like GD, these methods converge linearly for strongly convex and smooth problems and like, SGD, they calculate gradient using one (or few) data points and have low per-iteration complexity. Thus, the variance reduction methods enjoy best of GD and SGD. Please refer to, [16] for a review on optimization methods for solving large-scale machine learning problems. In this chapter, we have proposed new variants of SAAG-I and II, called SAAG-III and IV, as variance reduction techniques.

4.1.3 Contributions

The research contributions of the chapter are summarized below:

- Novel variants of SAAG-I and II are proposed, called SAAG-III and SAAG-IV, respectively. Unlike SAAG-I, for SAAG-III the starting point is set to the average of iterates of previous epoch except for the first one, $w_0^{s+1} = 1/m \sum_{i=1}^m w_i^s$, where m is number of inner iterations. Unlike SAAG-II, for SAAG-IV, the starting point and snap point are set to the last iterate and average of previous epoch except for the first one, $w_0^{s+1} = w_m^s$ and $\tilde{w}_0^s = 1/m \sum_{i=1}^m w_i^s$.

- SAAG-I and II, including SAAG-III and IV, are extended to solve problems with non-smooth regularizer by introducing two different update rules for smooth and non-smooth cases (refer to Sections 4.3 and 4.4, for details).

- Theoretical results prove linear convergence of SAAG-IV for all the four combinations of smoothness and strong-convexity in expectation.

- Finally, empirical results prove the efficacy of proposed methods against state-of-art methods, like, SVRG and VR-SGD.

4.2 NOTATIONS AND RELATED WORK

This section discusses notations used in the chapter and related work.

4.2.1 Notations

The training dataset is represented as $\{(x_1, y_1), (x_2, y_2), ..., (x_n, y_n)\}$, where n is the number of data points and $x_i \in \mathbb{R}^d$, d is the number of features. w denotes the parameter vector and λ_i, $i = 1, 2$ denotes the regularization parameter. $\| \cdot \|$ denotes Euclidean norm, also called l_2-norm, and $\| \cdot \|_1$ denotes l_1-norm. L and μ are used to denote L-smoothness and μ-strong convexity of problem, respectively. η_k^s denotes the learning rate, $s \in \{1, 2, ..., S\}$ denotes epoch number and S is the total number of epochs. b denotes the mini-batch size, $k \in \{1, 2, ..., m\}$ denotes the inner iterations, s.t., $n = mb$. The value of loss function at (x_i, y_i) is denoted by component function f_i. $w^* = \arg\min_w F(w)$ and $F(w^*)$ is the optimal objective function value, sometimes denoted as F^*.

4.2.2 Related Work

To solve problem (4.1) for smooth regularizer, a simple method is GD, given by [20], and it converges linearly for strongly-convex and smooth problems. For non-smooth regularizer, typically, proximal step is applied to GD step, called PGD method which converges at a rate of $O(1/k^2)$ for non-strongly convex problems. The per-iteration complexity of GD and PGD is $O(nd)$ which is very large for large-scale learning problems and results in slow training of models. Stochastic approximation is one of the approach to tackle this challenge. It was first introduced by Robbins and Monro [113] and is very effective to deal with problems with large number of data points because each iteration uses one (or few) data points, like in SGD [14]. In SGD, each iteration is n times faster than GD, as their per-iteration complexities are $O(d)$ and $O(nd)$, respectively. SGD need decreasing learning rates, i.e., $\eta_k \propto 1/\sqrt{k}$ for k^{th} iteration, because of variance in gradients, so it converges slower than GD, with sub-linear convergence rate $O(1/T)$ even for strongly convex problem [110]. There are several approaches to deal with stochastic noise but most important of these (as discussed in [34]) are: (a) using mini-batching [142], (b) decreasing learning rates[118], (c) variance reduction [74], and (d) importance sampling [34].

Variance reduction techniques, first introduced by [74], called SAG, converges linearly, like, GD for strongly convex and smooth problems, and uses one randomly selected data point, like SGD during each iteration. SAG enjoys benefits of both GD and SGD, as it converges linearly for strongly convex and smooth case like, GD but it has per-iteration complexity of SGD. Later, a lot of variance reduction methods were proposed, like, SVRG [63], SAGA [35], S2GD [71], SDCA [120], SPDC [149], Katyusha [4], Catalyst [87], SAAG-I, II [23], VR-SGD [39], etc. These variance reduction methods can use constant learning rate and can be divided into three categories (as discussed in [39]): (a) primal methods which can be applied to primal optimization problem, like, SAG, SAGA, SVRG, etc., (b) dual methods which can be applied to dual problems, like, SDCA, and (c) primal-dual methods which involve primal and dual variable both, like, SPDC, etc.

In this chapter, we have proposed novel variants of SAAG-I and II, named as SAAG-III and SAAG-IV, respectively. Unlike SAAG-I, for SAAG-III the starting point is set to the average of iterates of previous epoch except for the first one, $w_0^{s+1} = 1/m \sum_{i=1}^m w_i^s$, where m is number of inner iterations. Unlike SAAG-II, for SAAG-IV, the starting point and snap point are set to the last iterate and average of previous epoch except for the first one, $w_0^{s+1} = w_m^s$ and $\tilde{w}_0^s = 1/m \sum_{i=1}^m w_i^s$. [23] proposed Batch Block Optimization Framework (BBOF) to tackle the big data (large-scale learning) challenge in machine learning, along with two variance reduction methods SAAG-I and II. BBOF is based on best of stochastic approximation (SA) and best of coordinate descent (CD) (another approach which is very effective to deal with large-scale learning problems especially problems with high dimensions). Ideas based on best of SA and CD approaches are also used in [133, 140, 146, 152], [146] calls it doubly stochastic since both data points and coordinates are sampled during each iteration. It is observed that for ERM, it is difficult to get the advantage of BBOF in practice because results with CD or SGD are faster than BBOF setting as BBOF needs extra computations while sampling and updating the block of coordinate. When one block of coordinates is updated and as we move to another block, the partial gradients need dot product of parameter vector (w) and data points (like, in logistic regression). Since each update changes w so for each block of update need to calculate the dot product. On other hand, if all coordinates are updated in at a time, like in SGD, that would need to calculate dot product only once. Although, Gauss-Seidel-like update of parameters helps in faster convergence than SGD but the overall gain is less because of extra computational load. Moreover, SAAG-I and II have been proposed to work in BBOF (mini-batch and block-coordinate) setting as well as mini-batch (and considering all coordinates). Since BBOF is not very helpful for ERM so the SAAG-III and IV are proposed for mini-batch setting only. SAAGs (I, II, III and IV) can be extended to stochastic setting (consider one data point during each iteration) but SAAG-I and II are unstable for stochastic setting, and SAAG-III and IV, could not beat the existing methods in stochastic setting. SAAGs has been extended to deal with smooth and non-smooth regularizers, as we have used two different update rules, like [39] (refer to Section 4.3 for details).

4.3 SAAG-I, II AND PROXIMAL EXTENSIONS

Originally, [23] proposed SAAG-I and II for smooth problems, we have extended SAAG-I and II to non-smooth problems. Unlike proximal methods which use single update rule for both smooth and non-smooth problems, we have used two different update rules and introduced proximal step for non-smooth problem. For mini-batch B_k of size b, epoch s and inner iteration k, SAAG-I and II are given below:

SAAG-I:

$$\begin{aligned}
\text{smooth} \qquad & w_{k+1}^s = w_k^s - \eta_k^s \left[\sum_{i=1}^n \tau_i^{s,k} + \nabla g(w_k^s) \right], \\
\text{non-smooth} \qquad & w_{k+1}^s = Prox_{\eta_k^s}^g \left(w_k^s - \eta_k^s \sum_{i=1}^n \tau_i^{s,k} \right),
\end{aligned}$$
(4.5)

where $\tau_i^{s,k} = \begin{cases} \dfrac{1}{b} \nabla f_i(w_k^s) & \text{if } i \in B_k \\ \dfrac{1}{l} \tilde{\tau}_i^{s,k} & \text{otherwise} \end{cases}$ and $\tilde{\tau}_i^{s,k} = \begin{cases} \nabla f_i(w_k^s) & \text{if } i \in B_k \\ \tilde{\tau}_i^{s-1,k} & \text{otherwise.} \end{cases}$

SAAG-II:

$$\begin{aligned}
\text{smooth} \qquad & w_{k+1}^s = w_k^s - \eta_k^s \left[\tilde{\nabla} f_{B_k}(w_k^s) + \nabla g(w_k^s) \right], \\
\text{non-smooth} \qquad & w_{k+1}^s = Prox_{\eta_k^s}^g \left(w_k^s - \eta_k^s \tilde{\nabla} f_{B_k}(w_k^s) \right),
\end{aligned}$$
(4.6)

where $\tilde{\nabla} f_{B_k}(w_k^s) = 1/b \sum_{i \in B_k} \nabla f_i(w_k^s) - 1/n \sum_{i \in B_k} \nabla f_i(\tilde{w}^s) + \tilde{\mu}^s$ and $\tilde{\mu}^s = 1/n \sum_{i=1}^n \nabla f_i(\tilde{w}^s)$. Unlike SVRG and VRSGD, and like SAG and SAGA, SAAGs are biased gradient estimators because the expectation of gradient estimator is not equal to full gradient, i.e., $\mathbb{E}[\tilde{\nabla} f_{B_k}(w_k^s)] = \nabla f(w_k^s) + (m-1)/m \nabla f(\tilde{w}^{s-1})$, as detailed in Lemma 6.

SAAG-I algorithm, represented by Algorithm 10, divides the dataset into m minibatches of equal size (say) b and takes input S, number of epochs. During each inner iteration, it randomly selects one mini-batch of data points from $[n]$, calculates gradient over mini-batch, updates the total gradient value and performs stochastic backtracking-Armijo line search (SBAS) over B_k. Then parameters are updated using Option I for smooth regularizer and using Option II for non-smooth regularizer. Inner iterations are run m times where $n = mb$ and then last iterate is used as the starting point for next epoch.

SAAG-II algorithm, represented by Algorithm 11, takes input as number of epochs (S) and number of mini-batches (m) of equal size (say) b. It initializes $w_0^1 = \tilde{w}^0$. During each inner iteration, it randomly selects one mini-batch B_k, calculates two gradients over B_k at last iterate and snap-point, updates $\tilde{\nabla} f_{B_k}(w_k^s)$ and performs stochastic backtracking-Armijo line search (SBAS) over B_k. Then parameters are updated using Option I for smooth regularizer and using Option II for non-smooth regularizer. After inner iterations, it uses the last iterate to set the snap point and the starting point for the next epoch.

4.4 SAAG-III AND IV ALGORITHMS

SAAG-III algorithm, represented by Algorithm 12, divides the dataset into m minibatches of equal size (say) b and takes input S, number of epochs. During each inner iteration, it randomly selects one mini-batch of data points B_k from $[n]$, calculates gradient over mini-batch, updates the total gradient value and performs stochastic backtracking-Armijo line search (SBAS) over B_k. Then parameters are updated using Option I for smooth regularizer and using Option II for non-smooth regularizer. Inner iterations are run m times where $n = mb$ and then iterate average is calculated and used as the starting point for next epoch, $w_0^{s+1} = 1/m \sum_{i=1}^m w_i^s$.

Algorithm 10 SAAG-I

1: **Inputs:** $m = $ #mini-batches and $S = $ max #*epochs*.
2: **Initialize:** w_0^1
3: **for** $s = 1, 2, ..., S$ **do**
4:     **for** $k = 0, 1, ..., (m-1)$ **do**
5:         Randomly select one mini-batch B_k from [n].
6:         Update the gradient values, $\tau_i^{s,k}$ and $\tilde{\tau}_i^{s,k}$.
7:         Calculate η_k^s using stochastic backtracking line search on B_k.
8:         Option I (smooth): $w_{k+1}^s = w_k^s - \eta_k^s \left[\sum_{i=1}^n \tau_i^{s,k} + \nabla g(w_k^s) \right]$,
9:         Option II (non-smooth): $w_{k+1}^s = Prox_{\eta_k^s}^g \left(w_k^s - \eta_k^s \sum_{i=1}^n \tau_i^{s,k} \right)$,

$$\text{where } \tau_i^{s,k} = \begin{cases} \frac{1}{b} \nabla f_i(w_k^s) & \text{if } i \in B_k \\ \frac{1}{l} \tilde{\tau}_i^{s,k} & \text{otherwise} \end{cases} \quad \text{and } \tilde{\tau}_i^{s,k} = \begin{cases} \nabla f_i(w_k^s) & \text{if } i \in B_k \\ \tilde{\tau}_i^{s-1,k} & \text{otherwise.} \end{cases}$$

10:     **end for**
11: **end for**
12: **Output:** w_m^S

SAAG-IV algorithm, represented by Algorithm 13, takes input as number of epochs (S) and number of mini-batches (m) of equal size (say) b. It initializes $w_0^1 = \tilde{w}^0$. During each inner iteration, it randomly selects one mini-batch B_k, calculates two gradients over B_k at last iterate and snap-point, updates $\tilde{\nabla} f_{B_k}(w_k^s)$ and performs stochastic backtracking-Armijo line search (SBAS) over B_k. Then parameters are updated using Option I for smooth regularizer and using Option II for non-smooth regularizer. After inner iterations, it calculates average to set the snap point, and uses last iterate as the starting point for the new epoch, as $\tilde{w}^s = 1/m \sum_{i=1}^m w_i^s$ and $w_0^{s+1} = w_m^s$, respectively.

4.5 ANALYSIS

In general, SAAG-IV gives better results for large-scale learning problems as compared to SAAG-III. So, in this section, we provide convergence rates of SAAG-IV considering all cases of smoothness with strong convexity. Moreover, analysis of SAAG-III represents a typical case due to the biased nature of gradient estimator and the fact that the full gradient is incrementally maintained rather than being calculated at a fix point, like in SAAG-IV. So, analysis of SAAG-III is left open. The convergence rates for all the different combinations of smoothness and strong convexity are given below.

Following assumptions are considered in the chapter:

Assumption 1 (Smoothness) *Suppose function $f_i : \mathbb{R}^n \to \mathbb{R}$ is convex and differentiable, and that gradient ∇f_i, $\forall i$ is L-Lipschitz-continuous, where $L > 0$ is Lipschitz constant, then, we have,*

$$\|\nabla f_i(y) - \nabla f_i(x)\| \leq L\|y - x\|, \tag{4.7}$$

Algorithm 11 SAAG-II

1: **Inputs:** $m =$ #mini-batches and $S =$ max #epochs.
2: **Initialize:** w_0^1
3: **for** $s = 1, 2, ..., S$ **do**
4:     $\tilde{w}^s = w_0^s$
5:     $\tilde{\mu}^s = \frac{1}{n}\sum_{i=1}^n \nabla f_i(\tilde{w}^s)$ // calculate full gradient
6:     **for** $k = 0, 1, ..., (m-1)$ **do**
7:         Randomly select one mini-batch B_k from [n].
8:         Calculate $\tilde{\nabla} f_{B_k}(w_k^s) = \frac{1}{b}\sum_{i\in B_k} \nabla f_i(w_k^s) - \frac{1}{n}\sum_{i\in B_k} \nabla f_i(\tilde{w}^s) + \tilde{\mu}^s$.
9:         Calculate η_k^s using stochastic backtracking-Armijo line search on B_k.
10:         Option I (smooth): $w_{k+1}^s = w_k^s - \eta_k^s \left[\tilde{\nabla} f_{B_k}(w_k^s) + \nabla g(w_k^s)\right]$
11:         Option II (non-smooth): $w_{k+1}^s = Prox_{\eta_k^s}^g \left(w_k^s - \eta_k^s \tilde{\nabla} f_{B_k}(w_k^s)\right)$
12:     **end for**
13:     $w_0^{s+1} = w_m^s$
14: **end for**
15: **Output:** w_m^S

$$and, \quad f_i(y) \leq f_i(x) + \nabla f_i(x)^T(y-x) + \frac{L}{2}\|y-x\|^2. \tag{4.8}$$

Assumption 2 (Strong Convexity) *Suppose function* $F : \mathbb{R}^n \to \mathbb{R}$ *is* μ-*strongly convex function for* $\mu > 0$ *and* F^* *is the optimal value of* F, *then, we have,*

$$F(y) \geq F(x) + \nabla F(x)^T(y-x) + \frac{\mu}{2}\|y-x\|^2, \tag{4.9}$$

$$and, \quad F(x) - F^* \leq \frac{1}{2\mu}\|\nabla F(x)\|^2 \tag{4.10}$$

Assumption 3 (Assumption 3 in [39]) *For all* $s = 1, 2, ..., S$, *the following inequality holds*

$$\mathbb{E}\left[F(w_0^s) - F(w^*)\right] \leq c\mathbb{E}\left[F(\tilde{w}^{s-1}) - F(w^*)\right] \tag{4.11}$$

where $0 < c \ll m$ *is a constant.*

We derive our proofs by taking motivation from [39] and [138]. Before providing the proofs, we provide certain lemmas, as given below:

Lemma 1 (3-Point Property [73]) *Let* $\hat{z}$ *be the optimal solution of the following problem:* $\min_{z \in \mathbb{R}^d} \frac{\tau}{2}\|z - z_0\|^2 + r(z)$, *where* $\tau \geq 0$ *and* $r(z)$ *is a convex function (but possibly non-differentiable). Then for any* $z \in \mathbb{R}^d$, *then the following inequality holds,*

$$\frac{\tau}{2}\|\hat{z} - z_0\|^2 + r(\hat{z}) \leq r(z) + \frac{\tau}{2}\left(\|z - z_0\|^2 - \|z - \hat{z}\|^2\right) \tag{4.12}$$

Algorithm 12 SAAG-III

1: **Inputs:** $m = $ #mini-batches and $S = $max #epochs.
2: **Initialize:** w_0^1
3: **for** $s = 1, 2, ..., S$ **do**
4:     **for** $k = 0, 1, ..., (m - 1)$ **do**
5:         Randomly select one mini-batch B_k from [n].
6:         Update the gradient values, $\tau_i^{s,k}$ and $\tilde{\tau}_i^{s,k}$.
7:         Calculate η_k^s using stochastic backtracking line search on B_k.
8:         Option I (smooth): $w_{k+1}^s = w_k^s - \eta_k^s \left[\sum_{i=1}^n \tau_i^{s,k} + \nabla g(w_k^s) \right]$,
9:         Option II (non-smooth): $w_{k+1}^s = Prox_{\eta_k^s}^g \left(w_k^s - \eta_k^s \sum_{i=1}^n \tau_i^{s,k} \right)$,

$$\text{where } \tau_i^{s,k} = \begin{cases} \frac{1}{b} \nabla f_i(w_k^s) & \text{if } i \in B_k \\ \frac{1}{l} \tilde{\tau}_i^{s,k} & \text{otherwise} \end{cases} \quad \text{and } \tilde{\tau}_i^{s,k} = \begin{cases} \nabla f_i(w_k^s) & \text{if } i \in B_k \\ \tilde{\tau}_i^{s-1,k} & \text{otherwise.} \end{cases}$$

10:     **end for**
11:     $w_0^{s+1} = 1/m \sum_{i=1}^m w_i^s$ // iterate averaging
12: **end for**
13: **Output:** w_m^S

Lemma 2 (Theorem 4 in [70]) *For non-smooth problems, taking*

$\tilde{\nabla}'_{s,k} = \frac{1}{b} \sum_{i \in B_k} \nabla f_i(w_k^s) - \frac{1}{b} \sum_{i \in B_k} \nabla f_i(\tilde{w}^{s-1}) + \frac{1}{n} \sum_{i=1}^n f_i(\tilde{w}^{s-1})$, *we have* $\mathbb{E} \left[\tilde{\nabla}'_{s,k} \right] = \nabla f(w_k^s)$ *and the variance satisfies following inequality,*

$$\mathbb{E} \left[\|\tilde{\nabla}'_{s,k} - \nabla f(w_k^s)\|^2 \right] \leq 4L\alpha(b) \left[F(w_k^s) - F(w^*) + F(\tilde{w}^{s-1}) - F(w^*) \right], \quad (4.13)$$

where $\alpha(b) = (n - b)/(b(n - 1))$.

Following the Lemma 2 for non-smooth problems, one can easily prove the following results for the smooth problems,

Lemma 3 *For smooth problems, taking* $\tilde{\nabla}'_{s,k} = \frac{1}{b} \sum_{i \in B_k} \nabla f_i(w_k^s) - \frac{1}{b} \sum_{i \in B_k} \nabla f_i(\tilde{w}^{s-1})$

$+ \frac{1}{n} \sum_{i=1}^n f_i(\tilde{w}^{s-1})$, *we have* $\mathbb{E} \left[\tilde{\nabla}'_{s,k} \right] = \nabla f(w_k^s)$ *and the variance satisfies following inequality,*

$$\mathbb{E} \left[\|\tilde{\nabla}'_{s,k} - \nabla f(w_k^s)\|^2 \right] \leq 4L\alpha(b) \left[f(w_k^s) - f^* + f(\tilde{w}^{s-1}) - f^* \right], \quad (4.14)$$

where $\alpha(b) = (n - b)/(b(n - 1))$.

Lemma 4 (Extension of Lemma 3.4 in [138] to mini-batches) *Under Assumption 1 for smooth regularizer, we have*

$$\mathbb{E} \left[\|\nabla_{B_k} f(w_k^s) - \nabla_{B_k} f(w^*)\|^2 \right] \leq 2L \left[f(w_k^s) - f(w^*) \right] \quad (4.15)$$

Algorithm 13 SAAG-IV

1: **Inputs:** $m = $ #mini-batches and $S = $ max #epochs.
2: **Initialize:** $w_0^1 = \tilde{w}^0$
3: **for** $s = 1, 2, ..., S$ **do**
4:    $\tilde{\mu}^s = \dfrac{1}{n}\sum_{i=1}^n \nabla f_i(\tilde{w}^{s-1})$ // calculate full gradient
5:    **for** $k = 0, 1, ..., (m-1)$ **do**
6:       Randomly select one mini-batch B_k from [n].
7:       Calculate $\tilde{\nabla} f_{B_k}(w_k^s) = \dfrac{1}{b}\sum_{i \in B_k} \nabla f_i(w_k^s) - \dfrac{1}{n}\sum_{i \in B_k} \nabla f_i(\tilde{w}^{s-1}) + \tilde{\mu}^s$.
8:       Calculate η_k^s using stochastic backtracking-Armijo line search on B_k.
9:       Option I (smooth): $w_{k+1}^s = w_k^s - \eta_k^s \left[\tilde{\nabla} f_{B_k}(w_k^s) + \nabla g(w_k^s) \right]$
10:      Option II (non-smooth): $w_{k+1}^s = Prox_{\eta_k^s}^g \left(w_k^s - \eta_k^s \tilde{\nabla} f_{B_k}(w_k^s) \right)$
11:   **end for**
12:   $\tilde{w}^s = 1/m \sum_{i=1}^m w_i^s$ // iterate averaging
13:   $w_0^{s+1} = w_m^s$ //initialize starting point
14: **end for**
15: **Output:** w_m^S

Proof 4.1 *Given any $k = 0, 1, ..., (m-1)$, consider the function,*

$$\phi_{B_k}(w) = f_{B_k}(w) - f_{B_k}(w^*) - \nabla_{B_k} f(w^*)^T (w - w^*)$$

It is straightforward to check that $\nabla \phi_{B_k}(w^*) = 0$, hence $\min_w \phi_{B_k}(w) = \phi_{B_k}(w^*) = 0$. Since $\phi_{B_k}(w)$ is Lipschitz continuous so we have,

$$\frac{1}{2L}\|\nabla \phi_{B_k}(w)\|^2 \leq \phi_{B_k}(w) - \min_w \phi_{B_k}(w) = \phi_{B_k}(w) - \phi_{B_k}(w^*) = \phi_{B_k}(w)$$
$$\implies \|\nabla f_{B_k}(w) - \nabla f_{B_k}(w^*)\|^2 \leq 2L \left[f_{B_k}(w) - f_{B_k}(w^*) - \nabla_{B_k} f(w^*)^T (w - w^*) \right]$$

Taking expectation, we have

$$\mathbb{E}[\|\nabla f_{B_k}(w) - \nabla f_{B_k}(w^*)\|^2] \leq 2L \left[f(w) - f(w^*) - \nabla f(w^*)^T (w - w^*) \right] \quad (4.16)$$

By optimality, $\nabla f(w^*) = 0$, we have

$$\mathbb{E}[\|\nabla f_{B_k}(w) - \nabla f_{B_k}(w^*)\|^2] \leq 2L [f(w) - f(w^*)]$$

This proves the required lemma.

Lemma 5 (Extension of Lemma 3.4 in [138] to mini-batches) *Under Assumption 1 for non-smooth regularizer, we have*

$$\mathbb{E}\left[\|\nabla_{B_k} f(w_k^s) - \nabla_{B_k} f(w^*)\|^2 \right] \leq 2L [F(w_k^s) - F(w^*)] \quad (4.17)$$

Proof 4.2 *From inequality 4.16, we have*

$$\mathbb{E}[\|\nabla f_{B_k}(w) - \nabla f_{B_k}(w^*)\|^2] \leq 2L \left[f(w) - f(w^*) - \nabla f(w^*)^T(w - w^*) \right] \quad (4.18)$$

By optimality, there exist $\xi \in \partial g(w^*)$, such that, $\nabla F(w^*) = \nabla f(w^*) + \xi = 0$, we have

$$\mathbb{E}[\|\nabla f_{B_k}(w) - \nabla f_{B_k}(w^*)\|^2] \leq 2L \left[f(w) - f(w^*) + \xi^T(w - w^*) \right]$$
$$\leq 2L \left[f(w) - f(w^*) + g(w) - g(w^*) \right] \quad (4.19)$$
$$\leq 2L \left[F(w) - F(w^*) \right]$$

second inequality follows from the convexity of g. This proves the required lemma.

Lemma 6 (Variance bound for smooth problem) *Under the Assumption 1 and taking $\nabla_{B_k} f(w_k^s) = \frac{1}{b} \sum_{i \in B_k} \nabla f_i(w_k^s)$, $\nabla_{B_k'} f(\tilde{w}^{s-1}) = \frac{1}{n} \sum_{i \in B_k} \nabla f_i(\tilde{w}^{s-1})$, $\tilde{\mu}^s = \frac{1}{n} \sum_{i=1}^{n} \nabla f_i(\tilde{w}^{s-1})$ and the gradient estimator, $\tilde{\nabla}_{s,k} = \nabla_{B_k} f(w_k^s) - \nabla_{B_k'} f(\tilde{w}^{s-1}) + \tilde{\mu}^s$, then the variance satisfies the following inequality[1],*

$$\mathbb{E}\left[\|\tilde{\nabla}_{s,k} - \nabla f(w_k^s)\|^2 \right] \leq 8L\alpha(b) \left[f(w_k^s) - f^* \right] + \frac{8L \left(\alpha(b)m^2 + (m-1)^2 \right)}{m^2}$$
$$\times \left[f(\tilde{w}^{s-1}) - f^* \right] + R' \quad (4.20)$$

where $\alpha(b) = (n - b)/(b(n - 1))$ and R' is a constant.

Proof 4.3 *First the expectation of estimator is given by*

$$\mathbb{E}\left[\tilde{\nabla}_{s,k} \right] = \mathbb{E}\left[\nabla_{B_k} f(w_k^s) - \nabla_{B_k'} f(\tilde{w}^{s-1}) + \tilde{\mu}^s \right]$$
$$= \nabla f(w_k^s) - \frac{b}{n} \nabla f(\tilde{w}^{s-1}) + \nabla f(\tilde{w}^{s-1}) \quad (4.21)$$
$$= \nabla f(w_k^s) + \frac{m-1}{m} \nabla f(\tilde{w}^{s-1}),$$

second equality follows as $n = mb$. Now the variance bound is calculated as follows,

$$\mathbb{E}\left[\|\tilde{\nabla}_{s,k} - \nabla f(w_k^s)\|^2 \right]$$
$$= \mathbb{E}\left[\|\nabla_{B_k} f(w_k^s) - \nabla_{B_k'} f(\tilde{w}^{s-1}) + \nabla f(\tilde{w}^{s-1}) - \nabla f(w_k^s)\|^2 \right]$$
$$= \mathbb{E}\left[\|\nabla_{B_k} f(w_k^s) - \nabla_{B_k} f(\tilde{w}^{s-1}) + \nabla f(\tilde{w}^{s-1}) - \nabla f(w_k^s) + \frac{m-1}{m} \nabla_{B_k} f(\tilde{w}^{s-1})\|^2 \right]$$
$$\leq 2\mathbb{E}\left[\|\nabla_{B_k} f(w_k^s) - \nabla_{B_k} f(\tilde{w}^{s-1}) + \nabla f(\tilde{w}^{s-1}) - \nabla f(w_k^s)\|^2 \right]$$
$$+ \frac{2(m-1)^2}{m^2} \mathbb{E}\left[\|\nabla_{B_k} f(\tilde{w}^{s-1})\|^2 \right]$$
$$\leq 8L\alpha(b) \left[f(w_k^s) - f^* + f(\tilde{w}^{s-1}) - f^* \right] + \frac{2(m-1)^2}{m^2} \mathbb{E}\left[\|\nabla_{B_k} f(\tilde{w}^{s-1})\|^2 \right]$$
$$(4.22)$$

---

[1] For the simplification of proof, we take $f(w) = F(w)$, i.e., $f_i(w) = f_i(w) + g(w) \; \forall i$ and then $g(w) \equiv 0$

inequality follows from, $\|a + b\|^2 \leq 2 (\|a\|^2 + \|b\|^2)$ for $a, b \in \mathbb{R}^d$ and applying the Lemma 3.

$$Now, \quad \frac{2(m-1)^2}{m^2} \mathbb{E}\left[\|\nabla_{B_k} f(\tilde{w}^{s-1})\|^2\right]$$

$$\leq \frac{2(m-1)^2}{m^2} \left[2\mathbb{E}\|\nabla_{B_k} f(\tilde{w}^{s-1}) - \nabla_{B_k} f(w^*)\|^2 + 2\mathbb{E}\|\nabla_{B_k} f(w^*)\|^2\right] \quad (4.23)$$

$$\leq \frac{8L(m-1)^2}{m^2} \left[f(\tilde{w}^{s-1}) - f(w^*)\right] + R'$$

first inequality follows from, $\|a+b\|^2 \leq 2 (\|a\|^2 + \|b\|^2)$ for $a, b \in \mathbb{R}^d$, second inequality follows from Lemma 4 and assuming $\mathbb{E}\|\nabla_{B_k} f(w^*)\|^2 \leq R$, $\forall k$ and where taking $R' = \frac{2(m-1)^2}{m^2} * R$. Now, substituting the above inequality in 4.22, we have

$$\mathbb{E}\left[\|\tilde{\nabla}_{s,k} - \nabla f(w_k^s)\|^2\right]$$

$$\leq 8L\alpha(b) \left[f(w_k^s) - f^* + f(\tilde{w}^{s-1}) - f^*\right] + \frac{8L(m-1)^2}{m^2} \left[f(\tilde{w}^{s-1}) - f(w^*)\right] + R'$$

$$= 8L\alpha(b) \left[f(w_k^s) - f^*\right] + \frac{8L\left(\alpha(b)m^2 + (m-1)^2\right)}{m^2} \left[f(\tilde{w}^{s-1}) - f^*\right] + R',$$

$$(4.24)$$

This proves the required lemma.

Lemma 7 (Variance bound for non-smooth problem) *Under Assumption 1 and taking notations as in Lemma 6, the variance bound satisfies the following inequality,*

$$\mathbb{E}\left[\|\tilde{\nabla}_{s,k} - \nabla f(w_k^s)\|^2\right] \leq 8L\alpha(b) \left[F(w_k^s) - F^*\right] + \frac{8L\left(\alpha(b)m^2 + (m-1)^2\right)}{m^2}$$

$$\times \left[F(\tilde{w}^{s-1}) - F^*\right] + R', \quad (4.25)$$

where $\alpha(b) = (n - b)/(b(n - 1))$ and R' is constant.

Proof 4.4

$$\mathbb{E}\left[\|\tilde{\nabla}_{s,k} - \nabla f(w_k^s)\|^2\right]$$

$$= \mathbb{E}\left[\|\nabla_{B_k} f(w_k^s) - \nabla_{B_k'} f(\tilde{w}^{s-1}) + \nabla f(\tilde{w}^{s-1}) - \nabla f(w_k^s)\|^2\right]$$

$$= \mathbb{E}\left[\|\nabla_{B_k} f(w_k^s) - \nabla_{B_k} f(\tilde{w}^{s-1}) + \nabla f(\tilde{w}^{s-1}) - \nabla f(w_k^s) + \frac{m-1}{m}\nabla_{B_k} f(\tilde{w}^{s-1})\|^2\right]$$

$$\leq 2\mathbb{E}\left[\|\nabla_{B_k} f(w_k^s) - \nabla_{B_k} f(\tilde{w}^{s-1}) + \nabla f(\tilde{w}^{s-1}) - \nabla f(w_k^s)\|^2\right]$$

$$+ \frac{2(m-1)^2}{m^2}\mathbb{E}\left[\|\nabla_{B_k} f(\tilde{w}^{s-1})\|^2\right]$$

$$\leq 8L\alpha(b) \left[F(w_k^s) - F(w^*) + F(\tilde{w}^{s-1}) - F(w^*)\right] + \frac{2(m-1)^2}{m^2}\mathbb{E}\left[\|\nabla_{B_k} f(\tilde{w}^{s-1})\|^2\right]$$

$$(4.26)$$

inequality follows from, $\|a + b\|^2 \leq 2\left(\|a\|^2 + \|b\|^2\right)$ *for* $a, b \in \mathbb{R}^d$ *and applying the Lemma 2.*

$$Now, \frac{2(m-1)^2}{m^2}\mathbb{E}\left[\|\nabla_{B_k}f(\tilde{w}^{s-1})\|^2\right]$$

$$\leq \frac{2(m-1)^2}{m^2}\left[2\mathbb{E}\|\nabla_{B_k}f(\tilde{w}^{s-1}) - \nabla_{B_k}f(w^*)\|^2 + 2\mathbb{E}\|\nabla_{B_k}f(w^*)\|^2\right] \tag{4.27}$$

$$\leq \frac{8L(m-1)^2}{m^2}\left[F(\tilde{w}^{s-1}) - F(w^*)\right] + R' \tag{4.28}$$

first inequality follows from, $\|a + b\|^2 \leq 2\left(\|a\|^2 + \|b\|^2\right)$ *for* $a, b \in \mathbb{R}^d$, *second inequality follows from Lemma 5 and assuming* $\|\nabla_{B_k}f(w^*)\|^2 \leq R$, $\forall k$ *and taking* $R' = \frac{2(m-1)^2}{m^2} * R$. *Now, substituting the above inequality in 4.26, we have*

$$\mathbb{E}\left[\|\tilde{\nabla}_{s,k} - \nabla f(w_k^s)\|^2\right]$$

$$\leq 8L\alpha(b)\left[F(w_k^s) - F^* + F(\tilde{w}^{s-1}) - F^*\right] + \frac{8L(m-1)^2}{m^2}\left[F(\tilde{w}^{s-1}) - F(w^*)\right] + R'$$

$$= 8L\alpha(b)\left[F(w_k^s) - F^*\right] + \frac{8L\left(\alpha(b)m^2 + (m-1)^2\right)}{m^2}\left[F(\tilde{w}^{s-1}) - F^*\right] + R', \tag{4.29}$$

This proves the required lemma.

Theorem 2 *Under the assumptions of Lipschitz continuity with smooth regularizer, the convergence of SAAG-IV is given below:*

$$\mathbb{E}\left[f(\tilde{w}^s) - f^*\right] \leq C^s\left[f(\tilde{w}^0) - f^*\right] + V, \tag{4.30}$$

where, $C = \left[\dfrac{4\alpha(b)}{(\beta - 1 - 4\alpha(b))}\dfrac{c}{m} + \dfrac{4\left(\alpha(b)m^2 + (m-1)^2\right)}{m^2(\beta - 1 - 4\alpha(b))}\right] < 1$ *and* V *is constant.*

Proof 4.5 *By smoothness, we have,*

$$f(w_{k+1}^s) \leq f(w_k^s) + <\nabla f(w_k^s), w_{k+1}^s - w_k^s> + \frac{L}{2}\|w_{k+1}^s - w_k^s\|^2$$

$$= f(w_k^s) + <\nabla f(w_k^s), w_{k+1}^s - w_k^s> + \frac{L\beta}{2}\|w_{k+1}^s - w_k^s\|^2$$

$$- \frac{L(\beta - 1)}{2}\|w_{k+1}^s - w_k^s\|^2 \tag{4.31}$$

$$= f(w_k^s) + <\tilde{\nabla}_{s,k}, w_{k+1}^s - w_k^s> + \frac{L\beta}{2}\|w_{k+1}^s - w_k^s\|^2 + <\nabla f(w_k^s) -$$

$$- \tilde{\nabla}_{s,k}, w_{k+1}^s - w_k^s> - \frac{L(\beta - 1}{2}\|w_{k+1}^s - w_k^s\|^2,$$

where β *is appropriately chosen positive value. Now, separately simplifying the terms, we have*

$$\mathbb{E}\left[f(w_k^s) + <\tilde{\nabla}_{s,k}, w_{k+1}^s - w_k^s> + \frac{L\beta}{2}\|w_{k+1}^s - w_k^s\|^2\right]$$

$$= f(w_k^s) + \mathbb{E}\left[<\tilde{\nabla}_{s,k}, w_{k+1}^s - w_k^s>\right] + \frac{L\beta}{2}\|w_{k+1}^s - w_k^s\|^2$$

$$= f(w_k^s) + < \nabla f(w_k^s) + \frac{m-1}{m} \nabla f(\tilde{w}^{s-1}), w_{k+1}^s - w_k^s > + \frac{L\beta}{2} \|w_{k+1}^s - w_k^s\|^2$$

$$= f(w_k^s) + < \nabla f(w_k^s), w_{k+1}^s - w_k^s > + \frac{L\beta}{2} \|w_{k+1}^s - w_k^s\|^2 + \frac{m-1}{m}$$
$$< \nabla f(\tilde{w}^{s-1}), w_{k+1}^s - w_k^s >$$

$$\leq f(w_k^s) + < \nabla f(w_k^s), w^* - w_k^s > + \frac{L\beta}{2} \|w^* - w_k^s\|^2 - \frac{L\beta}{2} \|w^* - w_{k+1}^s\|^2$$
$$+ \frac{m-1}{m} < \nabla f(\tilde{w}^{s-1}), w_{k+1}^s - w_k^s >$$

$$= f(w_k^s) + < \nabla f(w_k^s), w^* - w_k^s > + \frac{L\beta}{2} \|w^* - w_k^s\|^2 - \frac{L\beta}{2} \|w^* - w_{k+1}^s\|^2$$
$$+ \frac{m-1}{m} \left[< \nabla f(\tilde{w}^{s-1}), w_{k+1}^s - w^* > - < \nabla f(\tilde{w}^{s-1}), w_k^s - w^* > \right]$$

$$\leq f(w^*) + \frac{L\beta}{2} \left[\|w^* - w_k^s\|^2 - \|w^* - w_{k+1}^s\|^2 \right]$$
$$+ \frac{m-1}{m} \left[\frac{1}{2\delta} \|\nabla f(\tilde{w}^{s-1})\|^2 + \frac{\delta}{2} \|w_{k+1}^s - w^*\|^2 \right.$$
$$\left. - \left[\frac{1}{2\delta} \|\nabla f(\tilde{w}^{s-1})\|^2 + \frac{\delta}{2} \|w_k^s - w^*\|^2 \right] \right]$$

$$= f(w^*) + \frac{L\beta}{2} \left[\|w^* - w_k^s\|^2 - \|w^* - w_{k+1}^s\|^2 \right]$$
$$+ \frac{\delta(m-1)}{2m} \left[\|w_{k+1}^s - w^*\|^2 - \|w_k^s - w^*\|^2 \right],$$

$$= f(w^*) + \left(\frac{L\beta}{2} - \frac{\delta(m-1)}{2m} \right) \left[\|w^* - w_k^s\|^2 - \|w^* - w_{k+1}^s\|^2 \right], \tag{4.32}$$
$$= f(w^*),$$

second equality follows from, $\mathbb{E}\left[\tilde{\nabla}_{s,k}\right] = \nabla f(w_k^s) + \frac{m-1}{m} \nabla f(\tilde{w}^{s-1})$, *first inequality follows from Lemma 1, second inequality follows from the convexity, i.e.,* $f(w^*) \geq f(w_k^s) + < \nabla f(w_k^s), w^* - w_k^s >$ *and Young's inequality, i.e.,* $x^T y \leq 1/(2\delta)\|x\|^2 + \delta/2\|y\|^2$ *for* $\delta > 0$, *and last equality follows by choosing* $\delta = \frac{mL\beta}{(m-1)}$.

and, $\mathbb{E}\left[< \nabla f(w_k^s) - \tilde{\nabla}_{s,k}, w_{k+1}^s - w_k^s > - \frac{L(\beta-1)}{2} \|w_{k+1}^s - w_k^s\|^2 \right]$

$$\leq \mathbb{E}\left[\frac{1}{2L(\beta-1)} \|\nabla f(w_k^s) - \tilde{\nabla}_{s,k}\|^2 + \frac{L(\beta-1)}{2} \|w_{k+1}^s - w_k^s\|^2 - \frac{L(\beta-1)}{2} \|w_{k+1}^s - w_k^s\|^2 \right]$$

$$= \frac{1}{2L(\beta-1)} \mathbb{E}\left[\|\tilde{\nabla}_{s,k} - \nabla f(w_k^s)\|^2 \right]$$

$$\leq \frac{1}{2L(\beta-1)} \left[8L\alpha(b) \left[f(w_k^s) - f^* \right] + \frac{8L\left(\alpha(b)m^2 + (m-1)^2\right)}{m^2} \left[f(\tilde{w}^{s-1}) - f^* \right] + R' \right]$$

$$= \frac{4\alpha(b)}{(\beta-1)} \left[f(w_k^s) - f^* \right] + \frac{4\left(\alpha(b)m^2 + (m-1)^2\right)}{m^2(\beta-1)} \left[f(\tilde{w}^{s-1}) - f^* \right] + R'' \tag{4.33}$$

first inequality follows from Young's inequality, second inequality follows from Lemma 6 and $R'' = R'/(2L(\beta - 1))$.

Now, substituting the values into 4.31 from inequalities 4.32 and 4.33, and taking expectation w.r.t. mini-batches, we have

$$\mathbb{E}\left[f(w_{k+1}^s)\right] \leq f(w^*) + \frac{4\alpha(b)}{(\beta - 1)}\left[f(w_k^s) - f^*\right] + \frac{4\left(\alpha(b)m^2 + (m-1)^2\right)}{m^2(\beta - 1)}\left[f(\tilde{w}^{s-1}) - f^*\right] + R''$$

$$\mathbb{E}\left[f(w_{k+1}^s) - f(w^*)\right] \leq \frac{4\alpha(b)}{(\beta - 1)}\left[f(w_k^s) - f^*\right] + \frac{4\left(\alpha(b)m^2 + (m-1)^2\right)}{m^2(\beta - 1)}\left[f(\tilde{w}^{s-1}) - f^*\right] + R''$$

$$(4.34)$$

Taking sum over $k = 0, 1, ..., (m-1)$ and dividing by m, we have

$$\frac{1}{m}\sum_{k=0}^{m-1}\mathbb{E}\left[f(w_{k+1}^s) - f^*\right]$$

$$\leq \frac{1}{m}\sum_{k=0}^{m-1}\left[\frac{4\alpha(b)}{(\beta - 1)}\left[f(w_k^s) - f^*\right] + \frac{4\left(\alpha(b)m^2 + (m-1)^2\right)}{m^2(\beta - 1)}\left[f(\tilde{w}^{s-1}) - f^*\right] + R''\right],$$

$$\frac{1}{m}\sum_{k=1}^{m}\mathbb{E}\left[f(w_k^s) - f^*\right]$$

$$\leq \frac{4\alpha(b)}{(\beta - 1)}\frac{1}{m}\sum_{k=1}^{m}\left[f(w_k^s) - f^*\right] + \frac{4\alpha(b)}{(\beta - 1)}\frac{1}{m}\left[f(w_0^s) - f^* - \{f(w_m^s) - f^*\}\right]$$

$$+ \frac{4\left(\alpha(b)m^2 + (m-1)^2\right)}{m^2(\beta - 1)}\left[f(\tilde{w}^{s-1}) - f^*\right] + R''$$

$$(4.35)$$

Subtracting $\frac{4\alpha(b)}{(\beta - 1)}\frac{1}{m}\sum_{k=1}^{m}\left[f(w_k^s) - f^*\right]$ from both sides, we have

$$\left(1 - \frac{4\alpha(b)}{(\beta - 1)}\right)\frac{1}{m}\sum_{k=1}^{m}\mathbb{E}\left[f(w_k^s) - f^*\right]$$

$$\leq \frac{4\alpha(b)}{(\beta - 1)}\frac{1}{m}\left[f(w_0^s) - f^* - \{f(w_m^s) - f^*\}\right] + \frac{4\left(\alpha(b)m^2 + (m-1)^2\right)}{m^2(\beta - 1)}\left[f(\tilde{w}^{s-1}) - f^*\right] + R''$$

$$(4.36)$$

Since $f(w_m^s) - f^* \geq 0$ so dropping this term and using Assumption 3, we have

$$\left(1 - \frac{4\alpha(b)}{(\beta - 1)}\right)\frac{1}{m}\sum_{k=1}^{m}\mathbb{E}\left[f(w_k^s) - f^*\right]$$

$$\leq \frac{4\alpha(b)}{(\beta - 1)}\frac{1}{m}\left[f(w_0^s) - f^*\right] + \frac{4\left(\alpha(b)m^2 + (m-1)^2\right)}{m^2(\beta - 1)}\left[f(\tilde{w}^{s-1}) - f^*\right] + R''$$

$$\leq \frac{4\alpha(b)}{(\beta - 1)}\frac{1}{m}\left[c\left(f(\tilde{w}^{s-1}) - f^*\right)\right] + \frac{4\left(\alpha(b)m^2 + (m-1)^2\right)}{m^2(\beta - 1)}\left[f(\tilde{w}^{s-1}) - f^*\right] + R''$$

$$= \left[\frac{4\alpha(b)}{(\beta - 1)}\frac{c}{m} + \frac{4\left(\alpha(b)m^2 + (m-1)^2\right)}{m^2(\beta - 1)}\right]\left[\left(f(\tilde{w}^{s-1}) - f^*\right)\right] + R'',$$

$$(4.37)$$

Dividing both sides by $\left(1 - \dfrac{4\alpha(b)}{(\beta-1)}\right)$, *and since* $\tilde{w}^s = 1/m \sum_{k=1}^{m} w_k^s$ *so by convexity,* $f(\tilde{w}^s) \leq 1/m \sum_{k=1}^{m} f(w_k^s)$, *we have*

$$\mathbb{E}\left[f(\tilde{w}^s) - f^*\right] \leq \left[\frac{4\alpha(b)}{(\beta-1-4\alpha(b))}\frac{c}{m} + \frac{4\left(\alpha(b)m^2 + (m-1)^2\right)}{m^2(\beta-1-4\alpha(b))}\right]\left[f(\tilde{w}^{s-1}) - f^*\right] + R''',$$

(4.38)

where $R''' = R''(\beta-1)/(\beta-1-4\alpha(b))$. *Now, applying this inequality recursively, we have*

$$\mathbb{E}\left[f(\tilde{w}^s) - f^*\right] \leq C^s \left[f(\tilde{w}^0) - f^*\right] + R'''', \tag{4.39}$$

inequality follows for $R'''' = R'''/(1-C)$, *since* $\sum_{i=0}^{k} r^i \leq \sum_{i=0}^{\infty} r^i = \dfrac{1}{1-r}$, $\|r\| < 1$

and $C = \left[\dfrac{4\alpha(b)}{(\beta-1-4\alpha(b))}\dfrac{c}{m} + \dfrac{4\left(\alpha(b)m^2 + (m-1)^2\right)}{m^2(\beta-1-4\alpha(b))}\right]$. *For certain choice of* β, *one can easily prove that* $C < 1$. *This proves linear convergence with some initial error.*

Theorem 3 *Under the assumptions of Lipschitz continuity and strong convexity with smooth regularizer, the convergence of SAAG-IV method is given below:*

$$\mathbb{E}\left[f(\tilde{w}^s) - f^*\right] \leq C^s \left[f(\tilde{w}^0) - f^*\right] + V, \tag{4.40}$$

where,

$$C = \left[\frac{cL\beta}{m\mu} + \frac{4\left(\alpha(b)m^2 + (m-1)^2\right)}{m^2(\beta-1)} - \frac{c(m-1)}{m^2} + \frac{4\alpha(b)}{(\beta-1)}\right]$$

$$\left(1 - \frac{4\alpha(b)}{(\beta-1)} - c\left(\frac{m-1}{m^2} - \frac{4\alpha(b)}{(\beta-1)}\frac{1}{m}\right)\right)^{-1} < 1 \text{ and } V \text{ is constant.}$$

Proof 4.6 *By smoothness, we have,*

$$f(w_{k+1}^s) \leq f(w_k^s) + <\nabla f(w_k^s), w_{k+1}^s - w_k^s > + \frac{L}{2}\|w_{k+1}^s - w_k^s\|^2$$

$$= f(w_k^s) + <\nabla f(w_k^s), w_{k+1}^s - w_k^s > + \frac{L\beta}{2}\|w_{k+1}^s - w_k^s\|^2 - \frac{L(\beta-1)}{2}\|w_{k+1}^s - w_k^s\|^2$$

$$= f(w_k^s) + <\tilde{\nabla}_{s,k}, w_{k+1}^s - w_k^s > + \frac{L\beta}{2}\|w_{k+1}^s - w_k^s\|^2 + <\nabla f(w_k^s)$$

$$- \tilde{\nabla}_{s,k}, w_{k+1}^s - w_k^s > - \frac{L(\beta-1)}{2}\|w_{k+1}^s - w_k^s\|^2$$

(4.41)

where β *is appropriately chosen positive value. Now, separately simplifying the terms, we have*

$$\mathbb{E}\left[f(w_k^s)+ < \tilde{\nabla}_{s,k}, w_{k+1}^s - w_k^s > +\frac{L\beta}{2}\|w_{k+1}^s - w_k^s\|^2\right]$$

$$= f(w_k^s) + \mathbb{E}\left[< \tilde{\nabla}_{s,k}, w_{k+1}^s - w_k^s >\right] + \frac{L\beta}{2}\|w_{k+1}^s - w_k^s\|^2$$

$$= f(w_k^s)+ < \nabla f(w_k^s) + \frac{m-1}{m}\nabla f(\tilde{w}^{s-1}), w_{k+1}^s - w_k^s > +\frac{L\beta}{2}\|w_{k+1}^s - w_k^s\|^2$$

$$= f(w_k^s)+ < \nabla f(w_k^s), w_{k+1}^s - w_k^s > +\frac{L\beta}{2}\|w_{k+1}^s - w_k^s\|^2 + \frac{m-1}{m}$$
$$< \nabla f(\tilde{w}^{s-1}), w_{k+1}^s - w_k^s >$$

$$\leq f(w_k^s)+ < \nabla f(w_k^s), w^* - w_k^s > +\frac{L\beta}{2}\|w^* - w_k^s\|^2 - \frac{L\beta}{2}\|w^* - w_{k+1}^s\|^2$$
$$+ \frac{m-1}{m} < \nabla f(\tilde{w}^{s-1}), w_{k+1}^s - w_k^s >$$

$$= f(w_k^s)+ < \nabla f(w_k^s), w^* - w_k^s > +\frac{L\beta}{2}\|w^* - w_k^s\|^2 - \frac{L\beta}{2}\|w^* - w_{k+1}^s\|^2$$
$$+ \frac{m-1}{m}\left[< \nabla f(\tilde{w}^{s-1}), w_{k+1}^s - \tilde{w}^{s-1} > - < \nabla f(\tilde{w}^{s-1}), w_k^s - \tilde{w}^{s-1} >\right]$$

$$\leq f(w^*) + \frac{L\beta}{2}\left[\|w^* - w_k^s\|^2 - \|w^* - w_{k+1}^s\|^2\right]$$
$$+ \frac{m-1}{m}\left[f(w_{k+1}^s) - f(\tilde{w}^{s-1}) - \left(f(w_k^s) - f(\tilde{w}^{s-1})\right)\right]$$

$$= f(w^*) + \frac{L\beta}{2}\left[\|w^* - w_k^s\|^2 - \|w^* - w_{k+1}^s\|^2\right] + \frac{m-1}{m}\left[f(w_{k+1}^s) - f(w_k^s)\right],$$

$$(4.42)$$

second equality follows from, $\mathbb{E}\left[\tilde{\nabla}_{s,k}\right] = \nabla f(w_k^s) + \frac{m-1}{m}\nabla f(\tilde{w}^{s-1})$, first inequality follows from Lemma 1 and second inequality follows from the convexity, i.e., $f(x) \geq f(y)+ < \nabla f(y), x - y >$.

and, $\mathbb{E}\left[< \nabla f(w_k^s) - \tilde{\nabla}_{s,k}, w_{k+1}^s - w_k^s > -\frac{L(\beta-1)}{2}\|w_{k+1}^s - w_k^s\|^2\right]$

$$\leq \mathbb{E}\left[\frac{1}{2L(\beta-1)}\|\nabla f(w_k^s) - \tilde{\nabla}_{s,k}\|^2 + \frac{L(\beta-1)}{2}\|w_{k+1}^s - w_k^s\|^2 - \frac{L(\beta-1)}{2}\|w_{k+1}^s - w_k^s\|^2\right]$$

$$\leq \frac{1}{2L(\beta-1)}\left[8L\alpha(b)\left[f(w_k^s) - f^*\right] + \frac{8L\left(\alpha(b)m^2 + (m-1)^2\right)}{m^2}\left[f(\tilde{w}^{s-1}) - f^*\right] + R'\right]$$

$$= \frac{4\alpha(b)}{(\beta-1)}\left[f(w_k^s) - f^*\right] + \frac{4\left(\alpha(b)m^2 + (m-1)^2\right)}{m^2(\beta-1)}\left[f(\tilde{w}^{s-1}) - f^*\right] + R''$$

$$(4.43)$$

first inequality follows from Young's inequality and second inequality follows from Lemma 6 and $R'' = R'/(2L(\beta-1))$.

Now, substituting the values into 4.41 from inequalities 4.42 and 4.43, and taking expectation w.r.t. mini-batches, we have

$$\mathbb{E}\left[f(w_{k+1}^s)\right]$$
$$\leq f(w^*) + \frac{L\beta}{2}\left[\|w^* - w_k^s\|^2 - \|w^* - w_{k+1}^s\|^2\right] + \frac{m-1}{m}\left[f(w_{k+1}^s) - f(w_k^s)\right]$$
$$+ \frac{4\alpha(b)}{(\beta-1)}\left[f(w_k^s) - f^*\right] + \frac{4\left(\alpha(b)m^2 + (m-1)^2\right)}{m^2(\beta-1)}\left[f(\tilde{w}^{s-1}) - f^*\right] + R'',$$

$$\mathbb{E}\left[f(w_{k+1}^s) - f(w^*)\right]$$
$$= \frac{L\beta}{2}\left[\|w^* - w_k^s\|^2 - \|w^* - w_{k+1}^s\|^2\right] + \frac{m-1}{m}\left[f(w_{k+1}^s) - f(w_k^s)\right]$$
$$+ \frac{4\alpha(b)}{(\beta-1)}\left[f(w_k^s) - f^*\right] + \frac{4\left(\alpha(b)m^2 + (m-1)^2\right)}{m^2(\beta-1)}\left[f(\tilde{w}^{s-1}) - f^*\right] + R''$$

$$(4.44)$$

Taking sum over $k = 0, 1, ..., (m-1)$ and dividing by m, we have

$$\frac{1}{m}\sum_{k=0}^{m-1}\mathbb{E}\left[f(w_{k+1}^s) - f(w^*)\right]$$
$$\leq \frac{1}{m}\sum_{k=0}^{m-1}\left\{\frac{L\beta}{2}\left[\|w^* - w_k^s\|^2 - \|w^* - w_{k+1}^s\|^2\right] + \frac{m-1}{m}\left[f(w_{k+1}^s) - f(w_k^s)\right]\right\}$$
$$+ \frac{1}{m}\sum_{k=0}^{m-1}\left\{\frac{4\alpha(b)}{(\beta-1)}\left[f(w_k^s) - f^*\right] + \frac{4\left(\alpha(b)m^2 + (m-1)^2\right)}{m^2(\beta-1)}\left[f(\tilde{w}^{s-1}) - f^*\right] + R''\right\},$$

$$\frac{1}{m}\sum_{k=1}^{m}\mathbb{E}\left[f(w_k^s) - f(w^*)\right]$$
$$\leq \frac{L\beta}{2m}\left[\|w^* - w_0^s\|^2 - \|w^* - w_m^s\|^2\right] + \frac{m-1}{m^2}\left[f(w_m^s) - f(w_0^s)\right]$$
$$+ \frac{4\alpha(b)}{(\beta-1)}\frac{1}{m}\left\{\sum_{k=1}^{m}\left[f(w_k^s) - f^*\right] + f(w_0^s) - f^* - (f(w_m^s) - f^*)\right\}$$
$$+ \frac{4\left(\alpha(b)m^2 + (m-1)^2\right)}{m^2(\beta-1)}\left[f(\tilde{w}^{s-1}) - f^*\right] + R''$$

$$(4.45)$$

Subtracting $\dfrac{4\alpha(b)}{(\beta-1)}\dfrac{1}{m}\sum_{k=1}^{m}[f(w_k^s)-f^*]$ *from both sides, we have*

$$\left(1-\frac{4\alpha(b)}{(\beta-1)}\right)\frac{1}{m}\sum_{k=1}^{m}\mathbb{E}\left[f(w_k^s)-f^*\right]$$

$$\leq \frac{L\beta}{2m}\left[\|w^*-w_0^s\|^2-\|w^*-w_m^s\|^2\right]-\left(\frac{m-1}{m^2}-\frac{4\alpha(b)}{(\beta-1)}\frac{1}{m}\right)[f(w_0^s)-f(w_m^s)]$$

$$+\frac{4\left(\alpha(b)m^2+(m-1)^2\right)}{m^2(\beta-1)}\left[f(\tilde{w}^{s-1})-f^*\right]+R''$$

$$\leq \frac{L\beta}{2m}\|w^*-w_0^s\|^2-\left(\frac{m-1}{m^2}-\frac{4\alpha(b)}{(\beta-1)}\frac{1}{m}\right)[f(w_0^s)-f^*-\{f(w_m^s)-f^*\}]$$

$$+\frac{4\left(\alpha(b)m^2+(m-1)^2\right)}{m^2(\beta-1)}\left[f(\tilde{w}^{s-1})-f^*\right]+R''$$

$$\leq \frac{L\beta}{2m}\frac{2}{\mu}\left(f(w_0^s)-f^*\right)-\left(\frac{m-1}{m^2}-\frac{4\alpha(b)}{(\beta-1)}\frac{1}{m}\right)\left[c\left[f(\tilde{w}^{s-1})-f^*\right]-c\left[f(\tilde{w}^s)-f^*\right]\right]$$

$$+\frac{4\left(\alpha(b)m^2+(m-1)^2\right)}{m^2(\beta-1)}\left[f(\tilde{w}^{s-1})-f^*\right]+R''$$

$$\leq \frac{L\beta}{2m}\frac{2}{\mu}c\left[f(\tilde{w}^{s-1})-f^*\right]-\left(\frac{m-1}{m^2}-\frac{4\alpha(b)}{(\beta-1)}\frac{1}{m}\right)\left[c\left[f(\tilde{w}^{s-1})-f^*\right]-c\left[f(\tilde{w}^s)-f^*\right]\right]$$

$$+\frac{4\left(\alpha(b)m^2+(m-1)^2\right)}{m^2(\beta-1)}\left[f(\tilde{w}^{s-1})-f^*\right]+R''$$

$$(4.46)$$

second inequality follows by dropping, $\|w^*-w_m^s\|^2>0$, *third inequality follows from the strong convexity, i.e.,* $\|w_0^s-w^*\|^2\leq 2/\mu\left(f(w_0^s)-f^*\right)$ *and application of Assumption 3 twice, and fourth inequality follows from Assumption 3.*

Since $\tilde{w}^s=1/m\sum_{k=1}^{m}w_k^s$ *so by convexity using,* $f(\tilde{w}^s)\leq 1/m\sum_{k=1}^{m}f(w_k^s)$, *we have*

$$\left(1-\frac{4\alpha(b)}{(\beta-1)}\right)\mathbb{E}\left[f(\tilde{w}^s)-f^*\right]$$

$$\leq \frac{L\beta}{2m}\frac{2}{\mu}c\left[f(\tilde{w}^{s-1})-f^*\right]-\left(\frac{m-1}{m^2}-\frac{4\alpha(b)}{(\beta-1)}\frac{1}{m}\right)\left[c\left[f(\tilde{w}^{s-1})-f^*\right]-c\left[f(\tilde{w}^s)-f^*\right]\right]$$

$$+\frac{4\left(\alpha(b)m^2+(m-1)^2\right)}{m^2(\beta-1)}\left[f(\tilde{w}^{s-1})-f^*\right]+R''$$

$$(4.47)$$

Subtracting, $c\left(\dfrac{m-1}{m^2}-\dfrac{4\alpha(b)}{(\beta-1)}\dfrac{1}{m}\right)\mathbb{E}\left[f(\tilde{w}^s)-f^*\right]$ *both sides, we have*

$$\left(1-\frac{4\alpha(b)}{(\beta-1)}-c\left(\frac{m-1}{m^2}-\frac{4\alpha(b)}{(\beta-1)}\frac{1}{m}\right)\right)\mathbb{E}\left[f(\tilde{w}^s)-f^*\right]$$

$$\leq \left[\frac{cL\beta}{m\mu}+\frac{4\left(\alpha(b)m^2+(m-1)^2\right)}{m^2(\beta-1)}-\frac{c(m-1)}{m^2}+\frac{4\alpha(b)}{(\beta-1)}\right]\left[f(\tilde{w}^{s-1})-f^*\right]+R''$$

$$(4.48)$$

Dividing both sides by $\left(1 - \dfrac{4\alpha(b)}{(\beta - 1)} - c\left(\dfrac{m - 1}{m^2} - \dfrac{4\alpha(b)}{(\beta - 1)}\dfrac{1}{m}\right)\right)$, *we have*

$$\mathbb{E}\left[f(\tilde{w}^s) - f^*\right] \leq C\left[f(\tilde{w}^{s-1}) - f^*\right] + R''' \tag{4.49}$$

where
$$C = \left[\frac{cL\beta}{m\mu} + \frac{4\left(\alpha(b)m^2 + (m-1)^2\right)}{m^2(\beta - 1)} - \frac{c(m-1)}{m^2} + \frac{4\alpha(b)}{(\beta - 1)}\right]$$
$$\left(1 - \frac{4\alpha(b)}{(\beta - 1)} - c\left(\frac{m - 1}{m^2} - \frac{4\alpha(b)}{(\beta - 1)}\frac{1}{m}\right)\right)^{-1}$$

and $R''' = R''\left(1 - \dfrac{4\alpha(b)}{(\beta - 1)} - c\left(\dfrac{m - 1}{m^2} - \dfrac{4\alpha(b)}{(\beta - 1)}\dfrac{1}{m}\right)\right)^{-1}$.

Now, recursively applying the inequality, we have

$$\mathbb{E}\left[f(\tilde{w}^s) - f^*\right] \leq C^s\left[f(\tilde{w}^0) - f^*\right] + R'''', \tag{4.50}$$

inequality follows for $R'''' = R'''/(1 - C)$, *since* $\sum_{i=0}^{k} r^i \leq \sum_{i=0}^{\infty} r^i = \dfrac{1}{1 - r}$, $\|r\| < 1$. *For certain choice of* β, *one can easily prove that* $C < 1$. *This proves linear convergence with some initial error.*

Theorem 4 *Under the assumptions of Lipschitz continuity with non-smooth regularizer, the convergence of SAAG-IV is given below:*

$$\mathbb{E}\left[F(\tilde{w}^s) - F(w^*)\right] \leq C^s\left[F(\tilde{w}^0) - F(w^*)\right] + V, \tag{4.51}$$

where,
$$C = \left(\frac{4\alpha(b)}{(\beta - 1 - 4\alpha(b))} \frac{c}{m} + \frac{4\left(\alpha(b)m^2 + (m-1)^2\right)}{m^2(\beta - 1 - 4\alpha(b))}\right) < 1 \text{ and } V \text{ is constant.}$$

Proof 4.7 *By smoothness, we have,*

$$f(w_{k+1}^s) \leq f(w_k^s) + <\nabla f(w_k^s), w_{k+1}^s - w_k^s> + \frac{L}{2}\|w_{k+1}^s - w_k^s\|^2 \tag{4.52}$$

Now, $F(w_{k+1}^s) = f(w_{k+1}^s) + g(w_{k+1}^s)$

$$\leq f(w_k^s) + g(w_{k+1}^s) + <\nabla f(w_k^s), w_{k+1}^s - w_k^s> + \frac{L}{2}\|w_{k+1}^s - w_k^s\|^2$$

$$= f(w_k^s) + g(w_{k+1}^s) + <\nabla f(w_k^s), w_{k+1}^s - w_k^s> + \frac{L\beta}{2}\|w_{k+1}^s - w_k^s\|^2$$

$$- \frac{L(\beta - 1)}{2}\|w_{k+1}^s - w_k^s\|^2 \tag{4.53}$$

$$= f(w_k^s) + g(w_{k+1}^s) + <\tilde{\nabla}_{s,k}, w_{k+1}^s - w_k^s> + \frac{L\beta}{2}\|w_{k+1}^s - w_k^s\|^2 +$$

$$< \nabla f(w_k^s) - \tilde{\nabla}_{s,k}, w_{k+1}^s - w_k^s> - \frac{L(\beta - 1)}{2}\|w_{k+1}^s - w_k^s\|^2$$

where β is appropriately chosen positive value. Now, separately simplifying the terms, we have

$$\mathbb{E}\left[f(w_k^s) + g(w_{k+1}^s) + <\tilde{\nabla}_{s,k}, w_{k+1}^s - w_k^s> + \frac{L\beta}{2}\|w_{k+1}^s - w_k^s\|^2\right]$$

$$= f(w_k^s) + g(w_{k+1}^s) + \mathbb{E}\left[<\tilde{\nabla}_{s,k}, w_{k+1}^s - w_k^s>\right] + \frac{L\beta}{2}\|w_{k+1}^s - w_k^s\|^2$$

$$= f(w_k^s) + g(w_{k+1}^s) + <\nabla f(w_k^s) + \frac{m-1}{m}\nabla f(\tilde{w}^{s-1}), w_{k+1}^s - w_k^s> + \frac{L\beta}{2}\|w_{k+1}^s - w_k^s\|^2$$

$$= f(w_k^s) + g(w_{k+1}^s) + <\nabla f(w_k^s), w_{k+1}^s - w_k^s> + \frac{L\beta}{2}\|w_{k+1}^s - w_k^s\|^2$$

$$+ \frac{m-1}{m} <\nabla f(\tilde{w}^{s-1}), w_{k+1}^s - w_k^s>$$

$$\leq f(w_k^s) + g(w^*) + <\nabla f(w_k^s), w^* - w_k^s> + \frac{L\beta}{2}\|w^* - w_k^s\|^2 - \frac{L\beta}{2}\|w^* - w_{k+1}^s\|^2$$

$$+ \frac{m-1}{m} <\nabla f(\tilde{w}^{s-1}), w_{k+1}^s - w_k^s>$$

$$= f(w_k^s) + g(w^*) + <\nabla f(w_k^s), w^* - w_k^s> + \frac{L\beta}{2}\|w^* - w_k^s\|^2 - \frac{L\beta}{2}\|w^* - w_{k+1}^s\|^2$$

$$+ \frac{m-1}{m}\left[<\nabla f(\tilde{w}^{s-1}), w_{k+1}^s - w^*> - <\nabla f(\tilde{w}^{s-1}), w_k^s - w^*>\right]$$

$$\leq f(w^*) + g(w^*) + \frac{L\beta}{2}\left[\|w^* - w_k^s\|^2 - \|w^* - w_{k+1}^s\|^2\right]$$

$$+ \frac{m-1}{m}\left[\frac{1}{2\delta}\|\nabla f(\tilde{w}^{s-1})\|^2 + \frac{\delta}{2}\|w_{k+1}^s - w^*\|^2 - \left[\frac{1}{2\delta}\|\nabla f(\tilde{w}^{s-1})\|^2 + \frac{\delta}{2}\|w_k^s - w^*\|^2\right]\right]$$

$$= F(w^*) + \frac{L\beta}{2}\left[\|w^* - w_k^s\|^2 - \|w^* - w_{k+1}^s\|^2\right] + \frac{\delta(m-1)}{2m}\left[\|w_{k+1}^s - w^*\|^2 - \|w_k^s - w^*\|^2\right],$$

$$= F(w^*) + \left(\frac{L\beta}{2} - \frac{\delta(m-1)}{2m}\right)\left[\|w^* - w_k^s\|^2 - \|w^* - w_{k+1}^s\|^2\right], \quad (4.54)$$

$$= F(w^*),$$

second equality follows from, $\mathbb{E}\left[\tilde{\nabla}_{s,k}\right] = \nabla f(w_k^s) + \frac{m-1}{m}\nabla f(\tilde{w}^{s-1})$, *first inequality follows from Lemma 1, second inequality follows from the convexity, i.e.,* $f(w^*) \geq f(w_k^s) + <\nabla f(w_k^s), w^* - w_k^s>$ *and Young's inequality, i.e.,* $x^T y \leq 1/(2\delta)\|x\|^2 +$

$\delta/2\|y\|^2$ *for* $\delta > 0$, *and last equality follows by choosing* $\delta = \dfrac{mL\beta}{(m-1)}$.

And, $\mathbb{E}\left[< \nabla f(w_k^s) - \tilde{\nabla}_{s,k}, w_{k+1}^s - w_k^s > -\dfrac{L(\beta-1)}{2}\|w_{k+1}^s - w_k^s\|^2\right]$

$\leq \mathbb{E}\left[\dfrac{1}{2L(\beta-1)}\|\nabla f(w_k^s) - \tilde{\nabla}_{s,k}\|^2 + \dfrac{L(\beta-1)}{2}\|w_{k+1}^s - w_k^s\|^2 - \dfrac{L(\beta-1)}{2}\|w_{k+1}^s - w_k^s\|^2\right]$

$= \dfrac{1}{2L(\beta-1)}\mathbb{E}\left[\|\tilde{\nabla}_{s,k} - \nabla f(w_k^s)\|^2\right]$

$\leq \dfrac{1}{2L(\beta-1)}\left[8L\alpha(b)\left[F(w_k^s) - F^*\right] + \dfrac{8L\left(\alpha(b)m^2 + (m-1)^2\right)}{m^2}\left[F(\tilde{w}^{s-1}) - F^*\right] + R'\right]$

$= \dfrac{4\alpha(b)}{(\beta-1)}\left[F(w_k^s) - F^*\right] + \dfrac{4\left(\alpha(b)m^2 + (m-1)^2\right)}{m^2(\beta-1)}\left[F(\tilde{w}^{s-1}) - F^*\right] + R''$

$$(4.55)$$

first inequality follows from Young's inequality and second inequality follows from Lemma 7 and $R'' = R'/(2L(\beta-1))$. *Now, substituting the values into 4.53 from inequalities 4.54 and 4.55, and taking expectation w.r.t. mini-batches, we have*

$$\mathbb{E}\left[F(w_{k+1}^s)\right] \leq F(w^*) + \dfrac{4\alpha(b)}{(\beta-1)}\left[F(w_k^s) - F^*\right]$$

$$+ \dfrac{4\left(\alpha(b)m^2 + (m-1)^2\right)}{m^2(\beta-1)}\left[F(\tilde{w}^{s-1}) - F^*\right] + R''$$

$$\mathbb{E}\left[F(w_{k+1}^s) - F(w^*)\right] \leq \dfrac{4\alpha(b)}{(\beta-1)}\left[F(w_k^s) - F^*\right]$$

$$+ \dfrac{4\left(\alpha(b)m^2 + (m-1)^2\right)}{m^2(\beta-1)}\left[F(\tilde{w}^{s-1}) - F^*\right] + R''$$

$$(4.56)$$

Taking sum over $k = 0, 1, ..., (m-1)$ *and dividing by* m, *we have*

$$\dfrac{1}{m}\sum_{k=0}^{m-1}\mathbb{E}\left[F(w_{k+1}^s) - F(w^*)\right]$$

$$\leq \dfrac{4\alpha(b)}{(\beta-1)}\dfrac{1}{m}\sum_{k=0}^{m-1}\left[F(w_k^s) - F(w^*)\right] + \dfrac{4\left(\alpha(b)m^2 + (m-1)^2\right)}{m^2(\beta-1)}\left[F(\tilde{w}^{s-1}) - F(w^*)\right] + R'',$$

$$\dfrac{1}{m}\sum_{k=1}^{m}\mathbb{E}\left[F(w_k^s) - F(w^*)\right]$$

$$\leq \dfrac{4\alpha(b)}{(\beta-1)}\dfrac{1}{m}\left\{\sum_{k=1}^{m}\left[F(w_k^s) - F(w^*)\right] + F(w_0^s) - F(w^*) - \{F(w_m^s) - F(w^*)\}\right\}$$

$$+ \dfrac{4\left(\alpha(b)m^2 + (m-1)^2\right)}{m^2(\beta-1)}\left[F(\tilde{w}^{s-1}) - F(w^*)\right] + R''$$

$$(4.57)$$

Subtracting $\dfrac{4\alpha(b)}{(\beta-1)}\dfrac{1}{m}\sum_{k=1}^{m}[F(w_k^s)-F(w^*)]$ *from both sides, we have*

$$\left(1-\frac{4\alpha(b)}{(\beta-1)}\right)\frac{1}{m}\sum_{k=1}^{m}\mathbb{E}\left[F(w_k^s)-F(w^*)\right]$$

$$\leq \frac{4\alpha(b)}{(\beta-1)}\frac{1}{m}\left[F(w_0^s)-F(w^*)-\{F(w_m^s)-F(w^*)\}\right] \tag{4.58}$$

$$+\frac{4\left(\alpha(b)m^2+(m-1)^2\right)}{m^2(\beta-1)}\left[F(\tilde{w}^{s-1})-F(w^*)\right]+R''$$

Since $F(w_m^s)-F(w^*)\geq 0$ *so dropping this term and using Assumption 3, we have*

$$\left(1-\frac{4\alpha(b)}{(\beta-1)}\right)\frac{1}{m}\sum_{k=1}^{m}\mathbb{E}\left[F(w_k^s)-F(w^*)\right]$$

$$\leq \frac{4\alpha(b)}{(\beta-1)}\frac{1}{m}\left[F(w_0^s)-F(w^*)\right]+\frac{4\left(\alpha(b)m^2+(m-1)^2\right)}{m^2(\beta-1)}\left[F(\tilde{w}^{s-1})-F(w^*)\right]+R''$$

$$\leq \frac{4\alpha(b)}{(\beta-1)}\frac{1}{m}\left[c\left(F(\tilde{w}^{s-1})-F(w^*)\right)\right]+\frac{4\left(\alpha(b)m^2+(m-1)^2\right)}{m^2(\beta-1)}\left[F(\tilde{w}^{s-1})-F(w^*)\right]+R''$$

$$=\left(\frac{4\alpha(b)}{(\beta-1)}\frac{c}{m}+\frac{4\left(\alpha(b)m^2+(m-1)^2\right)}{m^2(\beta-1)}\right)\left[(F(\tilde{w}^{s-1})-F(w^*))\right]+R'',$$

$$\tag{4.59}$$

Dividing both sides by $\left(1-\dfrac{4\alpha(b)}{(\beta-1)}\right)$, *and since* $\tilde{w}^s=1/m\sum_{k=1}^{m}w_k^s$ *so by convexity,*
$F(\tilde{w}^s)\leq 1/m\sum_{k=1}^{m}F(w_k^s)$, *we have*

$$\mathbb{E}\left[F(\tilde{w}^s)-F^*\right]\leq\left(\frac{4\alpha(b)}{(\beta-1-4\alpha(b))}\frac{c}{m}+\frac{4\left(\alpha(b)m^2+(m-1)^2\right)}{m^2(\beta-1-4\alpha(b))}\right)\left[F(\tilde{w}^{s-1})-F(w^*)\right]+R''',$$

$$\tag{4.60}$$

where $R'''=R''\left(1-\dfrac{4\alpha(b)}{(\beta-1)}\right)^{-1}$. *Now, applying above inequality recursively, we have*

$$\mathbb{E}\left[F(\tilde{w}^s)-F(w^*)\right]\leq C^s\left[F(\tilde{w}^0)-F(w^*)\right]+R'''', \tag{4.61}$$

inequality follows for $R''''=R'''/(1-C)$, *since* $\sum_{i=0}^{k}r^i\leq\sum_{i=0}^{\infty}r^i=\dfrac{1}{1-r}$, $\|r\|<1$

and $C=\left(\dfrac{4\alpha(b)}{(\beta-1-4\alpha(b))}\dfrac{c}{m}+\dfrac{4\left(\alpha(b)m^2+(m-1)^2\right)}{m^2(\beta-1-4\alpha(b))}\right)$. *For certain choice of* β, *one can easily prove that* $C<1$. *This proves linear convergence with some initial error.*

Theorem 5 *Under the assumptions of Lipschitz continuity and strong convexity with non-smooth regularizer, the convergence of SAAG-IV is given below:*

$$\mathbb{E}\left[F(\tilde{w}^s)-F^*\right]\leq C^s\left[F(\tilde{w}^0)-F^*\right]+V, \tag{4.62}$$

where,

$$C = \left(\frac{Lc\beta}{m\mu} + \frac{4c\alpha(b)}{m(\beta - 1)} - \frac{c(m-1)}{m^2} + \frac{4\left(\alpha(b)m^2 + (m-1)^2\right)}{m^2(\beta - 1)} \right)$$

$$\left(1 - \frac{4\alpha(b)}{(\beta - 1)} - \frac{c(m-1)}{m^2} + \frac{4c\alpha(b)}{m(\beta - 1)} \right)^{-1} < 1 \ and \ V \ is \ constant.$$

Proof 4.8 *By smoothness, we have,*

$$f(w_{k+1}^s) \leq f(w_k^s) + \ < \nabla f(w_k^s), w_{k+1}^s - w_k^s > + \frac{L}{2} \|w_{k+1}^s - w_k^s\|^2$$

Now,

$$F(w_{k+1}^s) = f(w_{k+1}^s) + g(w_{k+1}^s)$$

$$\leq f(w_k^s) + g(w_{k+1}^s) + \ < \nabla f(w_k^s), w_{k+1}^s - w_k^s > + \frac{L}{2} \|w_{k+1}^s - w_k^s\|^2$$

$$= f(w_k^s) + g(w_{k+1}^s) + \ < \nabla f(w_k^s), w_{k+1}^s - w_k^s > + \frac{L\beta}{2} \|w_{k+1}^s - w_k^s\|^2 - \frac{L(\beta - 1)}{2} \|w_{k+1}^s - w_k^s\|^2$$

$$= f(w_k^s) + g(w_{k+1}^s) + \ < \tilde{\nabla}_{s,k}, w_{k+1}^s - w_k^s > + \frac{L\beta}{2} \|w_{k+1}^s - w_k^s\|^2 +$$

$$< \nabla f(w_k^s) - \tilde{\nabla}_{s,k}, w_{k+1}^s - w_k^s > - \frac{L(\beta - 1)}{2} \|w_{k+1}^s - w_k^s\|^2$$

$$(4.63)$$

where β is appropriately chosen positive value. Now, separately simplifying the terms, *we have*

$$\mathbb{E}\left[f(w_k^s) + g(w_{k+1}^s) + <\tilde{\nabla}_{s,k}, w_{k+1}^s - w_k^s> + \frac{L\beta}{2}\|w_{k+1}^s - w_k^s\|^2\right]$$

$$= f(w_k^s) + g(w_{k+1}^s) + \mathbb{E}\left[<\tilde{\nabla}_{s,k}, w_{k+1}^s - w_k^s>\right] + \frac{L\beta}{2}\|w_{k+1}^s - w_k^s\|^2$$

$$= f(w_k^s) + g(w_{k+1}^s) + <\nabla f(w_k^s) + \frac{m-1}{m}\nabla f(\tilde{w}^{s-1}), w_{k+1}^s - w_k^s> + \frac{L\beta}{2}\|w_{k+1}^s - w_k^s\|^2$$

$$= f(w_k^s) + g(w_{k+1}^s) + <\nabla f(w_k^s), w_{k+1}^s - w_k^s> + \frac{L\beta}{2}\|w_{k+1}^s - w_k^s\|^2$$

$$\quad + \frac{m-1}{m}<\nabla f(\tilde{w}^{s-1}), w_{k+1}^s - w_k^s>$$

$$\leq f(w_k^s) + g(w^*) + <\nabla f(w_k^s), w^* - w_k^s> + \frac{L\beta}{2}\|w^* - w_k^s\|^2 - \frac{L\beta}{2}\|w^* - w_{k+1}^s\|^2$$

$$\quad + \frac{m-1}{m}<\nabla f(\tilde{w}^{s-1}), w_{k+1}^s - w_k^s>$$

$$= f(w_k^s) + g(w^*) + <\nabla f(w_k^s), w^* - w_k^s> + \frac{L\beta}{2}\|w^* - w_k^s\|^2 - \frac{L\beta}{2}\|w^* - w_{k+1}^s\|^2$$

$$\quad + \frac{m-1}{m}\left[<\nabla f(\tilde{w}^{s-1}), w_{k+1}^s - \tilde{w}^{s-1}> - <\nabla f(\tilde{w}^{s-1}), w_k^s - \tilde{w}^{s-1}>\right]$$

$$\leq f(w^*) + g(w^*) + \frac{L\beta}{2}\left[\|w^* - w_k^s\|^2 - \|w^* - w_{k+1}^s\|^2\right]$$

$$\quad + \frac{m-1}{m}\left[f(w_{k+1}^s) - f(\tilde{w}^{s-1}) - \left(f(w_k^s) - f(\tilde{w}^{s-1})\right)\right]$$

$$= f(w^*) + g(w^*) + \frac{L\beta}{2}\left[\|w^* - w_k^s\|^2 - \|w^* - w_{k+1}^s\|^2\right] + \frac{m-1}{m}\left[f(w_{k+1}^s) - f(w_k^s)\right],$$

$$= F(w^*) + \frac{L\beta}{2}\left[\|w^* - w_k^s\|^2 - \|w^* - w_{k+1}^s\|^2\right] + \frac{m-1}{m}\left[f(w_{k+1}^s) - f(w_k^s)\right],$$

$$(4.64)$$

second equality follows from, $\mathbb{E}\left[\tilde{\nabla}_{s,k}\right] = \nabla f(w_k^s) + \frac{m-1}{m}\nabla f(\tilde{w}^{s-1})$, *first inequality follows from Lemma 1 and second inequality follows from the convexity, i.e.,* $f(x) \geq f(y) + <\nabla f(y), x - y>$.

And, $\mathbb{E}\left[<\nabla f(w_k^s) - \tilde{\nabla}_{s,k}, w_{k+1}^s - w_k^s> - \frac{L(\beta-1)}{2}\|w_{k+1}^s - w_k^s\|^2\right]$

$$\leq \mathbb{E}\left[\frac{1}{2L(\beta-1)}\|\nabla f(w_k^s) - \tilde{\nabla}_{s,k}\|^2 + \frac{L(\beta-1)}{2}\|w_{k+1}^s - w_k^s\|^2 - \frac{L(\beta-1)}{2}\|w_{k+1}^s - w_k^s\|^2\right]$$

$$= \frac{1}{2L(\beta-1)}\mathbb{E}\left[\|\tilde{\nabla}_{s,k} - \nabla f(w_k^s)\|^2\right]$$

$$\leq \frac{1}{2L(\beta-1)}\left[8L\alpha(b)\left[F(w_k^s) - F^*\right] + \frac{8L\left(\alpha(b)m^2 + (m-1)^2\right)}{m^2}\left[F(\tilde{w}^{s-1}) - F^*\right] + R'\right]$$

$$= \frac{4\alpha(b)}{(\beta-1)}\left[F(w_k^s) - F^*\right] + \frac{4\left(\alpha(b)m^2 + (m-1)^2\right)}{m^2(\beta-1)}\left[F(\tilde{w}^{s-1}) - F^*\right] + R'', \quad (4.65)$$

first inequality follows from Young's inequality and second inequality follows from

Lemma 7 and $R'' = R'/(2L(\beta - 1))$. Now, substituting the values into 4.63 from inequalities 4.64 and 4.65, and taking expectation w.r.t. mini-batches, we have

$$\mathbb{E}\left[F(w_{k+1}^s)\right]$$

$$\leq F(w^*) + \frac{L\beta}{2}\left[\|w^* - w_k^s\|^2 - \|w^* - w_{k+1}^s\|^2\right] + \frac{m-1}{m}\left[f(w_{k+1}^s) - f(w_k^s)\right]$$

$$+ \frac{4\alpha(b)}{(\beta - 1)}\left[F(w_k^s) - F^*\right] + \frac{4\left(\alpha(b)m^2 + (m-1)^2\right)}{m^2(\beta - 1)}\left[F(\tilde{w}^{s-1}) - F^*\right] + R''$$

$$\mathbb{E}\left[F(w_{k+1}^s) - F(w^*)\right]$$

$$\leq \frac{L\beta}{2}\left[\|w^* - w_k^s\|^2 - \|w^* - w_{k+1}^s\|^2\right] + \frac{m-1}{m}\left[f(w_{k+1}^s) - f(w_k^s)\right]$$

$$+ \frac{4\alpha(b)}{(\beta - 1)}\left[F(w_k^s) - F^*\right] + \frac{4\left(\alpha(b)m^2 + (m-1)^2\right)}{m^2(\beta - 1)}\left[F(\tilde{w}^{s-1}) - F^*\right] + R''$$

$$(4.66)$$

Taking sum over $k = 0, 1, ..., (m-1)$ and dividing by m, we have

$$\frac{1}{m}\sum_{k=0}^{m-1}\mathbb{E}\left[F(w_{k+1}^s) - F(w^*)\right]$$

$$\leq \frac{1}{m}\sum_{k=0}^{m-1}\left\{\frac{L\beta}{2}\left[\|w^* - w_k^s\|^2 - \|w^* - w_{k+1}^s\|^2\right] + \frac{m-1}{m}\left[f(w_{k+1}^s) - f(w_k^s)\right]\right\}$$

$$+ \frac{1}{m}\sum_{k=0}^{m-1}\left\{\frac{4\alpha(b)}{(\beta - 1)}\left[F(w_k^s) - F^*\right] + \frac{4\left(\alpha(b)m^2 + (m-1)^2\right)}{m^2(\beta - 1)}\left[F(\tilde{w}^{s-1}) - F^*\right] + R''\right\},$$

$$\frac{1}{m}\sum_{k=1}^{m}\mathbb{E}\left[F(w_k^s) - F(w^*)\right]$$

$$\leq \frac{L\beta}{2m}\left[\|w^* - w_0^s\|^2 - \|w^* - w_m^s\|^2\right] + \frac{m-1}{m^2}\left[f(w_m^s) - f(w_0^s)\right]$$

$$+ \frac{4\alpha(b)}{(\beta - 1)}\frac{1}{m}\left\{\sum_{k=1}^{m}[F(w_k^s) - F(w^*)] + F(w_0^s) - F(w^*) - (F(w_m^s) - F(w^*))\right\}$$

$$+ \frac{4\left(\alpha(b)m^2 + (m-1)^2\right)}{m^2(\beta - 1)}\left[F(\tilde{w}^{s-1}) - F(w^*)\right] + R''$$

$$(4.67)$$

Subtracting, $\frac{4\alpha(b)}{(\beta - 1)}\frac{1}{m}\sum_{k=1}^{m}[F(w_k^s) - F(w^*)]$ from both sides, we have

$$t\left(1 - \frac{4\alpha(b)}{(\beta - 1)}\right)\frac{1}{m}\sum_{k=1}^{m}\mathbb{E}\left[F(w_k^s) - F(w^*)\right]$$

$$\leq \frac{L\beta}{2m}\left[\|w^* - w_0^s\|^2 - \|w^* - w_m^s\|^2\right] + \frac{m-1}{m^2}\left[f(w_m^s) - f(w_0^s)\right]$$

$$+ \frac{4\alpha(b)}{(\beta - 1)}\frac{1}{m}\left\{F(w_0^s) - F(w^*) - (F(w_m^s) - F(w^*))\right\}$$

$$+ \frac{4\left(\alpha(b)m^2 + (m-1)^2\right)}{m^2(\beta - 1)}\left[F(\tilde{w}^{s-1}) - F(w^*)\right] + R''$$

$$\leq \frac{L\beta}{2m}\left[\|w^* - w_0^s\|^2\right] + \frac{m-1}{m^2}\left[F(w_m^s) - F(w_0^s)\right]$$

$$+ \frac{4\alpha(b)}{(\beta - 1)}\frac{1}{m}\left\{F(w_0^s) - F(w^*) - (F(w_m^s) - F(w^*))\right\}$$

$$+ \frac{4\left(\alpha(b)m^2 + (m-1)^2\right)}{m^2(\beta - 1)}\left[F(\tilde{w}^{s-1}) - F(w^*)\right] + R'''$$

$$\leq \frac{L\beta}{2m}\frac{2}{\mu}\left[F(w_0^s) - F(w^*)\right] + \frac{m-1}{m^2}\left[F(w_m^s) - F(w_0^s)\right]$$

$$+ \frac{4\alpha(b)}{(\beta - 1)}\frac{1}{m}\left\{F(w_0^s) - F(w^*) - (F(w_m^s) - F(w^*))\right\}$$

$$+ \frac{4\left(\alpha(b)m^2 + (m-1)^2\right)}{m^2(\beta - 1)}\left[F(\tilde{w}^{s-1}) - F(w^*)\right] + R'''$$

$$= \left(\frac{L\beta}{m\mu} + \frac{4\alpha(b)}{m(\beta - 1)} - \frac{m-1}{m^2}\right)\left[F(w_0^s) - F(w^*)\right] + \left(\frac{m-1}{m^2} - \frac{4\alpha(b)}{m(\beta - 1)}\right)$$

$$\times \left[F(w_m^s) - F(w^*)\right] + \frac{4\left(\alpha(b)m^2 + (m-1)^2\right)}{m^2(\beta - 1)}\left[F(\tilde{w}^{s-1}) - F(w^*)\right] + R'''$$

$$\leq \left(\frac{L\beta}{m\mu} + \frac{4\alpha(b)}{m(\beta - 1)} - \frac{m-1}{m^2}\right)c\left[F(\tilde{w}^{s-1}) - F(w^*)\right]$$

$$+ \left(\frac{m-1}{m^2} - \frac{4\alpha(b)}{m(\beta - 1)}\right)c\left[F(\tilde{w}^s) - F(w^*)\right]$$

$$+ \frac{4\left(\alpha(b)m^2 + (m-1)^2\right)}{m^2(\beta - 1)}\left[F(\tilde{w}^{s-1}) - F(w^*)\right] + R'''$$

$$\leq \left(\frac{Lc\beta}{m\mu} + \frac{4c\alpha(b)}{m(\beta - 1)} - \frac{c(m-1)}{m^2} + \frac{4\left(\alpha(b)m^2 + (m-1)^2\right)}{m^2(\beta - 1)}\right)\left[F(\tilde{w}^{s-1}) - F(w^*)\right]$$

$$+ \left(\frac{m-1}{m^2} - \frac{4\alpha(b)}{m(\beta - 1)}\right)c\left[F(\tilde{w}^s) - F(w^*)\right] + R'''$$

(4.68)

second inequality follows from dropping, $\|w^* - w_m^s\|^2 \geq 0$ and converting, $f(w_m^s) - f(w_0^s)$ to $F(w_m^s) - F(w_0^s)$ by introducing some constant, third inequality follows from the strong convexity, i.e., $\|w_0^s - w^*\|^2 \leq 2/\mu\left(f(w_0^s) - f^*\right)$, fourth inequality follows from Assumption 3 and $R''' = R'' + (m-1)g(w_0^s)/m^2$.
Since $\tilde{w}^s = 1/m\sum_{k=1}^m w_k^s$ so by convexity using, $f(\tilde{w}^s) \leq 1/m\sum_{k=1}^m f(w_k^s)$, and subtracting $\left(\frac{m-1}{m^2} - \frac{4\alpha(b)}{m(\beta - 1)}\right)c\left[F(\tilde{w}^s) - F(w^*)\right]$ from both sides, we have

$$\left(1 - \frac{4\alpha(b)}{(\beta - 1)} - \frac{c(m-1)}{m^2} + \frac{4c\alpha(b)}{m(\beta - 1)}\right)\mathbb{E}\left[F(\tilde{w}^s) - F(w^*)\right]$$

$$\leq \left(\frac{Lc\beta}{m\mu} + \frac{4c\alpha(b)}{m(\beta - 1)} - \frac{c(m-1)}{m^2} + \frac{4\left(\alpha(b)m^2 + (m-1)^2\right)}{m^2(\beta - 1)}\right)\left[F(\tilde{w}^{s-1}) - F(w^*)\right] + R'''$$

(4.69)

Dividing both sides by $\left(1 - \dfrac{4\alpha(b)}{(\beta - 1)} - \dfrac{c(m-1)}{m^2} + \dfrac{4c\alpha(b)}{m(\beta - 1)}\right)$, *we have*

$$\mathbb{E}\left[F(\tilde{w}^s) - F(w^*)\right] \leq C\left[F(\tilde{w}^{s-1}) - F(w^*)\right] + R'''' \tag{4.70}$$

where

$$C = \left(\frac{Lc\beta}{m\mu} + \frac{4c\alpha(b)}{m(\beta - 1)} - \frac{c(m-1)}{m^2} + \frac{4\left(\alpha(b)m^2 + (m-1)^2\right)}{m^2(\beta - 1)}\right).$$

$$\left(1 - \frac{4\alpha(b)}{(\beta - 1)} - \frac{c(m-1)}{m^2} + \frac{4c\alpha(b)}{m(\beta - 1)}\right)^{-1}$$

and $R'''' = R'''\left(1 - \dfrac{4\alpha(b)}{(\beta - 1)} - \dfrac{c(m-1)}{m^2} + \dfrac{4c\alpha(b)}{m(\beta - 1)}\right)^{-1}$. *Now, applying this in-*
equality recursively, we have

$$\mathbb{E}\left[F(\tilde{w}^s) - F(w^*)\right] \leq C^s\left[F(\tilde{w}^0) - F(w^*)\right] + R''''', \tag{4.71}$$

inequality follows for $R''''' = R''''/(1 - C)$, *since* $\sum_{i=0}^{k} r^i \leq \sum_{i=0}^{\infty} r^i = \dfrac{1}{1 - r}$, $\|r\| <$
1. *For certain choice of* β, *one can easily prove that* $C < 1$. *This proves linear*
convergence with some initial error.

All the proofs given here prove linear convergence (as per definition of convergence) of SAAG-IV for all the four combinations of smoothness and strong-convexity with some initial errors due to the constant terms in the results. SAAGs are based on intuitions from practice [23] and they try to give more importance to the latest gradient values than the older gradient values, which make them biased techniques and results into this extra constant term. This constant term signifies that SAAGs converge to a region close to the solution, which is very practical because all the machine learning algorithms are used to solve the problems approximately and we never find an exact solution for the problem [15], because of computational difficulty. Moreover, the constant term pops up due to the mini-batched gradient value at optimal point, i.e., $\dfrac{1}{|B_k|}\sum_{i \in B_k} \nabla f_i(w^*)$. If the size of the mini-batch increases and eventually becomes equal to the dataset then this constant becomes equal to full gradient and vanishes, i.e., $\dfrac{1}{n}\sum_{i=1}^{n} \nabla f_i(w^*) = 0$.

The linear convergence for all combinations of strong convexity and smoothness of the regularizer, is the maximum rate exhibited by the first order methods without curvature information. SAG, SVRG, SAGA and VR-SGD also exhibit linear convergence for the strong convexity and smooth problem but except VR-SGD, they don't cover all the cases, e.g., SVRG does not cover the non-strongly convex cases. However, the theoretical results provided by VR-SGD, prove linear convergence for strongly convex cases, like our results, but VR-SGD provides only $O(1/T)$ convergence for non-strongly convex cases, unlike our linear convergence results.

4.6 EXPERIMENTAL RESULTS

In this section, we have presented the experimental results[2]. SAAG-III and IV are compared against the most widely used variance reduction method, SVRG and one of the latest method, VR-SGD, which has been proved to outperform existing techniques. The results have been reported in terms of suboptimality and accuracy against time, epochs and gradients/n. The SAAGs can be applied to strongly and non-strongly convex problems with smooth or non-smooth regularizers. But the results have been reported with strongly convex problems with and without smoothness because problems can be easily converted to strongly convex problems by adding l_2-regularization.

4.6.1 Experimental Setup

The experiments are reported using six different criteria which plot suboptimality (objective − best value) versus epochs (where one epoch refers to one pass through the dataset), suboptimality versus gradients/n, suboptimality versus time, accuracy versus time, accuracy versus epochs and accuracy versus gradients/n. The x-axis and y-axis data are represented in linear and log scale, respectively. The experiments use the following binary datasets: rcv1, news20, real-sim and Adult (also called as a9a), whose details are given in the Table 1.1. All the datasets are divided into 80% and 20% as training and test dataset, respectively. The value of regularization parameter is set as $\lambda = 1 * 10^{-5}$ (including λ_1, λ_2) for all the algorithms, unless specified. The parameters for, Stochastic Backtracking-Armijo line Search (SBAS), are set as: $\alpha = 0.1, \beta = 0.5$ and learning rate is initialized as, $\eta = 1.0$. The inner iterations are set as, $m = n/b$ (as used in [39]). Moreover, in SBAS, algorithms looks for maximum 10 iterations and after that it returns the current value of learning rate if it reduces the objective value otherwise it returns 0.0. This is done to avoid sticking in the algorithm because of stochastic line search. All the experiments have been conducted on MacBook Air (8 GB 1600 MHz DDR3, 1.6 GHz Intel Core i5 and 256GB SSD) using MEX files.

4.6.2 Results with Smooth Problem

The results are reported with l_2-regularized logistic regression problem as given below:

$$\min_{w} F(w) = \frac{1}{n} \sum_{i=1}^{n} \log \left(1 + \exp \left(-y_i w^T x_i \right) \right) + \frac{\lambda}{2} \|w\|^2. \qquad (4.72)$$

Figure 4.1 reports results with news20 dataset. SAAG-III and IV perform better than SVRG and VR-SGD, but SAAG-IV gives best results. This is because as the mini-batch size or the dataset size increases, SAAG-II and SAAG-IV perform better (as reported in [23]).

---

[2]for detailed experiments, like effect of regularization coefficient, please refer to the paper [28]

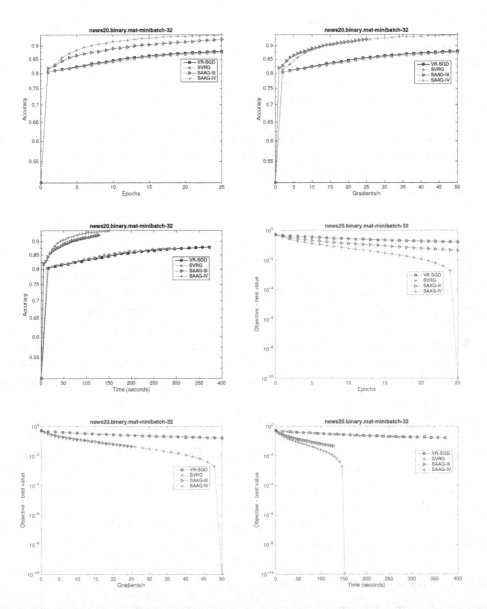

FIGURE 4.1 Comparison of SAAG-III, IV, SVRG and VR-SGD on smooth problem using news20 dataset with mini-batch of 32 data points.

4.6.3 Results with Non-smooth Problem

The results are reported with elastic-net-regularized logistic regression problem (non-smooth regularizer) as given below:

$$\min_{w} F(w) = \frac{1}{n} \sum_{i=1}^{n} \log \left(1 + \exp\left(-y_i w^T x_i\right)\right) + \frac{\lambda_1}{2} \|w\|^2 + \lambda_2 \|w\|_1, \qquad (4.73)$$

where $f(w) = \frac{1}{n} \sum_{i=1}^{n} \log \left(1 + \exp\left(-y_i w^T x_i\right)\right) + \frac{\lambda_1}{2} \|w\|^2$ and $g(w) = \lambda_2 \|w\|_1$.

Figure 4.2 represents the comparative study of SAAG-III, IV, SVRG and VR-SGD on rcv1 dataset. As it is clear from the figure, for all the six criteria plots, SAAG-III and IV outperform SVRG and VR-SGD, SAAG-IV giving best results in terms of suboptimality but in terms of accuracy, SAAG-III and IV have close performance except for accuracy versus gradients/n, where SAAG-III gives better results because SAAG-III calculates gradients at last iterate only unlike SAAG-IV which calculates gradients at snap point and last iterate.

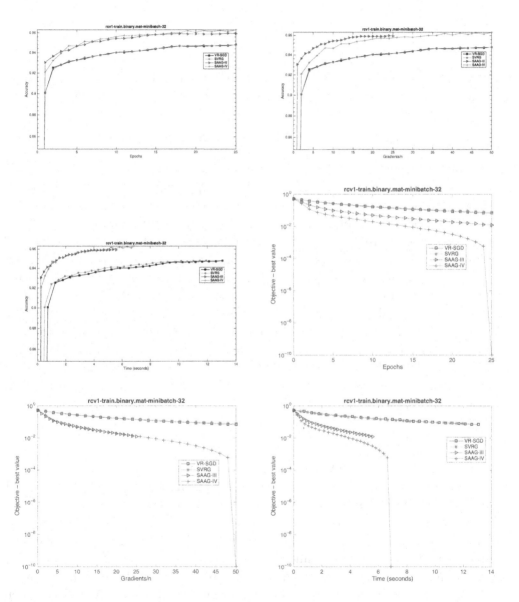

FIGURE 4.2 Comparison of SAAG-III, IV, SVRG and VR-SGD on non-smooth problem using rcv1 dataset with mini-batch of 32 data points.

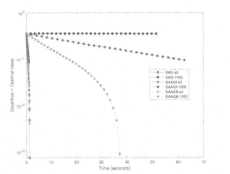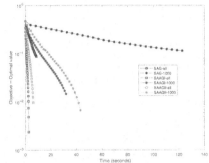

FIGURE 4.3 Comparison of BBOF setting with mini-batch setting on rcv1 (first) and real-sim (second) datasets using all features and a block size of 1000.

4.6.4 Mini-batch Block-coordinate versus Mini-batch setting

This subsection provides empirical evidence for the observation that mini-batch block-coordinate setting (BBOF), i.e., using stochastic approximation and coordinate together does not work well. Figure 4.3 compares three methods, namely, SAG, SAAG-I and SAAG-II without sampling features, i.e., using all features and using a block of 1000 features, and mini-batch of 1000 data points. Figure plots suboptimality against training time on rcv1 and real-sim datasets and uses stochastic backtracking line search method to find the learning rate. It is clear from the figure that doubly sampled methods, i.e., methods using BBOF setting lag far behind the singly sampled methods, i.e., methods using only data sampling and all features. Thus, it is not suitable to use stochastic approximation and coordinate descent approaches together because the advantage of having low per-iteration complexity is lost in the implementation overhead due to double sampling. But if we could find ways to reduce the implementation overhead then BBOF could be very effective to solve big data problems.

4.6.5 Results with SVM

This subsection compares SAAGs against SVRG and VR-SGD on SVM problem with mushroom and gisette datasets. Methods use stochastic backtracking line search method to find the step size. Figure 4.4 presents the results and compares the suboptimality against the training time (in seconds). Results are similar to experiments with logistic regression but are not that smooth. SAAGs outperform other methods on mushroom dataset (first row) and gisette dataset (second row) for suboptimality against training time and accuracy against time but all methods give almost similar results on accuracy versus training time for mushroom dataset. SAAG-IV outperforms other method and SAAG-III sometimes lags behind VR-SGD method. It is also observed that results with logistic regression are better than the results with the

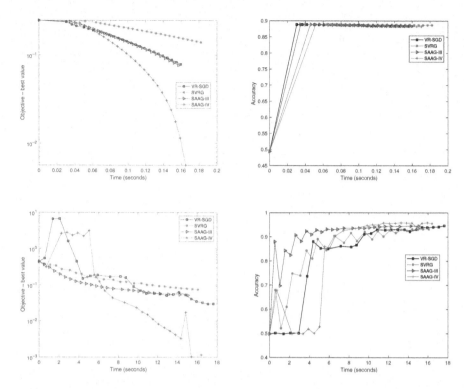

FIGURE 4.4 Results with SVM using mini-batch of 1000 data points on mushroom (first row) and gisette (second row) datasets.

SVM problem. The optimization problem for SVM is given below:

$$\min_{w} F(w) = \frac{1}{n} \sum_{i=1}^{n} \max\left(0, 1 - y_i w^T x_i\right)^2 + \frac{\lambda}{2} \|w\|^2, \tag{4.74}$$

where λ is the regularization coefficient (also penalty parameter) which balances the trade-off between margin size and error [25].

4.7 CONCLUSION

We have proposed novel variants of SAAG-I and II, called SAAG-III and IV, respectively, by using average of iterates for SAAG-III as a starting point, and average of iterates and last iterate for SAAG-IV as the snap point and starting point, respectively, for new epoch, except the first one. SAAGs (I, II, III and IV) are also extended to solve non-smooth problems by using two different update rules and introducing proximal step for non-smooth problem. Theoretical results proved linear convergence of SAAG-IV for all the four combinations of smoothness and strong-convexity with some initial errors, in expectation. The empirical results proved the efficacy of proposed methods against existing variance reduction methods in terms of, accuracy and suboptimality, against training time, epochs and gradients/n.

CHAPTER 5

Learning and Data Access

The training time of models has two major components time to access the data and time to process (learn from) the data. So far, the research has focused only on the second part, i.e., learning from the data. In this chapter, we have proposed one possible solution to handle the big data problems in machine learning. The idea is to reduce the training time through reducing data access time by proposing systematic sampling and cyclic/sequential sampling to select mini-batches from the dataset. To prove the effectiveness of proposed sampling techniques, we have used empirical risk minimization, which is commonly used machine learning problem, for strongly convex and smooth case. The problem has been solved using SAG, SAGA, SVRG, SAAG-II and MBSGD (Mini-batched SGD), each using two step determination techniques, namely, constant step size and backtracking line search method. Theoretical results prove similar convergence for systematic and cyclic sampling as the widely used random sampling technique, in expectation. Empirical results with benchmarked datasets prove the efficacy of the proposed sampling techniques and show up to six times faster training.

5.1 INTRODUCTION

Nowadays, the major challenge is to develop efficient and scalable learning algorithms for dealing with big data problems, as discussed in detail in Section 3.1. The training time of models have two major components [144] as:

$$training\ time = time\ to\ access\ data + time\ to\ process\ data. \qquad (5.1)$$

As it is known that for processing any data or running any program, it should be first brought into memory, more precisely into RAM (Random Access Memory), from hard disk. The time taken in bringing the data or program from hard disk into memory is called access time. Access time has, further, three components, namely, seek time (it is the time taken by the reading head to move from current position up to the track containing the data), rotational latency time (it is the time taken by the reading head from the current position to reach up to the sector/block containing the data) and transfer time (it is the time taken to transfer data from sector/block over the disk to memory). Moreover, data is not read content wise rather block-wise,

DOI: 10.1201/9781003240167-5

where each block can have multiple sectors. Now, it is interesting to note that for data stored on the contiguous memory or in the close proximity, has lesser data access time as compared with the data dispersed far away from each other. This is due to lesser seek, latency and transfer times. In case of SSD (Solid State Disk) and RAM (Random Access Memory), there are no seek and latency times because they do not have moving parts and they are based on direct access mechanism, but transfer time still plays its role. Since data are read/written block-wise so for contiguous data access, there would be one or two transfer times but dispersed data access would require more number of transfer times. Moreover, cache memory strategies also favor the contiguous memory access and make it faster as compared to dispersed data access. Thus, contiguous data access time is faster than dispersed data access, in all the cases whether data is stored on RAM, SSD or HDD. But the difference in access time would be more prominent for HDD.

The second component of training time is processing (learning) time which is the time taken by the CPU (Central Processing Unit) to process the data to solve for model parameters. Due to mini-batching and iterative learning algorithms, the accessing and processing of data is intermixed and occurs quite frequently. The data access time is dependent on the sampling technique and processing time is dependent on the method used to solve the problem. Till this date, to improve the training time, most of the focus is given only to improve the processing time by using different methods. The training time is dependent on both data accessing time and data processing time, and this is to be noted that, generally, data access time is very high as compared to the data processing time. Thus, efforts should be equally done to improve the data accessing time. This chapter has tried to reduce the training time for big data problems by reducing the data access time using systematic sampling technique [93, 94] and cyclic sampling to select mini-batches of data points from the dataset.

5.1.1 Optimization Problem

Empirical risk minimization (ERM) problem [111] is a commonly used problem in machine learning and statistics, which typically consists of a loss function and a regularization term. In this chapter, $l2$-regularized ERM problem with the assumptions of strong convexity and smoothness, is used for demonstrating the effectiveness of proposed sampling techniques. For the training data $\{(x_1, y_1), (x_2, y_2), ..., (x_l, y_l)\}$, where $x_i \in \mathbb{R}^n$, $y_i \in \mathbb{R}$, and for loss functions $f_1, f_2, ..., f_l : \mathbb{R}^n \to \mathbb{R}$, model parameter vector $w \in \mathbb{R}^n$ and regularization coefficient $C > 0$, $l2$-regularized ERM problem is given by

$$\min_{w} \ f(w) = \frac{1}{l} \sum_{i=1}^{l} f_i(w) + \frac{C}{2} \|w\|^2, \tag{5.2}$$

where first term is the data fitting term and second term is used for avoiding the overfitting of data. Commonly used loss functions are the square loss $(w^T x_i - y_i)^2$, the logistic loss $\log (1 + exp (-y_i w^T x_i))$ and the hinge loss $\max (0, 1 - y_i w^T x_i)$. In this chapter, experimentation uses logistic loss function. When problem represented by eq.(5.2) is a large-scale or big data problem then per iteration complexity of learning algorithms with traditional methods like Gradient Descent is $O(nl)$ which is very high. This is because, such problems have large number of data points (l) or large number of features (n), or both, and each iteration updates n variables over l data points. Because of this high computational complexity per iteration it would be very expensive or even infeasible for single machine to process a single iteration of learning algorithm. Stochastic approximation approach is widely used for handling such cases (e.g., [148, 63, 35, 19, 115, 23]), which uses one data point or mini-batch of data points during each iteration. The reduced subproblem with mini-batch B_j of data points for j^{th} inner iteration is given by

$$\min_w \frac{1}{|B_j|} \sum_{i \in B_j} f_i(w) + \frac{C}{2}\|w\|^2, \quad j = 1, 2, ..., m. \tag{5.3}$$

The iteration complexity for solving this reduced subproblem is $O(n)$ (for one data point) or $O(n|B_j|)$ (for mini-batch of data points) where $|B_j|$ is the size of mini-batch, which is very low and independent of l. Since it is easier to solve the problem (5.3) and this is widely used approach to handle large-scale problems so the chapter uses this reduced subproblem approach.

5.1.2 Literature Review

Big data challenge is one of the major challenge in machine learning and stochastic approximation is one of the important approach to deal with large-scale learning problems, as discussed in detail in Chapter 3. Sampling plays an important role in the convergence and training time of learning algorithms. For selecting one data point or mini-batch of data points from the dataset in stochastic approximation approach, random sampling (e.g., [19, 35, 63, 115, 148]) is widely used, and other sampling techniques are importance sampling (e.g., [34, 151]), stratified sampling [150] and adaptive sampling [48]. Importance sampling is a non-uniform sampling technique, which uses properties of data for finding probabilities of selection of data points in the iterative process, leading to the acceleration of training process. Importance sampling involves some overhead in calculating the probabilities and the average computational complexity per iteration of importance sampling could be more than the computational complexity of the iteration in some cases, like, when it is implemented dynamically. Stratified sampling technique divides the dataset into clusters of similar data points and then mini-batch of data points are selected from the clusters. In adaptive sampling [48], information about the classes, i.e., data-labels is used for selecting the data points; this technique gives good results for problems with large number of classes. Random sampling is widely used in mini-batching for large-scale learning problems (e.g., [19]), as only [34] is known importance sampling technique in mini-batching. In this chapter, we have focused on simple sampling techniques which do not involve any extra overhead and can be effective for dealing with large-scale learning problems. Two simple sampling techniques, namely, systematic sampling and cyclic/sequential sampling techniques have been proposed for selecting mini-batches. To the best of our knowledge, systematic sampling is not used in machine learning for selecting data points. We are the first to introduce systematic sampling in machine learning for the selection of mini-batches of data points from the dataset. Before this, cyclic sampling was used in coordinate descent and block coordinate descent methods (e.g.,[137]) for selecting one coordinate or block of coordinates, respectively, and to the best of our knowledge, cyclic sampling is not used for selecting mini-batches. Both sampling techniques are simple, effective and easy to implement. The proposed sampling techniques try to reduce the training time of models by reducing the data access time because these are based on contiguous access of data. Before this, for reducing the training time of models, the focus is mainly given on reducing the processing time, but this chapter has focused on reducing the data access time by changing the sampling techniques.

5.1.3 Contributions

The contributions of the article are summarized below:

- Novel systematic sampling and sequential/cyclic sampling techniques have been proposed for selecting mini-batches of data points from the dataset for solving large-scale learning problems. The proposed techniques focus on reducing the training time of learning algorithms by reducing the data access time, and are based on simple observations that data stored on the contiguous memory locations are faster to access as compared with data stored on dispersed memory locations. To the best of our knowledge, this chapter is the first to focus on reducing data access time to reduce the overall training time for machine learning algorithms.

- Proposed ideas are independent of problem and method used to solve problem as it focuses on data access only. So, it can be extended to other machine learning problems.

- Experimental results prove the efficacy of systematic sampling and cyclic sampling in reducing the training time, and show up to six times faster training. The results have been provided using five different methods (SAG, SAGA, SVRG, SAAG-II and MBSGD) each using two step determination techniques (constant step size and backtracking line search methods) over eight bench marked datasets.

- Theoretical results prove similar convergence for learning algorithms using cyclic and systematic sampling, as for widely used random sampling technique, in expectation.

5.2 SYSTEMATIC SAMPLING

Sampling is the way of selecting one mini-batch of data points (or one data point) from the whole dataset. Iterative approximation methods used for solving the problem use sampling again and again during each iteration/epoch. The convergence of learning algorithm depends upon the type of sampling used since sampling controls two things:

data access time and diversity of data. In general, when consecutive data points are used they reduce the data access time which reduces the training time but selected data points might not be diverse which affects the convergence of learning algorithm. On the other hand, when data is used from different locations then the data access time is more which increases the training time but selected data points might be diverse which can improve the convergence. Thus, sampling has a significant role in the learning algorithms. Three sampling techniques, namely, random sampling, cyclic sampling and systematic sampling are discussed below and used in learning algorithm as they are simple, easy to implement and do not involve any extra overhead and thus effective in handling large-scale problems.

5.2.1 Definitions

Suppose a mini-batch B of m data points is to be selected from a training dataset $\{(x_1, y_1), (x_2, y_2), ..., (x_l, y_l)\}$ of l data points.

(a) *Random Sampling:* Random sampling (RS) can be of two types, RS with replacement and RS without replacement. RS with replacement first selects one data point randomly from the whole dataset where each data point has equal probability of selection, then, similarly, second data point is selected randomly from the whole dataset where previously selected point has equal probability of selection, and so on to select m data points. RS without replacement first selects one data point randomly from the whole dataset where each data point has equal probability of selection, then, similarly, second data point is selected randomly from the remaining $l-1$ points without considering the previously selected point, and so on to select m data points.

(b) *Cyclic/Sequential Sampling:* First mini-batch is selected by taking the first 1 to m points. Second mini-batch is selected by taking next $m+1$ to $2m$ points and so on until all data points are covered. Then again start with the first data point.

(c) *Systematic Sampling:* [93, 94] It randomly selects the first point and then selects the remaining points according to a fixed pattern, e.g., it randomly selects a data point, say i, and then selects data points as $i, i+k, ..., i+(m-1)k$ as mini-batch where k is some positive integer. For simplicity, $k=1$ can be taken.

Example: Suppose the training dataset is given by $S = \{1, 2, 3, ..., 20\}$ and size of mini-batch to be selected is $m = 5$, then four mini-batches can be selected/drawn from S using different sampling techniques as follows: mini-batches selected using random sampling with replacement are – $B_1 = \{15, 2, 20, 2, 1\}$, $B_2 = \{3, 10, 20, 6, 1\}$, $B_3 = \{5, 9, 19, 2, 7\}$ and $B_4 = \{1, 11, 18, 3, 16\}$; mini-batches selected using random sampling without replacement are – $B_1 = \{15, 2, 20, 11, 6\}$, $B_2 = \{3, 10, 8, 14, 1\}$, $B_3 = \{16, 4, 17, 7, 19\}$ and $B_4 = \{9, 5, 12, 18, 13\}$; mini-batches selected using cyclic sampling are – $B_1 = \{1, 2, 3, 4, 5\}$, $B_2 = \{6, 7, 8, 9, 10\}$, $B_3 = \{11, 12, 13, 14, 15\}$ and $B_4 = \{16, 17, 18, 19, 20\}$; and mini-batches selected using systematic sampling are – $B_1 = \{16, 17, 18, 19, 20\}$, $B_2 = \{1, 2, 3, 4, 5\}$, $B_3 = \{6, 7, 8, 9, 10\}$ and

$B_4 = \{11, 12, 13, 14, 15\}$. As it is clear from the above examples, in random sampling with replacement, points are selected randomly with repetition inside the mini-batch or within mini-batches. CS is the simplest and non-probabilistic sampling, and selects the points in a sequential manner. For systematic sampling, first point is selected randomly then the remaining points are selected back to back, here idea of replacement and without replacement can be applied between mini-batches but only sampling without replacement within mini-batches is demonstrated.

It is interesting to note that for RS, data points of the mini-batch are dispersed over the different sectors of the disk, so every data point needs its own seek time and latency time. Since the data is read block-wise and not content-wise so it is possible that each data point is present in a different block and thus needs its own transfer time also. For CS, only one seek time is needed for one mini-batch because it starts with first data point and then moves till end and for SS, one seek time is needed per mini-batch because only first element is determined randomly but rest points of the mini-batch are stored on contiguous memory locations. So, seek time is the least for CS and the most for RS. The transfer time is almost equal for CS and SS but less as compared with RS because in RS, generally, each data point needs a separate transfer time but for other case it needs as many transfer times as the number of blocks required to fit the mini-batch of data points. Thus, the overall access time to access one mini-batch of data points is minimum for CS and is maximum for RS. It is observed that RS gives the best solution as compared with the CS for a given number of epochs but the access time of RS is the most. On the other hand for CS the access time is the least for a given number of epoch but the convergence is the slowest. So, there is a trade-off between reducing the data access time and convergence of learning algorithm. SS balances this trade-off since SS has the best of both techniques, like CS the data points are stored on the contiguous memory locations and like RS it has some randomness as it draws the first point randomly. Overall, methods using CS and SS converges faster as compared with methods using RS, as discussed in Sec. 5.4.

5.2.2 Learning Using Systematic Sampling

A general learning algorithm with systematic sampling to solve large-scale problems is given by Algorithm 14. Similar learning algorithms can be obtained for cyclic and random sampling techniques by using the corresponding sampling technique for selecting the mini-batch at Step 5 of Algorithm 14. The algorithm starts with the initial solution. It divides the dataset into m mini-batches using systematic sampling for selecting mini-batches. Inside the inner loop, it takes one mini-batch B_j, formulates a subproblem over B_j and solves the sub-problem thus formed. This process is repeated until all the sub-problems over all m mini-batches are solved. Then this solution process is repeated for the given number of epochs or other stopping criteria can be used in the algorithm. At Step 7 of Algorithm 14, different solvers can be used to update the solution, like, SAG (Stochastic Average Gradient) [115], SAGA [35], SVRG (Stochastic Variance Reduced Gradient) [63], SAAG-II (Stochastic Average Adjusted Gradient) [23] and MBSGD (Mini-Batch Stochastic Gradient Descent) [23, 32].

Algorithm 14 A General Learning Algorithm with Systematic Sampling

---

1: **Inputs:** $m = $ #mini-batches and $p = $max #*epochs*.
2: **Initialize:** Take initial solution w^0.
3: **for** $k = 1, 2, ..., p$ **do**
4:    **for** $j = 1, 2, ..., m$ **do**
5:       Select one mini-batch B_j using systematic sampling without replacement.
6:       Formulate a subproblem using mini-batch B_j as given below:

$$\min_{w} \frac{1}{|B_j|} \sum_{i \in B_j} f_i(w) + \frac{C}{2}\|w\|^2$$

7:       Solve the subproblem and update the solution using appropriate method.
8:    **end for**
9: **end for**

5.3 ANALYSIS

The proposed sampling techniques are simple but effective for solving large-scale learning problems with different solvers, as discussed in Section 5.4. The convergence proof of learning algorithms have been provided using the simplest solver MBSGD (mini-batched Stochastic Gradient Descent) method with constant step size, for the simplicity of proofs as the focus of study is only on sampling techniques and not on solvers. $l2$-regularized ERM problem has been solved under the following assumptions to demonstrate the efficacy of proposed sampling techniques. It is assumed that the regularization term is hidden inside the loss function term for notational convenience otherwise it needs to write separate gradients for regularization term.

Assumption 4 (Lipschitz Continuous Gradient) *Suppose function $f : \mathbb{R}^n \to \mathbb{R}$ is convex and differentiable on S, and that gradient ∇f is L-Lipschitz-continuous, where $L > 0$ is Lipschitz constant, then, we have,*

$$\|\nabla f(y) - \nabla f(x)\| \leq L\|y - x\|, \tag{5.4}$$

$$and, \quad f(y) \leq f(x) + \nabla f(x)^T(y - x) + \frac{L}{2}\|y - x\|^2. \tag{5.5}$$

Assumption 5 (Strong Convexity) *Suppose function $f : \mathbb{R}^n \to \mathbb{R}$ is μ-strongly convex function for $\mu > 0$ on S and p^* is the optimal value of f, then, we have,*

$$f(y) \geq f(x) + \nabla f(x)^T(y - x) + \frac{\mu}{2}\|y - x\|^2, \tag{5.6}$$

$$and, \quad f(x) - p^* \leq \frac{1}{2\mu}\|\nabla f(x)\|^2 \tag{5.7}$$

Theorem 6 *Suppose for function given by eq. (5.2), under Assumptions 4, 5 and constant step size α, and taking solver MBSGD, Algorithm 14, converges linearly in expectation for cyclic, systematic and sequential sampling techniques.*

Proof 5.1 *By definition of MBSGD, we have,*

$$w^{k+1} = w^k - \frac{\alpha}{|B_j|} \sum_{i \in B_j} \nabla f_i(w^k) \tag{5.8}$$

By L-Lipschitz continuity of gradients,

$$f(w^{k+1}) \le f(w^k) + \nabla f(w^k)^T (w^{k+1} - w^k) + \frac{L}{2} \|w^{k+1} - w^k\|^2$$
$$= f(w^k) - \alpha \nabla f(w^k)^T \left[\frac{1}{|B_j|} \sum_{i \in B_j} \nabla f_i(w^k) \right] + \frac{L\alpha^2}{2} \left\| \frac{1}{|B_j|} \sum_{i \in B_j} \nabla f_i(w^k) \right\|^2,$$

equality follows from the definition of MBSGD.

Case-I: Mini-batch B_j is selected using random sampling (RS) without replacement or Systematic Sampling (SS) without replacement

Taking expectation on both sides over mini-batches B_j and subtracting optimal value (p^*), we have,

$$E_{B_j} \left[f(w^{k+1}) - p^* \right] \le f(w^k) - p^* - \alpha \nabla f(w^k)^T E_{B_j} \left[\frac{1}{|B_j|} \sum_{i \in B_j} \nabla f_i(w^k) \right]$$
$$+ \frac{L\alpha^2}{2} E_{B_j} \left\| \frac{1}{|B_j|} \sum_{i \in B_j} \nabla f_i(w^k) \right\|^2$$
$$\le f(w^k) - p^* - \alpha \nabla f(w^k)^T \nabla f(w^k) + \frac{L\alpha^2}{2} \|R_0\|^2,$$

inequality follows using $E_{B_j} \left[\frac{1}{|B_j|} \sum_{i \in B_j} \nabla f_i(w^k) \right] = \nabla f(w^k)$ and taking

$$\left\| \frac{1}{|B_j|} \sum_{i \in B_j} \nabla f_i(w^k) \right\|^2 \le R_0, \ \forall j, w.$$

$$E_{B_j} \left[f(w^{k+1}) - p^* \right] \le f(w^k) - p^* - \alpha \|\nabla f(w^k)\|^2 + \frac{L\alpha^2 R_0^2}{2},$$
$$\le f(w^k) - p^* - \alpha.2\mu \left(f(w^k) - p^* \right) + \frac{L\alpha^2 R_0^2}{2},$$

inequality follows from strong convexity results.

$$E_{B_j} \left[f(w^{k+1}) - p^* \right] \le (1 - 2\alpha\mu) \left(f(w^k) - p^* \right) + \frac{L\alpha^2 R_0^2}{2}$$

Applying inequality recursively, we have,

$$E_{B_j} \left[f(w^{k+1}) - p^* \right] \le (1 - 2\alpha\mu)^{k+1} \left(f(w^0) - p^* \right) + \frac{L\alpha^2 R_0^2}{2} \sum_{i=0}^{k} (1 - 2\alpha\mu)^i$$
$$\le (1 - 2\alpha\mu)^{k+1} \left(f(w^0) - p^* \right) + \frac{L\alpha^2 R_0^2}{2} \cdot \frac{1}{2\alpha\mu},$$

inequality follows since $\sum_{i=0}^{k} r^i \le \sum_{i=0}^{\infty} r^i = \dfrac{1}{1-r}$, $\quad \|r\| < 1$.

$$E_{B_j}\left[f(w^{k+1}) - p^* \right] \le (1 - 2\alpha\mu)^{k+1}\left(f(w^0) - p^* \right) + \frac{L\alpha R_0^2}{4\mu}.$$

Thus, algorithm converges linearly with initial error proportional to α.

Case-II: Mini-batch B_j *is selected using Cyclic/Sequential Sampling (SS)*

Taking summation over number of mini-batches and dividing by number of mini-batches (m), *and subtracting* p^*, *we have,*

$$\frac{1}{m}\sum_{j=1}^{m}\left[f(w^{k+1}) - p^* \right]$$

$$\le \frac{1}{m}\sum_{j=1}^{m}\left[f(w^k) - p^* \right] - \alpha \nabla f(w^k)^T \frac{1}{m}\sum_{j=1}^{m}\left[\frac{1}{\|B_j\|}\sum_{i\in B_j} \nabla f_i(w^k) \right]$$

$$+ \frac{L\alpha^2}{2}\frac{1}{m}\sum_{j=1}^{m}\left\| \frac{1}{|B_j|}\sum_{i\in B_j} \nabla f_i(w^k) \right\|^2,$$

$$\le f(w^k) - p^* - \alpha \nabla f(w^k)^T \nabla f(w^k) + \frac{L\alpha^2}{2}R_0^2,$$

inequality follows since $\dfrac{1}{m}\sum_{j=1}^{m}\left[\dfrac{1}{\|B_j\|}\sum_{i\in B_j} \nabla f_i(w^k) \right] = \nabla f(w^k)$

and $\left\| \dfrac{1}{|B_j|}\sum_{i\in B_j} \nabla f_i(w^k) \right\| \le R_0$.

$$\frac{1}{m}\sum_{j=1}^{m}\left[f(w^{k+1}) - p^* \right] \le (1 - 2\alpha\mu)^{k+1}\left(f(w^0) - p^* \right) + \frac{L\alpha R_0^2}{4\mu},$$

inequality follows from the Case-I derivation. Thus, algorithm converges linearly with initial error proportional to α. *Hence, theorem is proved.*

5.4 EXPERIMENTS

5.4.1 Experimental Setup

Experiments have been performed using five methods, namely, SAG, SAGA, SAAG-II, SVRG and MBSGD with eight bench marked datasets (details are given in the Table 1.1). Each method has been run with two mini-batches of size 500 and 1000 data points, and two techniques to find step size, namely, constant step size method and backtracking line search (LS) method for a predefined number of epochs. Constant step size method uses Lipschitz constant L and takes step size as $1/L$ for all methods. Backtracking line search is performed approximately only using the selected mini-batch of data points because performing backtracking line search on whole dataset could hurt the convergence of learning algorithm for large-scale problems by taking huge time. For one dataset, one method runs for 12 times (3(sampling techniques) ×

2(mini-batches) × 2(step size finding techniques)), and for one dataset, three sampling techniques are compared on 20 different settings (5(methods) × 2(mini-batches) × 2(step size finding techniques)). Thus, 160(20 × 8(datasets)) settings have been used to compare the results for three sampling techniques. As training time depends on the configuration of machine over which experiments are performed so this is to be noted that all the experiments have been conducted on MacBook Air (8GB 1600 MHz DDR3, 256GB SSD, 1.6 GHz Intel Core i5).

5.4.2   Implementation Details

For each sampling technique, i.e., Random Sampling (RS), Cyclic Sampling (CS) and Systematic Sampling (SS), same algorithmic structure is used with difference only in selecting the mini-batch for each sampling technique. And for each sampling technique, the dataset is divided into predefined number of mini-batches, as per the Algorithm 14. For simplicity, dataset has been divided into equal sized mini-batches except the last mini-batch which might has data points less than or equal to other mini-batches. For RS, during each epoch, an array of size equal to the number of data points in the dataset is taken and this array contains the randomized indexes of data points. To select the mini-batches, array contents equal to mini-batch size or till the end of array, are selected sequentially. For CS, during each epoch, an array of size equal to the number of data points in the dataset is taken, containing indexes of data points in sorted order. To select the mini-batches, array contents equal to mini-batch size or till the end of array, are selected sequentially. For SS, during each epoch, an array of size equal to the number of mini-batches is taken and this array contains the randomized indexes of mini-batches. To select a mini-batch, an array element is selected in the sequence. This array element gives us the first index of data point in the selected mini-batch. The other data points are selected sequentially from the starting index of the mini-batch equal to the size of a mini-batch or till the last data point in the dataset.

5.4.3   Results

Experimental results[1] plot the difference between objective function and optimum value against training time for three sampling techniques, namely, Random Sampling (RS), Cyclic/Sequential Sampling (CS) and Systematic Sampling (SS), which are represented by Figs.5.1–5.2. To save space, results for different samplings with constant step size and backtracking line search methods are plotted in same figure (red color for constant step size and blue for line search (LS)). As it is clear from figures, 20 different settings over one dataset compare CS, SS and RS, and prove that methods with CS and SS converges faster than with RS. In general, SS gives the best results as per the intuition but sometimes CS produces better results than SS since CS and SS are quite similar. The results with constant step size and backtracking line search methods show similar results. For larger datasets, like SUSY and HIGGS, SS and CS show clear advantage over RS, than for smaller dataset and thus prove the

---

[1]for detailed experiments, please refer to [26]

efficacy/suitability of CS and SS for large-scale learning problems. For some of the results, like, with HIGGS dataset and SAG method, learning algorithms with all the sampling techniques converge quickly to same value but careful examination reveals that CS and SS converges earlier than RS.

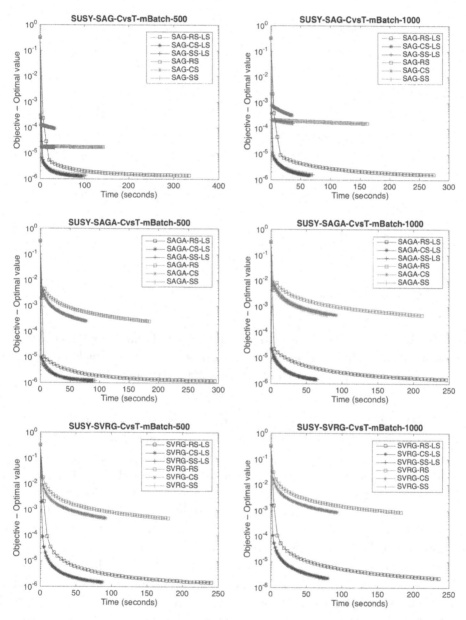

FIGURE 5.1 RS, CS and SS are compared using SAG, SAGA and SVRG, each with two step determination techniques, namely, constant step and backtracking line search, over SUSY dataset with mini-batch of 500 and 1000 data points.

Experimental results can be presented using tables comparing the training time and objective function value, for given number of epochs (number of passes through

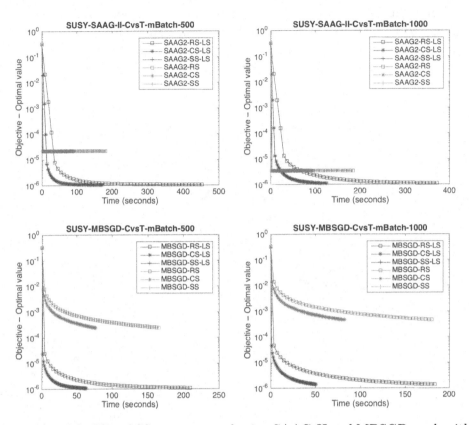

FIGURE 5.2 RS, CS and SS are compared using SAAG-II and MBSGD, each with two step determination techniques, namely, constant step and backtracking line search, over SUSY dataset with mini-batch of 500 and 1000 data points.

dataset), for CS, SS and RS. Since it is easy to understand the graphs so experiments are documented using figures. Results HIGGS is represented using Table **??**, which proves faster training for CS and SS than RS, while their values are same up to certain decimal places. As it is clear from the table, SAG method with mini-batch of size 200 and constant step size, the training time for Systematic Sampling (SS) and Cyclic Sampling (CS) are faster than for Random Sampling (RS) by a factor of more than three while the values of objective function are same up to four decimal places. The training times for SS and CS are very close as expected. For mini-batch of 1000 data points and constant step size, SAG method runs three and half times faster for SS and CS as compared with RS while the values of objective function are same up to six decimal places. With backtracking line search for determining the step size, SAG method runs more than two times faster with mini-batch of 200 and more than three and half times with mini-batch of size 1000, for SS and CS as compared with RS while the values of objective function are same up to eight decimal places. SAGA with constant step size runs more than two times faster with mini-batches of 200 and 1000 for CS and SS as compared with RS while the values of objective function are same up to five and four decimal places for mini-batches of 200 and 1000, respectively.

With backtracking line search, SAGA performs even better for CS and SS and runs more than two times faster with mini-batch of 200 and more than three and half times with mini-batch of size 1000 as compared with RS while the values of objective function are same up to eight decimal places with mini-batch of size 200 and up to six decimal places with mini-batch of size 1000. Similar trend are followed for SAAG-II, SVRG and MBSGD methods where CS and SS are around two to more than three and half times faster and objective values are same up to six to nine decimal places as compared with RS with constant step and backtracking line search (LS).

TABLE 5.1 Comparison of Training Time (in seconds) and Objective Function Values after 30 Epochs Using Dataset HIGGS

Method	Sampling	Batch	Constant Step		Line Search	
			Time	Objective	Time	Objective
SAG	RS	200	229.220102	0.3258410619	495.873963	0.3258353956
	CS		66.378361	0.3258375894	214.083371	0.3258353935
	SS		67.867812	0.3258410840	214.533017	0.3258353956
	RS	1000	234.129248	0.3258356616	535.821883	0.3258354793
	CS		63.957239	0.3258358353	126.807235	0.3258354785
	SS		65.908254	0.3258356562	148.786983	0.3258354792
SAGA	RS	200	302.318358	0.3258637650	432.787547	0.3258353922
	CS		147.235962	0.3258659974	182.545531	0.3258353924
	SS		148.402540	0.3258636638	177.698227	0.3258353937
	RS	1000	301.003253	0.3259746991	445.741781	0.3258354946
	CS		145.917197	0.3259814282	112.433248	0.3258355048
	SS		147.646753	0.3259748885	120.481113	0.3258354828
SAAG-II	RS	200	297.134694	0.3263398874	708.881659	0.3258353918
	CS		174.232600	0.3263398971	380.852014	0.3258353920
	SS		176.845275	0.3263398982	338.122579	0.3258353920
	RS	1000	299.840227	0.3258550019	687.638964	0.3258354037
	CS		171.384496	0.3258550023	209.564000	0.3258354039
	SS		172.268358	0.3258550036	213.877001	0.3258354041
SVRG	RS	200	297.620959	0.3258923266	406.229956	0.3258354055
	CS		172.405902	0.3258923398	213.151577	0.3258354059
	SS		172.612984	0.3258923141	185.538374	0.3258354064
	RS	1000	297.259155	0.3261069018	497.501496	0.3258357363
	CS		172.227776	0.3261069217	159.518159	0.3258357365
	SS		172.601618	0.3261068804	151.230547	0.3258357352
MBSGD	RS	200	267.252470	0.3258635308	312.865696	0.3258353862
	CS		144.769059	0.3258635315	121.004686	0.3258353865
	SS		140.241334	0.3258635313	122.396247	0.3258353867
	RS	1000	268.102817	0.3259704996	306.236327	0.3258354906
	CS		139.586141	0.3259704998	82.340378	0.3258354912
	SS		135.646766	0.3259704994	81.486252	0.3258354909

5.5 CONCLUSION

In this chapter, novel systematic sampling and cyclic sampling techniques have been proposed, for solving large-scale learning problems, for improving the training time by reducing the data access time. Methods have similar convergence in expectation for systematic and cyclic sampling, as for widely used random sampling, but with cyclic and systematic sampling the training is up to six times faster than widely used random sampling technique, at the expense of fractionally small difference in the minimized objective function value, for a given number of epochs. Thus, systematic sampling technique is suitable for solving large-scale problems with low accuracy solution. Random shuffling of data can be used before the data is fed to the learning algorithms with systematic and cyclic sampling to improve their results for the cases where similar data points are grouped together. These sampling techniques can be extended to parallel and distributed learning algorithms because of mini-batching.

III

SECOND ORDER METHODS

CHAPTER 6

Mini-batch Block-coordinate Newton Method

N owadays, big data challenge is one of the major challenge in machine learning. Stochastic approximation and coordinate descent approaches are very effective to deal with the challenge, as they make each iteration of the learning algorithm independent of number of data points and number of features, respectively. In this chapter, we have combined the best of stochastic approximation and coordinate descent approaches with second order methods to propose mini-bath block-coordinate Newton (MBN) method. We find that MBN does not perform well as per the expectations and lags behind even the pure Newton method in term of training time. This is due to the double sampling of data points and features, and associated implementation overheads.

6.1 INTRODUCTION

In this chapter, we consider the empirical risk minimization problem (ERM), as given below:

$$\min_{w} \ F(w) = \frac{1}{l} \sum_{i=1}^{l} f_i(w), \tag{6.1}$$

The general solution of (6.1), using Newton method is given by

$$w_{k+1} = w_k - \alpha_k \nabla^2 F(w_k)^{-1} \nabla F(w_k), \tag{6.2}$$

where α_k is the learning rate. The per-iteration complexity of this iteration is $O(n^2 l + n^3)$ which is huge for large-scale learning problems. The major issues with Newton method are the need to calculate and store a large Hessian matrix and calculation of Hessian inverse.

For large-scale learning problems or big data problems in machine learning, number of data points and/or number of features are large, which lead to high per-iteration complexity for the iterative algorithms. To deal with the large-scale problems or big data problems in machine learning, stochastic approximation and coordinate descent

DOI: 10.1201/9781003240167-6

are very effective. Stochastic approximation randomly samples one or few data points during each iteration and makes each iteration independent of number of data points in the dataset. It has been widely and successfully used with first and second order methods.

Similarly, coordinate descent (CD) approach samples one or block of features as variables and rest as constants, which makes each iteration independent of number of features. So, CD is very effective to deal with the high dimensional problems. It is clear that SA and CD are very effective to deal with big data problems. Now, it is interesting to study these techniques together because they can make each iteration independent of n and l and that can provide an efficient and scalable solution. The combination of SA and CD has been studied for first order methods, e.g., [133, 140, 146, 152], and to the best of our knowledge not studied for second order methods. We studied it and proposed BBOF (batch block optimization framework) and SAAG-I and II (stochastic average adjusted gradient methods) to work with BBOF [23]. We observed that SA and CD approaches do not work well together [28]. This is because of the extra computational overhead to implement, dominates the advantage of using SA and CD together.

In this chapter, we have studied SA and CD together with second order method. We observe similar results as observed with first order methods. The advantage of low and controllable per-iteration complexity is lost in the extra-overhead to implement the learning algorithm due to double sampling, i.e., sampling of data and features, and associated implementation issues.

6.1.1 Contributions

The contributions of the chapter are given below:

- We have studied mini-batch block-coordinate setting, i.e., BBOF framework with second order methods, with an intention to solve the issues related with the Newton method.

- Empirical results have proved that BBOF does not help with second order methods, i.e., proposed reduced per iteration complexity is not able to get the overall benefit in training on a large-scale problem.

6.2 MBN

MBN (mini-batch block-coordinate Newton) method is based on the best of SA and CD approaches with Newton method to solve problem (6.1). The idea of the method is to reduce the per-iteration complexity and make it controllable by using subsampling of data points and features. This looks to solve the major issues with the Newton method, as is clear from the update rule of MBN.

$$w_{k+1} = w_k - \alpha_k \left[\nabla^2_{C_k} F_{B_k}(w_k)^{-1} \nabla_{C_k} F_{B_k}(w_k) \right] e_{C_k}, \tag{6.3}$$

where

$$e_{C_k}[i] = \begin{cases} 1 & \text{if } i \in C_k \\ 0 & \text{else} \end{cases},$$

$$\nabla^2_{C_k} F_{B_k}(w_k) = \frac{1}{|B_k|} \sum_{i \in B_k} \nabla^2_{C_k} f_i(w_k),$$

$$\nabla_{C_k} F_{B_k}(w_k) = \frac{1}{|B_k|} \sum_{i \in B_k} \nabla_{C_k} f_i(w_k), \qquad (6.4)$$

$\nabla_{C_k} F_{B_k}(w_k)$ represents partial gradient over the selected block C_k and $\nabla^2_{C_k} F_{B_k}(w_k)$ represents partial Hessian over C_k and is of size $|C_k| \times |C_k|$. Thus, the per-iteration complexity of (6.3) is $O(|C_k|^2 |B_k| + |C_k|^3)$ which is much smaller and controllable than per-iteration complexity of Newton method. MBN looks to solve the problems related to Newton method and is presented using the Algorithm 15. This algorithm

---

Algorithm 15 MBN

1: **Inputs**: $m = $ #mini-batches, $s = $ #blocks, $n = $ #epochs and $\alpha = $ step size.
2: **Initialize**: w^0
3: **for** $k = 1, 2, \dots$ **do**
4:     Sample mini-batch of data points B_k
5:     Sample block of features C_k
6:     Formulate a subproblem using mini-batch B_k and block of features C_k
7:     Update parameter using eq. (6.3)
8: **end for**

---

is similar to BBOF when used with Newton method. The algorithm samples a mini-batch of data points and a block of features during each iteration and formulates a reduced subproblem, which is then solved using parameter update rule similar to Newton's method. Since it works with a subsample of data with subsample of features, this leads to reduction in per-iteration complexity. The size of Hessian used in the subproblem is $|C_k|^2$, which is much smaller and controllable.

6.3 EXPERIMENTS

In this section, we present the experimental results. We have used following datasets: mushroom and real-sim, whose details are given in the Table 1.1, and compared the following methods:

MBN: This is the proposed method.

SNewton: This is subsampled Newton method which uses progressive subsampling for gradient and Hessian calculations.

Newton: This is exact Newton method.

TRON: This is trust region Newton method which uses PCG (preconditioned conjugate gradient) method to solve the trust region subproblem. This is one of the widely used method to solve large-scale classification problems and is available in LIBLINEAR library [38].

SVRG-SQN: This is a stochastic quasi-Newton method [99].

6.3.1 Experimental Setup

The regularization parameter is set as $\lambda = 1/l$ for all the methods and learning rate is determined using stochastic backtracking line search for subsampled methods, i.e., MBN, SNewton and SVRG-SQN, and deterministic backtracking line search is used with Newton method. MBN and SNewton methods use progressive subsampling with initial mini-batch size of 10%. SVRG-SQN uses sample size of 10% and memory size (M) and update frequency (L) are set to a value of 10. All the methods are implemented using MATLAB and executed on MacBook Air (8 GB 1600 MHz DDR3, 1.6 GHz Intel Core i5 and 256GB SSD).

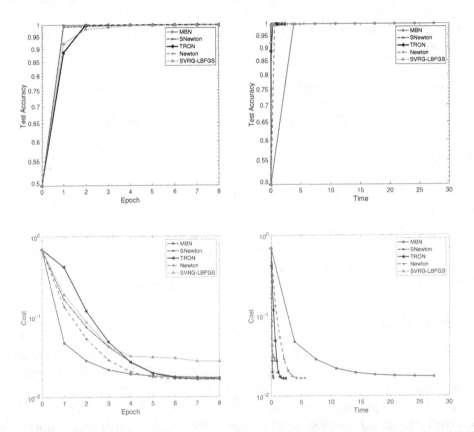

FIGURE 6.1 Comparison of MBN, SNewton, TRON, Newton and SVRG-SQN on mushroom dataset.

6.3.2 Comparative Study

Results compare MBN, SNewton, Newton, TRON and SVRG-SQN by plotting cost and test accuracy against training time (in seconds) and epochs. Figures 6.1–6.2 depict the results on two different datasets. For mushroom dataset (Fig. 6.1), MBN performs similar to Newton for results on epochs and outperform all other methods but lags behind other methods on training time. SNewton beats all methods in terms

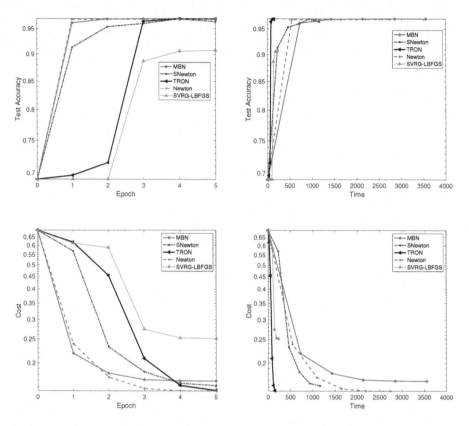

FIGURE 6.2 Comparison of MBN, SNewton, TRON, Newton and SVRG-SQN on real-sim dataset.

of training time. For real-sim (Fig. 6.2), we observe similar results where Newton and MBN outperform others on epochs but lags on the training time.

6.4 CONCLUSION

We have proposed to use Newton methods with best of stochastic approximation, i.e., mini-batching and best of coordinate descent, i.e., block-coordinates, with hope to reduce the per-iteration complexity and develop scalable and efficient method. But it is observed that inspite of reduced and controllable per-iteration complexity, MBN failed to perform as per the expectations due to double sampling of data points and features and associated overhead of implementation, and lags behind (singly) sampled stochastic Newton and pure Newton method. Thus, it is not suitable to use stochastic approximation and coordinate descent approaches together until we find a way to reduce the overhead associated with double sampling.

CHAPTER 7

Stochastic Trust Region Inexact Newton Method

N owadays stochastic approximation methods are one of the major research direction to deal with the large-scale machine learning problems. From stochastic first order methods, now the focus is shifting to stochastic second order methods due to their faster convergence and availability of computing resources. In this chapter, we have proposed a novel Stochastic Trust RegiOn Inexact Newton method, called as STRON, which uses conjugate gradient (CG) to inexactly solve trust region subproblem. The method uses progressive subsampling in the calculation of gradient and Hessian values to take the advantage of both, stochastic and full-batch regimes. We have extended STRON using existing variance reduction techniques to deal with the noisy gradients and using preconditioned conjugate gradient (PCG) as subproblem solver, and empirically proved that they do not work as expected, for the large-scale learning problems. Finally, our empirical results prove efficacy of the proposed method against existing methods with bench marked datasets.

7.1 INTRODUCTION

Machine learning involves data intensive optimization problems which have large number of component functions corresponding to large amount of data available. Traditional/classical methods, like Newton method, fail to perform well on such optimization problems due to large per-iteration complexity. So, nowadays one of the major challenge in machine learning is to develop scalable and efficient algorithms to deal with these large-scale learning problems [25].

To solve the machine learning problems, gradient descent (GD) [20] is the classical method of choice but it trains slowly while dealing with large-scale learning problems due to high per-iteration cost. Stochastic approximation based methods [113] can be quite effective in such situations but they converge slowly due to the noisy approximations of gradient. So, a variety of stochastic variance reduction techniques came to existence, e.g., [39]. But the major limitation of these methods is that they can converge up to linear rate only.

DOI: 10.1201/9781003240167-7

Newton method is another classical method to solve optimization problems, which can give up to quadratic convergence rate [17]. But again (pure) Newton method is not feasible with large-scale learning problems due to huge per-iteration computational complexity and need to store a huge Hessian matrix. So, nowadays one of the most significant open question in optimization for machine learning is: 'Can we develop stochastic second order methods with quadratic convergence, like Newton method but has low per-iteration complexity, like stochastic approximation methods?'. After success in the stochastic first order methods, the research is shifting its focus towards the stochastic second order methods to leverage the faster convergence of second order methods and the available computing power.

Inexact Newton (also called truncated Newton or Hessian free) methods and quasi-Newton methods are among the major research directions for developing second order methods [10]. Inexact Newton methods try to solve the Newton equation approximately without calculating and storing the Hessian matrix. On the other hand, quasi-Newton methods try to approximate the Hessian inverse and avoid the need to store the Hessian matrix. Thus, both the methods try to resolve the issues with Newton method. The stochastic variants of inexact Newton and quasi-Newton, further reduce the complexity of these methods by using subsampled gradient and Hessian calculations. In this chapter, we have proposed a novel stochastic trust region inexact Newton (STRON) method which introduces subsampling to gradient and Hessian calculations. It uses progressive subsampling to enjoy the benefits of both the regimes, stochastic approximation and full-batch learning. We further extend the method using existing variance reduction techniques to deal with noise produced by subsampling of gradient values, and by proposing PCG for solving the trust region subproblem.

7.1.1 Optimization Problem

We consider unconstrained convex optimization problem of expected risk, as given below:

$$\min_{w} R(w) = \mathbb{E}\left[f\left(w; \xi\right)\right], \qquad (7.1)$$

where $f\left(w; \xi\right) = f\left(w; x_i, y_i\right) = f\left(h\left(w; x_i\right), y_i\right)$ is a smooth composition of linear prediction model h and loss function f over randomly selected data point (x_i, y_i) from the unknown distribution $P\left(x_i, y_i\right)$, parameterized by the model parameter $w \in \mathbb{R}^n$. Since it is not feasible to solve (7.1) as P is unknown so the model is approximated by taking a set $N = \{(x_1, y_1), ..., (x_l, y_l)\}$ of l data points from the unknown distribution P and then solving the empirical risk minimization problem, as given below:

$$\min_{w} F(w) = \frac{1}{l} \sum_{i=1}^{l} f(w; x_i, y_i). \qquad (7.2)$$

For simplicity, we take $f\left(w; x_i, y_i\right) = f_i(w)$. Finite sum optimization problems of type (7.2) exists across different fields, like signal processing, statistics, operation research, data science and machine learning, e.g., logistic regression and SVM in machine learning.

7.1.2 Solution Techniques

Simple iterative classical method to solve (7.2) is gradient descent (GD) [20], as given below:

$$w^{k+1} = w^k - \alpha_k \nabla F(w_k), \tag{7.3}$$

where $(k + 1)$ is iteration number and α_k is called learning rate or step size. The complexity of this iteration is $O(nl)$ which is large for large-scale learning problems due to large number of data points. Stochastic gradient descent (SGD) [113] is very effective to deal with such problems due to its low per-iteration complexity, as given below:

$$w^{k+1} = w^k - \alpha_k \nabla f_{i_k}(w_k), \tag{7.4}$$

where i_k is randomly selected data point. But convergence can't be guaranteed in SGD because of noisy gradient values.

Another classical second order method to solve (7.2) is Newton method, as given below:

$$w^{k+1} = w^k - \alpha_k \nabla^2 F(w_k)^{-1} \nabla F(w_k). \tag{7.5}$$

The complexity of this iteration is $O(n^2 l + n^3)$ and it needs to store and invert the Hessian matrix $\nabla^2 F(w_k)$, which is computationally very expensive and needs large memory, respectively. That's why first order methods and their stochastic variants have been studied very extensively, during the last decade, to solve large-scale learning problems but not second order methods. As stochastic first order methods have hit their limits and due to the availability of better computing power, the main focus started shifting towards stochastic second order methods, and nowadays one important open question is to find stochastic second order methods with quadratic convergence rates.

There are two major research directions for second order methods: quasi-Newton methods and inexact Newton methods, both of which try to resolve the issues associated with the Newton method. Quasi-Newton methods try to approximate the Hessian matrix during each iteration, as given below:

$$w^{k+1} = w^k - \alpha_k B_k \nabla F(w_k), \tag{7.6}$$

where B_k is an approximate of $\nabla^2 F(w_k)^{-1}$, e.g., Broyden-Fletcher-Goldfarb-Shanno (BFGS) algorithm is one such method [42]. On the other hand, inexact Newton methods try to solve the Newton system approximately, e.g., Newton-CG [124]. Both the methods try to resolve the issues related with Newton method but still their complexities are large for large-scale problems. So, a number of stochastic variants of these methods have been proposed, e.g., [18, 19, 11, 8] which introduce subsampling to gradient and Hessian calculations.

7.1.3 Contributions

The contributions of the chapter are listed below:

- The chapter highlights the recent shift of stochastic methods from first order to second order methods and raises an open question that we need stochastic second order methods with quadratic convergence rate to solve large-scale machine learning problems.

- We have proposed a novel subsampled variant of trust region inexact Newton method, which is called STRON and is first stochastic variant of trust region inexact Newton methods. STRON uses progressive subsampling scheme for gradient and Hessian calculations to enjoy the benefits of both stochastic and full batch regimes. STRON can converge up to quadratic rate and answers the raised open question.

- STRON has been extended using existing variance reduction techniques to deal with the noisy approximations of the gradient calculations. The extended method uses stochastic variance reduced gradient (SVRG) for variance reduction with static batching for gradient calculations and progressive batching for the Hessian calculations. The empirical results prove that this does not work as expected for large-scale learning.

- We further extend STRON and use PCG, instead of CG method, to solve the Newton system inexactly. We have used weighted average of identity matrix and diagonal matrix as the preconditioner. But even this fails to work as expected for large-scale learning.

- Finally, our empirical experiments prove the efficacy of STRON against existing techniques with bench marked datasets.

7.2 LITERATURE REVIEW

Stochastic approximation methods are very effective to deal with the large-scale learning problems due to their low per-iteration cost, e.g., SGD [113], but they lead to slow convergence rates due to the noisy approximation. To deal with the noise issue, a number of techniques have been proposed and some of the important techniques (as discussed in [34]) are: (a) decreasing learning rates [118], (b) using mini-batching [26], (c) importance sampling [34], and (d) variance reduction [115]. The variance reduction methods can further be classified into three categories: primal methods [115], dual methods [120] and primal-dual methods [149]. The variance reduction techniques are effective to deal with the large-scale learning problems because of low per-iteration complexity, like SGD, and have fast linear convergence, like GD. These techniques exploit the best of SGD and GD but for these stochastic variants of first order methods the convergence is limited to linear rate only, unlike the second order methods which can give up to quadratic rate.

Second order methods utilize the curvature information to guide the step direction towards the solution and exhibit faster convergence than the first order methods. But huge per-iteration cost due to the huge Hessian matrix and its inversion make the training of models slow for large-scale problems. So, certain techniques have been developed to deal with the issues related to Hessian matrix, e.g., quasi-Newton methods and inexact Newton methods are two major directions to deal with the huge computational cost of Newton method. Quasi-Newton methods approximate the Hessian matrix during each iteration, e.g., BFGS [42] and its limited memory variant, called L-BFGS [89], are examples of the quasi-Newton class which use gradient and parameter values from the previous iterations to approximate the Hessian inverse. L-BFGS uses only recent information from previous M-iterations. On the other hand, inexact Newton methods try to solve the Newton system approximately, e.g., Newton-CG [124].

Recently, several stochastic variants of BFGS and L-BFGS have been proposed to deal with large-scale problems. [117] proposed stochastic variants of BFGS and L-BFGS for the online setting, known as oBFGS. [98] extended oBFGS by adding regularization which enforces upper bound on the eigen values of the approximate Hessian, known as RES (Regularized Stochastic BFGS). Stochastic quasi-Newton (SQN) [19] is another stochastic variant of L-BFGS which collects curvature information at regular intervals, instead of at each iteration. Variance-reduced Stochastic Newton (VITE) [91] extended RES and proposed to use variance reduction for the subsampled gradient values for solving smoothly strongly convex problems. [69] provided another stochastic L-BFGS method with variance reduction using SVRG (referred as SVRG-LBFGS). [99] proposed Stochastic L-BFGS (SLBFGS) using SVRG for variance reduction and using Hessian-vector product to approximate the gradient differences for calculating the Hessian approximations, also referred as SVRG-SQN. SVRG-LBFGS and SVRG-SQN differ in how the curvature is approximated (i.e. how Hessian is approximated), former collects the curvature information once during each epoch (outer iterations) using gradient differences but later collects the curvature information after regular intervals inside the inner-iterations using Hessian-vector products. [9] proposed multi-batch scheme into stochastic L-BFGS where batch sample changes with some overlaps with previous iteration. [11] proposed progressive batching, stochastic line search and stable Newton updates for L-BFGS. [10] studies the conditions on the subsample sizes to get the different convergence rates.

Stochastic inexact Newton methods are also explored extensively. [18] proposed stochastic variants of Newton-CG along with L-BFGS method. [10] studies subsampled Newton methods and find conditions on subsample sizes and forcing term (constant used with the residual condition), for linear convergence of Newton-CG method. [8] studies the effect of forcing term and line search to find linear and super-linear convergence of Newton-CG method. Newton-SGI (stochastic gradient iteration) is another way of solving the linear system approximately and is studied in [3].

Trust Region Newton (TRON) method is one of the most efficient solver for solving large-scale linear classification problems [85]. This is trust region inexact Newton method which does not use any subsampling and is present in LIBLINEAR library [38]. [52] extends TRON by improving the trust region radius value. [51] further extends TRON and uses preconditioned conjugate gradient (PCG) which uses weighted average of identity matrix and diagonal matrix as a preconditioner, to solve the trust region subproblem. Since subsampling is an effective way to deal with the large-scale problems so in this chapter, we have proposed a stochastic variant of trust region inexact Newton method, which have not been studied so far to the best of our knowledge.

7.3 TRUST REGION INEXACT NEWTON METHOD

Inexact Newton methods, also called as Truncated Newton or Hessian free methods, solve the Newton equation (linear system) approximately. CG method is a commonly used technique to solve the trust region subproblem approximately. In this section, we discuss inexact Newton method and its trust region variation.

7.3.1 Inexact Newton Method

The quadratic model $m_k(p)$ obtained using Taylor's theorem is given below:

$$F(w_k + p) - F(w_k) \approx m_k(p) \equiv \nabla F(w_k)^T p + \frac{1}{2} p^T \nabla^2 F(w_k) p. \qquad (7.7)$$

Taking derivative of $m_k(p)$ w.r.t. p and equating to zero, we get,

$$\nabla^2 F(w_k) p = -\nabla F(w_k), \qquad (7.8)$$

which is Newton system and its solution gives Newton method, as given below:

$$w^{k+1} = w^k + p_k = w^k - \nabla^2 F(w_k)^{-1} \nabla F(w_k). \qquad (7.9)$$

The computational complexity of this iteration is $O(n^2 l + n^3)$ which is very expensive. This iteration involves the calculation and inversion of a large Hessian matrix which is not only very expensive to calculate but expensive to store also. CG method approximately solves the subproblem (7.8) without forming the Hessian matrix, which solves the issues related to large computational complexity and need to store the large Hessian matrix. Each iteration runs for a given number of CG iterations or until the residual condition is satisfied, as given below:

$$\|r_k\| \leq \eta_k' \|\nabla F(w_k)\|, \qquad (7.10)$$

where $r_k = \nabla^2 F(w_k) p + \nabla F(w_k)$ and η_k' is a small positive value, known as forcing term [103].

7.3.2 Trust Region Inexact Newton Method

Trust region is a region in which the approximate quadratic model of the given function gives correct approximation for that function. In trust region methods, we don't need to calculate the step size (also called learning rate) directly but they indirectly adjust the step size as per the trust region radius. Trust region method solves the following subproblem to get the step direction p_k:

$$\min_p m_k(p) \quad \text{s.t.} \quad \|p\| \leq \triangle_k, \qquad (7.11)$$

where $m_k(p)$ is a quadratic model of $F(w_k + p) - F(w_k)$, as given in (7.7) and $\triangle_k$ is the trust region radius. This subproblem can be solved similar to Newton-CG, except that now we need to take care of the extra constraint of p. TRON (trust region Newton method) [85] is one of the most famous and widely used such method, which is used in LIBLINEAR [38] to solve l_2-regularized logistic regression and l_2-SVM problems. [52] extends TRON by proposing better trust region radius. [51] further extends TRON using PCG subproblem solver which uses average of identity matrix and diagonal matrix as preconditioner, to solve the trust region subproblem and shows that PCG could be effective to solve ill-conditioned problems.

Then the ratio of actual and predicted reductions of the model is calculated, as given below:

$$\rho_k = \frac{F(w_k + p_k) - F(w_k)}{m_k(p_k)}. \tag{7.12}$$

The parameters are updated for the $(k+1)$th iteration as given below:

$$w_{k+1} = \begin{cases} w_k + p_k, & \text{if } \rho_k > \eta_0, \\ w_k, & \text{if } \rho_k \le \eta_0, \end{cases} \tag{7.13}$$

where $\eta_0 > 0$ is a given constant. Then the trust region radius $\triangle_k$ is updated as per the ratio of actual reduction and predicted reduction, and a framework for updating $\triangle_k$ as given in [83], is given below:

$$\triangle_{k+1} \in \begin{cases} [\gamma_1 \min\{\|p_k\|, \triangle_k\}, \gamma_2 \triangle_k], & \text{if } \rho_k \le \eta_1, \\ [\gamma_1 \triangle_k, \gamma_3 \triangle_k], & \text{if } \rho_k \in (\eta_1, \eta_2), \\ [\triangle_k, \gamma_3 \triangle_k], & \text{if } \rho_k \ge \eta_2, \end{cases} \tag{7.14}$$

where $0 < \eta_1 < \eta_2 \le 1$ and $0 < \gamma_1 < \gamma_2 < 1 < \gamma_3$. If $\rho_k \le \eta_1$ then the Newton step is considered unsuccessful and the trust region radius is shrunk. On the other hand if $\rho_k \ge \eta_2$ then the step is successful and the trust region radius is enlarged. We have implemented this framework as given in the LIBLINEAR library [38] and chose the following pre-defined values for the above constants: $\eta_0 = 1e-4$, $\eta_1 = 0.25$, $\eta_2 = 0.75$, $\gamma_1 = 0.25$, $\gamma_2 = 0.5$ and $\gamma_3 = 4$.

7.4 STRON

STRON exploits the best of both, stochastic and batch regimes, using progressive sub-sampling. As stochastic gradient descent (SGD) trains faster for large-scale learning problems than gradient descent (GD) due to low computations per iteration but GD is more accurate than SGD due to batch calculations, similarly STRON takes benefit of low computation during initial iterations and as it reaches the solution region it uses batch calculations to find accurate solution like TRON. The major challenge with STRON is to decide when to switch from stochastic to full-batch regime, i.e., to tune the subsampling rate.

STRON introduces stochasticity into the trust region inexact Newton method and calculates subsampled function, gradient and Hessian values to solve the trust region subproblem, as given below:

$$\min_p m_k(p) = \nabla F_{X_k}(w_k)^T p + \frac{1}{2} p^T \nabla^2 F_{S_k}(w_k) p, \quad \text{s.t. } \|p\| \le \triangle_k, \tag{7.15}$$

where $\nabla^2 F_{S_k}(w_k)$ and $\nabla F_{X_k}(w_k)$ are subsampled Hessian and gradient values over the subsamples S_k and X_k, respectively, as defined below:

$$\nabla^2 F_{S_k}(w_k) = \frac{1}{|S_k|} \sum_{i \in S_k} \nabla^2 f_i(w_k),$$

$$\nabla F_{X_k}(w_k) = \frac{1}{|X_k|} \sum_{i \in X_k} \nabla f_i(w_k), \qquad (7.16)$$

$$F_{X_k}(w_k) = \frac{1}{|X_k|} \sum_{i \in X_k} f_i(w_k),$$

where subsamples are increasing, i.e., $|X_k| < |X_{k+1}|$, $|S_k| < |S_{k+1}|$ and F_{X_k} is subsampled function value used for calculating ρ_k. STRON solves (7.15) approximately for given number of CG iterations or until the following residual condition is satisfied:

$$\|r_k\| \leq \eta_k' \|\nabla F_{X_k}(w_k)\|, \qquad (7.17)$$

where $r_k = \nabla^2 F_{S_k}(w_k) p + \nabla F_{X_k}(w_k)$.

STRON is presented by Algorithm 16. It randomly selects subsamples S_k and X_k for

---

Algorithm 16 STRON

1: **Input:** w_0
2: **Result:** $w = w_k$
3: **for** $k = 0, 1, \ldots$ **do**
4:     Randomly select subsamples S_k and X_k
5:     Calculate subsampled gradient $\nabla F_{X_k}(w_k)$
6:     Solve the trust region subproblem using Algorithm 17, to get the step direction p_k
7:     Calculate the ratio $\rho_k = (F_{X_k}(w_k + p_k) - F_{X_k}(w_k)) / m_k(p_k)$
8:     Update the parameters using (7.13)
9:     Update the trust region radius $\triangle_k$ using (7.14)
10: **end for**

---

the kth iteration (outer iterations). X_k and S_k are used for calculating the gradient and Hessian values, respectively. Then it solves the trust region subproblem using CG solver (inner iterations) which uses subsampled Hessian in calculating Hessian-vector products. CG stops when residual condition, same as (7.17), satisfies, it reaches maximum #CG iterations or it reaches the trust region boundary. The ratio of reduction in actual and predicted reduction is calculated similar to (7.12) but using subsampled function, and is used for updating the parameters as given in (7.13). Then trust region radius $\triangle_k$ is updated as per ρ_k as given in (7.14) and these steps are repeated for a given number of iterations or until convergence.

STRON uses progressive subsampling, i.e., dynamic subsampling to calculate function, gradient and Hessian values, and solves the Newton system approximately. It is effective to deal with large-scale problems since it uses subsampling and solves the subproblem approximately, without forming the Hessian matrix but using only Hessian-vector products. So, it handles the complexity issues related with the Newton method.

Algorithm 17 CG Subproblem Solver

1: **Inputs:** $\triangle_k > 0$, $\eta_k' \in (0, 1)$
2: **Result:** $p_k = p_j$
3: Initialize $p_0 = 0, r_0 = d_0 = -\nabla F_{X_k}(w_k)$
4: **for** $j = 1, 2, \ldots$ **do**
5:     **if** $\|r_{j-1}\| < \eta_k' \|\nabla F_{X_k}(w_k)\|$ **then**
6:         return $p_k = p_{j-1}$
7:     **end if**
8:     Calculate subsampled Hessian-vector product $v_j = \nabla^2 F_{S_k}(w_k)d_{j-1}$
9:     $\alpha_j = \|r_{j-1}\|^2 / \left(d_{j-1}^T v_j\right)$
10:     $p_j = p_{j-1} + \alpha_j d_{j-1}$
11:     **if** $\|p_j\| \geq \triangle_k$ **then**
12:         Calculate τ_j such that $\|p_{j-1} + \tau_j d_{j-1}\| = \triangle_k$
13:         return $p_k = p_{j-1} + \tau_j d_{j-1}$
14:     **end if**
15:     $r_j = r_{j-1} - \alpha_j v_j$,
16:     $\beta_j = \|r_j\|^2 / \|r_{j-1}\|^2, d_j = r_j + \beta_j d_{j-1}$
17: **end for**

7.4.1 Complexity

The complexity of trust region inexact Newton (TRON) method depends on function, gradient and CG subproblem solver. This is dominated by CG subproblem solver and is given by $O(nl) \times$ #CG iterations, and for sparse data, $O(\#nnz) \times$ #CG iterations, where #nnz is number of non-zeros values in the dataset. For subsampled trust region inexact Newton (STRON) method, the complexity per-iteration is given by $O(n|S_k|) \times$ #CG iterations, and for sparse data, $O(\#nnz_{S_k}) \times$ #CG iterations, where #nnz_{S_k} is number of non-zeros values in the subsample S_k. Since #CG iterations taken by TRON and STRON do not differ much so the per-iteration complexity of STRON is smaller than TRON in the initial iterations and later becomes equal to TRON due to progressive subsampling, i.e., when $|S_k| = N$.

7.4.2 Analysis

STRON method uses progressive subsampling with the assumption that eventually mini-batch size becomes equal to the whole dataset, i.e., for some value of $k \geq \bar{k} > 0$, STRON becomes TRON. So, we can follow the theoretical results given in TRON, which itself refers the results from [83]. For $k \geq \bar{k}$, we get different convergence depending upon the value of η_k': If $\eta_k' < 1$ then STRON converges Q-linearly, if $\eta_k' \to 0$ as $k \to \infty$ then STRON has Q-superlinear convergence and when $\eta_k' \leq \kappa_0 \|\nabla F(w_k)\|$ for $\kappa_0 > 0$ then STRON converges at quadratic rate.

7.5 EXPERIMENTAL RESULTS

In this section, we discuss experimental settings and results[1]. The experiments have been conducted with the bench marked binary datasets as given in the Table 1.1. We use following methods in experimentation:

TRON [51]: This is a trust region inexact Newton method without any subsampling. It uses preconditioned CG method to solve the trust region subproblem and it is present in the current version of LIBLINEAR library [38].

STRON: This is the proposed stochastic trust region inexact Newton method with progressive subsampling technique for gradient and Hessian calculations. It uses CG method to solve the trust region subproblem.

STRON-PCG: This is an extension of STRON using PCG for solving the trust region subproblem, as discussed in the Subsection 7.6.1.

STRON-SVRG: This is another extension of STRON using variance reduction for subsampled gradient calculations, as discussed in Subsection 7.6.2.

Newton-CG [18]: This is stochastic inexact Newton method which uses CG method to solve the subproblem. It uses progressive subsampling similar to STRON.

SVRG-SQN [99]: This is stochastic L-BFGS method with variance reduction for gradient calculations.

SVRG-LBFGS [69]: This is another stochastic L-BFGS method with variance reduction. It differs from SVRG-SQN method in approach by which Hessian information is sampled.

7.5.1 Experimental Setup

The datasets have been divided into 80% and 20%, for training and testing datasets, respectively to plot the convergence, and 5-fold cross-validation has been used to present results in Table 7.1. We have used $\lambda = 1/l$ for all methods because generally it gives good results and at the same time helps to reduce number of tunable hyper-parameters. #CG iterations has been set to a sufficiently large value of 25, as all the inexact Newton methods use 5–10 iterations and hardly go beyond 20 iterations. Progressive batching scheme uses initial batch size of 1% for all datasets except ijcnn which uses 10% of dataset and the subsample size is increased linearly for all datasets, except covtype where exponential rate is used. Moreover we set the rate such that subsample size equals dataset size in 5 epochs because, generally second order methods reach the solution region in 4–5 epochs and converge in 8–10 epochs. For the sake of simplicity and to avoid extra sampling, we take same subsample for Hessian and gradient calculations, i.e, $S_k = X_k$. Quasi-Newton methods (SVRG-SQN and SVRG-LBFGS) use mini-batch size of 10% with stochastic backtracking line search to find the step size, and same size mini-batches are taken for gradient and Hessian subsampling. Memory of $M = 5$ is used in quasi-Newton methods with $L = 5$ as update frequency of Hessian inverse approximation for SVRG-SQN method. All the algorithms use similar exit criterion of decrease in gradient value where we calculate gradient ($\|g_0\|$) at w_0 and run the algorithms until $\|g_k\| \leq \epsilon\|g_0\|$, where

---

[1]for detailed experiments, please refer to [29]

$\|g_k\|$ is gradient value at k^{th}-iteration and ϵ is the given tolerance level. Moreover all the methods are implemented in C++[2] with MATLAB interface and experiments have been executed on MacBook Air (8 GB 1600 MHz DDR3, 1.6 GHz Intel Core i5 and 256GB SSD).

7.5.2 Comparative Study

The experiments have been performed with strongly convex and smooth l_2-regularized logistic regression problem as given below:

$$\min_{w} F(w) = \frac{1}{l} \sum_{i=1}^{l} \log \left(1 + \exp \left(-y_i w^T x_i \right) \right) + \frac{\lambda}{2} \|w\|^2. \qquad (7.18)$$

The results have been plotted as optimality $(F(w) - F(w^*))$ versus training time (in seconds) and accuracy versus training time for high $\epsilon(=10^{-10})$-accuracy solutions, as given in the Fig. 7.1. As it is clear from the results, STRON converges faster than all other methods and shows improvement against TRON on accuracy vs. time plots. Moreover, quasi-Newton methods converges slower than inexact Newton methods as already established in the literature [85]. As per the intuitions, STRON takes initial advantage over TRON due to subsampling and as it reaches the solution region the progressive batching scheme reaches the full batching scheme and converges with same rate as TRON. That's why, in most of the figures, we can observe STRON and TRON converging in parallel lines. Moreover, we observe a horizontal line for accuracy vs. time plot with covtype dataset because all methods give 100% accuracy. Generally, the models are trained for low $\epsilon(=10^{-02})$-accuracy solutions. So we present the results for such a case using Table 7.1, which reports results using 5-fold cross validation. As it is clear from the table, STRON either outperforms other solvers or shows results pretty close to the best method.

7.5.3 Results with SVM

We extend STRON to solve l_2-SVM problem which is a non-smooth problem, as given below:

$$\min_{w} F(w) = \frac{1}{l} \sum_{i=1}^{l} \max(0, 1 - y_i w^T x_i)^2 + \frac{\lambda}{2} \|w\|^2. \qquad (7.19)$$

The results are reported in the Fig. 7.2 with news20 dataset. As it is clear from the figure, STRON shows results similar to logistic regression problem and outperforms all other methods.

7.6 EXTENSIONS

In this section, we discuss extensions of the proposed method with PCG for solving the trust region subproblem, and with variance reduction technique.

---

[2]experimental results can be reproduced using the library [27]: https://github.com/jmdvinodjmd/LIBS2ML.

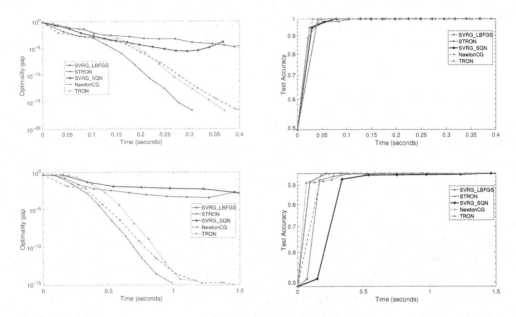

FIGURE 7.1 First column presents optimality versus training time (in seconds) and second column presents accuracy versus training time, on mushroom (first row) and rcv1 (second row) datasets.

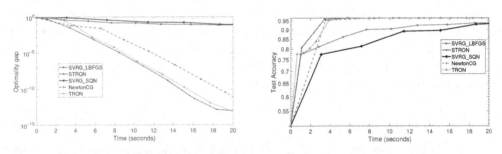

FIGURE 7.2 Experiments with l₂-SVM on news20 dataset.

7.6.1 PCG Subproblem Solver

Number of iterations required by CG method to solve the subproblem depends on the condition number of the Hessian matrix. So, for ill-conditioned problems CG method converges slowly. To avoid such situations, generally a non-singular matrix M, called preconditioner, is used as follow. For the linear system $\nabla^2 F(w)p = -\nabla F(w)$, we solve following system:

$$M^{-1}\nabla^2 F(w)p = -M^{-1}\nabla F(w). \tag{7.20}$$

Generally, $M^{-1} = LL^T$ is taken to ensure the symmetry and positive definiteness of $M^{-1}\nabla^2 F(w)$. PCG can be useful for solving the ill-conditioned problems but it involves extra computational overhead. We follow [51] to use PCG as a weighted average of identity matrix and diagonal matrix of Hessian, as given below:

$$M = \alpha \times diag(H) + (1 - \alpha) \times I, \qquad (7.21)$$

where H is a Hessian matrix and $0 \leq \alpha \leq 1$. For $\alpha = 0$, there is no preconditioning and for $\alpha = 1$ it is a diagonal preconditioner. In the experiments, we have taken $\alpha = 0.01$ for TRON and STRON-PCG [51]. To apply PCG to trust region subproblem, we can use Algorithm 17 without any modifications, after changing the trust region subproblem (7.11), as given below [124]:

$$\min_{\hat{p}} \left(L^{-1} \nabla F_{X_k} (w_k) \right)^T \hat{p} + \frac{1}{2} \hat{p}^T \left(L^{-1} \nabla^2 F_{S_k} (w_k) L^{-T} \right) \hat{p}, \;\; \text{s.t.} \;\; \|\hat{p}\| \leq \triangle_k, \quad (7.22)$$

where $\hat{p} = L^T p$. STRON using PCG as a trust region subproblem solver is denoted by STRON-PCG and the results are reported in Fig. 7.3. It compares TRON, STRON and STRON-PCG on Adult dataset. As it is clear from the figure, both STRON and STRON-PCG outperform TRON.

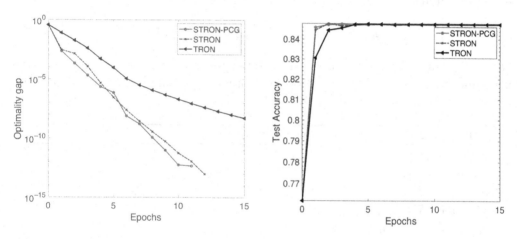

FIGURE 7.3 Comparative study of STRON_PCG, STRON and TRON on Adult dataset.

PCG trust region subproblem solver involves extra cost for calculating the preconditioner, and for TRON the overhead due to preconditioner is given by

$$O(n) \times \#\text{CG iterations} + O(nl). \qquad (7.23)$$

And for STRON-PCG, preconditioner involves extra cost as given below:

$$O(n) \times \#\text{CG iterations} + O(n|S_k|). \qquad (7.24)$$

7.6.2 Stochastic Variance Reduced Trust Region Inexact Newton Method

Recently, researchers have proposed stochastic variants of second order methods with variance reduction. So, it is an interesting question to know that how will variance reduction work with stochastic trust region inexact Newton methods, as this is not studied yet. Our empirical results prove that variance reduction does not work in this case, even after using progressive subsampling for Hessian calculation.

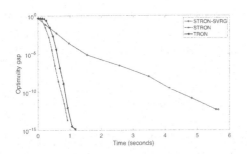 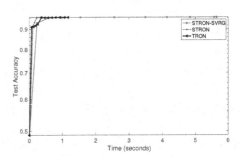

FIGURE 7.4 Comparative study of STRON-SVRG, STRON and TRON rcv1 dataset.

To improve the quality of search direction, we have used SVRG as variance reduction technique for gradient calculations, as given below:

$$g_k = \nabla F_{S_k}(w_k) - \nabla F_{S_k}(\bar{w}) + \nabla F(\bar{w}), \tag{7.25}$$

where $\bar{w}$ is parameter value at the start of outer iteration. STRON-SVRG uses variance reduction for gradient calculations and progressive batching for Hessian calculations, as given in the Algorithm 18.

Algorithm 18 STRON with Variance Reduction

1: **Inputs:** w_0, m
2: **Result:** $w = w_k$
3: **for** $i = 0, 1, 2, \ldots$ **do**
4:     Calculate $\nabla F(w_i)$ and set $\bar{w} = w_i$
5:     **for** $k = 0, 1, \ldots, (m-1)$ **do**
6:         Randomly select subsamples S_k and X_k
7:         Calculate subsampled gradient $\nabla F_{X_k}(w_k)$
8:         Calculate variance reduced gradient using (7.25)
9:         Solve the trust region subproblem using Algorithm 17 with variance reduced gradient, instead of subsampled gradient, to get the step direction p_k
10:        Calculate the ratio $\rho_k = (F_{X_k}(w_k + p_k) - F_{X_k}(w_k))/m_k(p_k)$
11:        Update the parameters using (7.13)
12:        Update the trust region $\triangle_k$ using (7.14)
13:     **end for**
14: **end for**

The experimental results are presented in Fig. 7.4 with rcv1 datasets. As it is clear from the figures, STRON-SVRG lags behind STRON and TRON, i.e., variance reduction in STRON-SVRG is not sufficient to beat the progressive batching in gradient calculations of STRON. This is because both, STRON-SVRG and STRON, are stochastic/subsampled variants of TRON and to compensate for the noisy gradient calculations, former uses well-known variance reduction strategy but later uses progressive subsampling strategy. STRON is able to beat TRON but STRON-SVRG fails and lags behind both.

7.7 CONCLUSION

We proposed a novel stochastic trust region inexact Newton method, called as STRON. The proposed method used progressive batching scheme to deal with noisy approximations of gradient and Hessian, and enjoyed the benefits of both stochastic and full batch regimes. STRON has been extended to use preconditioned CG as trust region subproblem solver and to use variance reduction for noisy gradient calculations. Our empirical results proved the efficacy of STRON against the state-of-art techniques with bench marked datasets.

TABLE 7.1 Comparison of Training Time for Low Accuracy ($\epsilon=0.01$) Solution

Datasets↓	Methods→	SVRG_LBFGS	STRON	SVRG_SQN	Newton_CG	TRON
covtype	Time	0.8440±0.1770	**0.0620±0.0045**	0.4140±0.0397	0.9740±0.1907	0.7294±0.0162
	Accuracy	**1.00±0.0**	**1.00±0.0**	**1.00±0.0**	**1.00±0.0**	**1.00±0.0**
real-sim	Time	1.5920±0.5867	0.9340±0.1258	2.3480±0.5909	**0.68±0.01**	0.88±0.10
	Accuracy	0.9670±0.0055	0.9697±0.0017	0.9670±0.0029	0.9688±0.0022	**0.9698±0.0015**
rcv1	Time	2.1780±0.1813	**0.5700±0.0200**	3.2840±0.0270	0.5860±0.0167	0.6589±0.0866
	Accuracy	**0.9641±0.0023**	0.9640±0.0025	0.9637±0.0024	0.9640±0.0024	0.9639±0.0027
news20	Time	42.8960±2.5993	6.9620±1.3534	84.0520±2.2915	**6.764±0.0074**	7.2470±0.3567
	Accuracy	0.9333±0.0079	0.9337±0.0076	**0.9339±0.0072**	0.9338±0.0074	0.9338±0.0077
mushroom	Time	0.1540±0.01340	0.0820±0.0268	0.1820±0.01920	**0.072±0.0045**	0.1316±0.0169
	Accuracy	0.9995±0.0007	0.9992±0.0005	0.9986±0.0026	**0.9996±0.0005**	0.9995±0.0005
ijcnn1	Time	0.3460±0.1390	**0.2560±0.03780**	0.3600±0.1158	0.3120±0.0795	0.2564±0.0185
	Accuracy	0.9235±0.0022	0.9232±0.0021	0.9237±0.0018	**0.9238±0.0025**	0.9233±0.0185
Adult	Time	0.3620±0.0981	**0.2000±0.0187**	0.3100±0.0644	0.2380±0.0084	0.2139±0.0046
	Accuracy	**0.8479±0.0028**	0.8470±0.0028	0.8469±0.0031	0.8473±0.0030	0.8477±0.0028
gisette	Time	9.5620±0.9891	**8.1800±0.4260**	10.7020±1.1314	41.6480±36.1190	10.4277±0.1709
	Accuracy	0.9725±0.0036	0.9730±0.0045	0.9690±0.0026	0.9701±0.0057	**0.9755±0.0028**
webspam	Time	6.0480±2.2814	6.3720±0.9942	7.6080±2.1462	**3.272±0.2141**	9.0548±1.2572
	Accuracy	0.9139±0.0033	0.9214±0.0019	0.9158±0.0036	0.9219±0.0017	**0.9227±0.0009**

IV

CONCLUSION

CHAPTER 8

Conclusion and Future Scope

The advancements in the technology and the availability of data sources have led us to the 'Big Data' era. One side, this large data has potential to uncover more fine-grained patterns, take timely and accurate decisions, but on the other side it creates a lot of challenges to make a sense of it, like, slow training and scalability of machine learning models etc. So, one of the major challenges in machine learning is to develop efficient and scalable learning algorithms, i.e., optimization techniques to solve large-scale learning problems.

We can tackle the challenge by working in following areas: problem formulations, problem solvers, optimization strategies to improve the solvers and utilizing computing resources, like graphics processing unit (GPUs), parallel and distributed computing. But out of these potential areas, recently, researchers have focused on stochastic approximation algorithms, coordinate descent algorithms, proximal algorithms and parallel and distributed algorithms to tackle the challenge.

We have provided solutions to tackle the challenge by focusing on both parts of the training time of models, i.e., time to access the data and time to learn from the data. To improve the data access time, we have proposed to use the systematic sampling and sequential sampling techniques to sample mini-batches of data points from the dataset, which are based on contiguous memory access. This is a general observation that data access is faster from contiguous memory than from the dispersed memory. This solution to the big data challenge is independent of problem or solver used, as it is based on the data access. This helped to achieve up to six times faster training.

To improve the learning time from the data, we have used stochastic approximation and coordinate descent approaches, which are very effective to deal with the big data problems because they make each iteration independent of number of data points and number of features, respectively. First, we utilize the best of stochastic approximation and coordinate descent approaches to propose a batch block optimization framework to solve the big data problems. We used batch block optimization framework with first and second order methods and proposed SAAG-I and II and MBN, respectively. But it is observed that the stochastic approximation and coordinate descent, do not work well when combined together because the advantage is lost in extra overhead to implement batch block optimization framework. Since a batch block optimization framework uses double sampling, i.e., sampling of data points and that of features so it also involves data access related issues, due to sparse representations of data.

We have also provided solutions to the big data challenge using stochastic approximation because nowadays this is one of the most popular approach to solve large scale problems. We have proposed SAAG-III and IV, as extensions of SAAG-I and II, respectively. These are stochastic variance reduction techniques based on iterate averaging and solve both smooth and non-smooth problems with linear convergence. With second order methods, we have utilized the best of stochastic and full-batch regimes to propose stochastic trust region inexact Newton method based on progressive subsampling. The second order methods converge faster than first order methods which are limited to linear convergence only. We have also used CG and PCG with STRON to solve the trust region subproblem.

It is observed that the stochastic approximation and coordinate descent, do not work well when combined together because the advantage is lost in extra overhead to implement batch block optimization framework due to double sampling, i.e., sampling of data points and that of features. Although, stochastic approximation based first and second order methods are very effective to solve large-scale problems, where later ones can converge faster but need more computations.

8.1 FUTURE SCOPE

Optimization is the backbone of machine learning. Due to increasing data set sizes and increasing popularity of deep learning the importance of optimization methods have increased even more. The current research work to solve large-scale learning problems can be extended, as discussed below:

1. *Theoretical Insights*

   Although, theory is lagging behind practice in most of the areas of machine learning but this is very important as it helps to realize the actual potential of a learning algorithm. In current work, the main focus was on empirical study but finding convergence rates and theoretical properties of a learning algorithm will help to further improve the methods and propose new ones.

2. *Complex (non-convex) Problems*

   Deep learning has revolutionized the field of machine learning and opened many opportunities to solve challenging real life problems. It involves non-convex large scale problems which are complex to solve. So, efficient and scalable optimization methods are required to solve deep learning problems. The current work focuses only on convex problems so the next hurdle is to extend the current work to solve non convex problems.

3. *Parallel and Distributed Algorithms*

   Parallel and distributed algorithms are the future of machine learning because the increasing data set sizes are difficult to process on single machines. The current work deals with the development of optimization techniques to solve large-scale problems on single machine. But work has used mini-batching scheme in proposed techniques so it has potential to extend the work to parallel and distributed setting. The research has already picked up the pace in this direction. This is one of the most fascinating research directions, as it offers truly scalable solutions to solve the big data challenge.

4. *Non-linear Models*
   During the last decade, the main focus has been on the linear models. Non-linear models are more accurate than the linear models, so another interesting but even more complex problem is to extend the work to non-linear models.

Bibliography

[1] Shigeo Abe. Fuzzy support vector machines for multilabel classification. *Pattern Recognition*, 48(6):2110 – 2117, 2015.

[2] Shigeo Abe and Takuya Inoue. Fuzzy support vector machines for multiclass problems. In *in European Symposium on Artificial Neural Networks, 2002*, pages 113–118, 2002.

[3] Naman Agarwal, Brian Bullins, and Elad Hazan. Second-order stochastic optimization for machine learning in linear time. *Journal of Machine Learning Research*, 18(116):1–40, 2017.

[4] Zeyuan Allen-Zhu. Katyusha: The First Direct Acceleration of Stochastic Gradient Methods. *Journal of Machine Learning Research*, 18(1):8194–8244, 2017.

[5] P Baldi, P Sadowski, and D Whiteson. Searching for exotic particles in high-energy physics with deep learning. *Nat. Commun.*, 5:4308, Jul 2014.

[6] Amir Beck and Luba Tetruashvili. On the convergence of block coordinate descent type methods. *SIAM Journal on Optimization*, 23(4):2037–2060, 2013.

[7] Stephen Becker and Mohamed-Jalal Fadili. A quasi-newton proximal splitting method. In *Advances in Neural Information Processing Systems 25: 26th Annual Conference on Neural Information Processing Systems 2012. Proceedings of a meeting held December 3-6, 2012, Lake Tahoe, Nevada, United States.*, pages 2627–2635, 2012.

[8] Stefania Bellavia, Nataša Krejic, and Nataša Krklec Jerinkic. Subsampled inexact newton methods for minimizing large sums of convex functions. *Optimization Online*, 2018.

[9] Albert S Berahas, Jorge Nocedal, and Martin Takac. A multi-batch l-bfgs method for machine learning. In *Advances in Neural Information Processing Systems 29*, pages 1055–1063. 2016.

[10] R. Bollapragada, R. Byrd, and J. Nocedal. Exact and Inexact Subsampled Newton Methods for Optimization. *IMA Journal of Numerical Analysis*, 39(2):545–578, 2019.

[11] Raghu Bollapragada, Jorge Nocedal, Dheevatsa Mudigere, Hao-Jun Shi, and Ping Tak Peter Tang. A progressive batching l-BFGS method for machine learning. In *Proceedings of the 35th International Conference on Machine Learning*,

volume 80 of *Proceedings of Machine Learning Research*, pages 620–629. PMLR, 2018.

[12] Bernhard E. Boser, Isabelle M. Guyon, and Vladimir N. Vapnik. A training algorithm for optimal margin classifiers. In *Proceedings of the 5th Annual ACM Workshop on Computational Learning Theory*, pages 144–152. ACM Press, 1992.

[13] L Bottou and C J Lin. Support Vector Machine Solvers. *Science*, 3(1)7477:1–27, 2007.

[14] Léon Bottou. Large-scale machine learning with stochastic gradient descent. In Yves Lechevallier and Gilbert Saporta, editors, *Proceedings of the 19th International Conference on Computational Statistics (COMPSTAT'2010)*, pages 177–187, Paris, France, August 2010. Springer.

[15] Leon Bottou and Olivier Bousquet. The tradeoffs of large scale learning. In *Proceedings of the 20th International Conference on Neural Information Processing Systems*, NIPS'07, pages 161–168, USA, 2007. Curran Associates Inc.

[16] Léon Bottou, Frank E. Curtis, and Jorge Nocedal. Optimization Methods for Large-Scale Machine Learning. 2016.

[17] Stephen Boyd and Lieven Vandenberghe. *Convex Optimization*. Cambridge University Press, New York, NY, USA, 2004.

[18] R. Byrd, G. Chin, W. Neveitt, and J. Nocedal. On the use of stochastic hessian information in optimization methods for machine learning. *SIAM Journal on Optimization*, 21(3):977–995, 2011.

[19] Richard H. Byrd, S. L. Hansen, Jorge Nocedal, and Yoram Singer. A stochastic quasi-newton method for large-scale optimization. *SIAM Journal on Optimization*, 26(2):1008–1031, 2016.

[20] Augustin-Louis Cauchy. Méthode générale pour la résolution des systèmes d'équations simultanées. *Compte Rendu des S'eances de L'Acad'emie des Sciences XXV*, S'erie A(25):536–538, October 1847.

[21] Chih-Chung Chang and Chih-Jen Lin. LIBSVM: A library for support vector machines. *ACM Transactions on Intelligent Systems and Technology*, 2:27:1–27:27, 2011.

[22] Kai-Wei Chang, Cho-Jui Hsieh, and Chih-Jen Lin. Coordinate descent method for large-scale l2-loss linear support vector machines. *J. Mach. Learn. Res.*, 9:1369–1398, June 2008.

[23] Vinod Kumar Chauhan, Kalpana Dahiya, and Anuj Sharma. Mini-batch block-coordinate based stochastic average adjusted gradient methods to solve big data problems. In *Proceedings of the Ninth Asian Conference on Machine Learning*, volume 77, pages 49–64. PMLR, 2017.

[24] Vinod Kumar Chauhan, Kalpana Dahiya, and Anuj Sharma. Trust region levenberg-marquardt method for linear svm. In *2017 Ninth International Conference on Advances in Pattern Recognition (ICAPR)*, pages 1–6, Dec 2017.

[25] Vinod Kumar Chauhan, Kalpana Dahiya, and Anuj Sharma. Problem formulations and solvers in linear svm: a review. *Artificial Intelligence Review*, 52(2):803–855, 2019.

[26] Vinod Kumar Chauhan, Anuj Sharma, and Kalpana Dahiya. Faster learning by reduction of data access time. *Applied Intelligence*, 48(12):4715–4729, Dec 2018.

[27] Vinod Kumar Chauhan, Anuj Sharma, and Kalpana Dahiya. Libs2ml: A library for scalable second order machine learning algorithms. *arXiv preprint arXiv:1904.09448*, 2019.

[28] Vinod Kumar Chauhan, Anuj Sharma, and Kalpana Dahiya. Saags: Biased stochastic variance reduction methods for large-scale learning. *Applied Intelligence*, 49(9):3331–3361, 2019.

[29] Vinod Kumar Chauhan, Anuj Sharma, and Kalpana Dahiya. Stochastic trust region inexact newton method for large-scale machine learning. *International Journal of Machine Learning and Cybernetics*, 11(7):1541–1555, 2020.

[30] Yan-cheng Chen and Chao-ton Su. Distance-based margin support vector machine for classification. *Applied Mathematics and Computation*, 283:141–152, 2016.

[31] Corinna Cortes and Vladimir Vapnik. Support-vector networks. *Machine Learning*, 20(3):273–297, 1995.

[32] Andrew Cotter, Ohad Shamir, Nathan Srebro, and Karthik Sridharan. Better Mini-Batch Algorithms via Accelerated Gradient Methods. *Nips*, pages 1–9, 2011.

[33] Koby Crammer and Yoram Singer. On the learnability and design of output codes for multiclass problems. *Machine Learning*, 47(1995):201–233, 2002.

[34] Dominik Csiba and Peter Richt. Importance Sampling for Minibatches. pages 1–19, 2016.

[35] Aaron Defazio, Francis Bach, and Simon Lacoste-Julien. Saga: A fast incremental gradient method with support for non-strongly convex composite objectives. In *Proceedings of the 27th International Conference on Neural Information Processing Systems*, NIPS'14, pages 1646–1654, Cambridge, MA, USA, 2014. MIT Press.

[36] Marco F Duarte and Yu Hen Hu. Vehicle classification in distributed sensor networks. *Journal of Parallel and Distributed Computing*, 64(7):826 – 838, 2004. Computing and Communication in Distributed Sensor Networks.

[37] Theodoros Evgeniou and Massimiliano Pontil. Regularized multi–task learning. In *Proceedings of the Tenth ACM SIGKDD International Conference on Knowledge Discovery and Data Mining*, KDD '04, pages 109–117, New York, NY, USA, 2004. ACM.

[38] R. Fan, K. Chang, C. Hsieh, X. Wang, and C. Lin. Liblinear: A library for large linear classification. *JMLR*, 9:1871–1874, 2008.

[39] Shang Fanhua, Kaiwen Zhou, James Cheng, Ivor W. Tsang, Lijun Zhang, and Dacheng Tao. Vr-sgd: A simple stochastic variance reduction method for machine learning. *IEEE Transactions on Knowledge and Data Engineering*, 32(1):188–202, 2018.

[40] Jason D. R. Farquhar, Hongying Meng, Sandor Szedmak, David R. Hardoon, and John Shawe-taylor. Two view learning: Svm-2k, theory and practice. In *Advances in Neural Information Processing Systems*. MIT Press, 2006.

[41] Michael C. Ferris and Todd S. Munson. Interior-Point Methods for Massive Support Vector Machines. *SIAM Journal on Optimization*, 13(3):783–804, 2002.

[42] R Fletcher. Practical methods of optimization, vol. 1, unconstrained optimization, 1980.

[43] R. Fletcher and C. M. Reeves. Function minimization by conjugate gradients. *The Computer Journal*, 7(2):149–154, February 1980.

[44] J. Friedman. Another approach to polychotomous classification. *Dept. Statistics, Stanford Univ., Tech. Rep*, 1996.

[45] Glenn Fung and Olvi L. Mangasarian. Proximal support vector machine classifiers. In *Proceedings of the Seventh ACM SIGKDD International Conference on Knowledge Discovery and Data Mining*, KDD '01, pages 77–86, New York, NY, USA, 2001. ACM.

[46] Y. Gao and S. Sun. An empirical evaluation of linear and nonlinear kernels for text classification using support vector machines. In *2010 Seventh International Conference on Fuzzy Systems and Knowledge Discovery*, volume 4, pages 1502–1505, Aug 2010.

[47] NL Gibson. Gradient-based methods for optimization. part i & ii., 2011.

[48] Siddharth Gopal. Adaptive Sampling for SGD by Exploiting Side Information. *International Conference on Machine Learning*, 364–372, 2016.

[49] Hans Peter Graf, Eric Cosatto, Leon Bottou, Igor Durdanovic, and Vladimir Vapnik. Parallel Support Vector Machines : The Cascade SVM. *In Advances in Neural Information Processing Systems*, pages 521–528, 2005.

[50] Magnus R. Hestenes and Eduard Stiefel. Methods of Conjugate Gradients for Solving Linear Systems. *Journal of Research of the National Bureau of Standards*, 49(6):409–436, December 1952.

[51] Chih-Yang Hsia, Wei-Lin Chiang, and Chih-Jen Lin. Preconditioned conjugate gradient methods in truncated newton frameworks for large-scale linear classification. In *Proceedings of the Tenth Asian Conference on Machine Learning*, Proceedings of Machine Learning Research. PMLR, 2018.

[52] Chih-Yang Hsia, Ya Zhu, and Chih-Jen Lin. A study on trust region update rules in newton methods for large-scale linear classification. In *Proceedings of the Ninth Asian Conference on Machine Learning*, volume 77 of *Proceedings of Machine Learning Research*, pages 33–48. PMLR, 2017.

[53] Cho-Jui Hsieh, Kai-Wei Chang, Chih-Jen Lin, S. Sathiya Keerthi, and S. Sundararajan. A dual coordinate descent method for large-scale linear svm. In *Proceedings of the 25th International Conference on Machine Learning*, ICML '08, pages 408–415, New York, NY, USA, 2008. ACM.

[54] Cho-Jui Hsieh, Si Si, and Inderjit Dhillon. A Divide-and-Conquer Solver for Kernel Support Vector Machines. *JMLR W&Cp*, 32(1):566–574, 2014.

[55] Chih-Wei Hsu and Chih-Jen Lin. A comparison of methods for multiclass support vector machines. *IEEE Transactions on Neural Networks*, 13(2):415–425, Mar 2002.

[56] Jayadeva, R. Khemchandani, and Suresh Chandra. Twin support vector machines for pattern classification. *IEEE Transactions on Pattern Analysis and Machine Intelligence*, 29(5):905–910, 2007.

[57] Jayadeva, Reshma Khemchandani, and Suresh Chandra. Fast and robust learning through fuzzy linear proximal support vector machines. *Neurocomput.*, 61(C):401–411, October 2004.

[58] Jayadeva, Reshma Khemchandani, and Suresh Chandra. *Twin Support Vector Machines - Models, Extensions and Applications*, volume 659 of *Studies in Computational Intelligence*. Springer, 2017.

[59] Y. Ji and S. Sun. Multitask multiclass support vector machines. In *2011 IEEE 11th International Conference on Data Mining Workshops*, pages 512–518, Dec 2011.

[60] You Ji and Shiliang Sun. Multitask multiclass support vector machines: Model and experiments. *Pattern Recognition*, 46(3):914 – 924, 2013.

[61] Thorsten Joachims. Transductive inference for text classification using support vector machines. In *Proceedings of the Sixteenth International Conference on Machine Learning*, ICML '99, pages 200–209, San Francisco, CA, USA, 1999. Morgan Kaufmann Publishers Inc.

[62] Thorsten Joachims. Training linear svms in linear time. In *Proceedings of the 12th ACM SIGKDD International Conference on Knowledge Discovery and Data Mining*, KDD '06, pages 217–226, 2006.

[63] Rie Johnson and Tong Zhang. Accelerating stochastic gradient descent using predictive variance reduction. In C. J. C. Burges, L. Bottou, M. Welling, Z. Ghahramani, and K. Q. Weinberger, editors, *Advances in Neural Information Processing Systems 26*, pages 315–323. Curran Associates, Inc., 2013.

[64] Wc Kao, Km Chung, Cl Sun, and Cj Lin. Decomposition methods for linear support vector machines. *Neural Computation*, 16:1689–1704, 2004.

[65] S. Sathiya Keerthi and Dennis DeCoste. A modified finite newton method for fast solution of large scale linear svms. *JMLR*, 6:341–361, December 2005.

[66] S Sathiya Keerthi and Dennis Decoste. Building Support Vector Machines with Reduced Classifier Complexity. *JMLR*, 7:1493–1515, 2006.

[67] J. Kiefer and J. Wolfowitz. Stochastic estimation of the maximum of a regression function. *The Annals of Mathematical Statistics*, 23:462–466, 1952.

[68] S. Knerr, L. Personnaz, and G. Dreyfus. *Neurocomputing: Algorithms, Architectures and Applications*, chapter Single-layer learning revisited: a stepwise procedure for building and training a neural network, pages 41–50. Springer Berlin Heidelberg, Berlin, Heidelberg, 1990.

[69] Ritesh Kolte, Murat Erdogdu, and Ayfer Ozgur. Accelerating svrg via second-order information. In *NIPS Workshop on Optimization for Machine Learning*, 2015.

[70] Jakub Konečný, Jie Liu, Peter Richtárik, and Martin Takáč. Mini-Batch Semi-Stochastic Gradient Descent in the Proximal Setting. *IEEE J. Sel. Top. Signal Process.*, 10(2):242–255, 2016.

[71] Jakub Konečný and Peter Richtárik. Semi-Stochastic Gradient Descent Methods. 1:19, 2013.

[72] Ulrich H.-G. Kressel. Advances in kernel methods. chapter Pairwise Classification and Support Vector Machines, pages 255–268. MIT Press, Cambridge, MA, USA, 1999.

[73] Guanghui Lan. An optimal method for stochastic composite optimization. *Math. Program.*, 133(1):365–397, Jun 2012.

[74] Nicolas Le Roux, Mark Schmidt, and Francis Bach. A Stochastic Gradient Method with an Exponential Convergence Rate for Strongly-Convex Optimization with Finite Training Sets. Technical report, INRIA, 2012.

[75] Y LeCun, L Bottou, Y Bengio, and P Haffner. Gradient-based learning applied to document recognition. *Proceedings of the IEEE*, pages 2278–2324, 1998.

[76] C.-P. Lee and C.-J. Lin. A study on l2-loss (squared hinge-loss) multi-class svm. *Neural Computation*, 25:1302–1323, 2013.

[77] Yuh-Jye Lee and O.L. Mangasarian. Ssvm: A smooth support vector machine for classification. *Computational Optimization and Applications*, 20(1):5–22, 2001.

[78] K. Levenberg. A method for the solution of certain problems in least squares. *Quart. Appl. Math.*, 2:164–168, 1944.

[79] David D. Lewis, Yiming Yang, Tony G. Rose, and Fan Li. Rcv1: A new benchmark collection for text categorization research. *JMLR*, 5:361–397, December 2004.

[80] Lijuan Li, Youfeng Li, Hongye Su, and Jian Chu. *Intelligent Computing: International Conference on Intelligent Computing, ICIC 2006, Kunming, China, August 16-19, 2006. Proceedings, Part I*, chapter Least Squares Support Vector Machines Based on Support Vector Degrees, pages 1275–1281. Springer Berlin Heidelberg, Berlin, Heidelberg, 2006.

[81] Mu Li, Tong Zhang, Yuqiang Chen, and Alexander J. Smola. Efficient mini-batch training for stochastic optimization. In *Proceedings of the 20th ACM SIGKDD International Conference on Knowledge Discovery and Data Mining*, KDD '14, pages 661–670, 2014.

[82] M. Lichman. UCI machine learning repository, 2013.

[83] C. Lin and J. Moré. Newton's method for large bound-constrained optimization problems. *SIAM Journal on Optimization*, 9(4):1100–1127, 1999.

[84] Chieh-Yen Lin, Cheng-Hao Tsai, Ching-Pei Lee, and Chih-Jen Lin. Large-scale logistic regression and linear support vector machines using spark. *2014 IEEE International Conference on Big Data (Big Data)*, pages 519–528, 2014.

[85] Chih-Jen Lin, Ruby C. Weng, and S. Sathiya Keerthi. Trust region newton method for logistic regression. *JMLR*, 9:627–650, June 2008.

[86] Chun-Fu Lin and Sheng-De Wang. Fuzzy support vector machines. *IEEE Transactions on Neural Networks*, 13(2):464–471, Mar 2002.

[87] Hongzhou Lin, Julien Mairal, and Zaid Harchaoui. A universal catalyst for first-order optimization. In *Proceedings of the 28th International Conference on Neural Information Processing Systems*, NIPS'15, pages 3384–3392, 2015.

[88] Dalian Liu, Yong Shi, Yingjie Tian, and Xiankai Huang. Ramp loss least squares support vector machine. *Journal of Computational Science*, 14:61–68, 2016.

[89] Dong C. Liu and Jorge Nocedal. On the limited memory bfgs method for large scale optimization. *Mathematical Programming*, 45(1):503–528, 1989.

[90] Zhaosong Lu and Lin Xiao. On the complexity analysis of randomized block-coordinate descent methods. *Math. Program.*, 152(1):615–642, 2015.

[91] Aurélien Lucchi, Brian McWilliams, and Thomas Hofmann. A variance reduced stochastic newton method. *arXiv*, 2015.

[92] Ronny Luss and Alexandre d'Aspremont. Support vector machine classification with indefinite kernels. *Mathematical Programming Computation*, 1(2):97–118, 2009.

[93] William G. Madow. On the theory of systematic sampling, ii. *The Annals of Mathematical Statistics*, 20:333–354, 1949.

[94] William G. Madow and Lillian H. Madow. On the theory of systematic sampling, i. *The Annals of Mathematical Statistics*, 15:1–24, March 1944.

[95] O. L. Mangasarian and David R. Musicant. Lagrangian support vector machines. *JMLR*, 1:161–177, September 2001.

[96] Olvi L. Mangasarian and Edward W. Wild. Multisurface proximal support vector machine classification via generalized eigenvalues. *IEEE Trans. Pattern Anal. Mach. Intell.*, 28(1):69–74, January 2006.

[97] D. Marquardt. An algorithm for least-squares estimation of nonlinear parameters. *SIAM J. Appl. Math.*, 11:431–441, 1963.

[98] A. Mokhtari and A. Ribeiro. Res: Regularized stochastic bfgs algorithm. *IEEE Transactions on Signal Processing*, 62(23):6089–6104, 2014.

[99] Philipp Moritz, Robert Nishihara, and Michael I. Jordan. A linearly-convergent stochastic l-bfgs algorithm. In *AISTATS*, 2016.

[100] Yu. Nesterov. Efficiency of coordinate descent methods on huge-scale optimization problems. *SIAM Journal on Optimization*, 22(2):341–362, 2012.

[101] Feiping Nie, Yizhen Huang, Xiaoqian Wang, and Heng Huang. New primal svm solver with linear computational cost for big data classifications. In *Proceedings of the 31st International Conference on International Conference on Machine Learning - Volume 32*, ICML'14, pages II–505–II–513. JMLR.org, 2014.

[102] Feiping Nie, Xiaoqian Wang, and Heng Huang. Multiclass capped lp-norm svm for robust classifications, 2017.

[103] Nocedal and S.J. Wright. *Numerical Optimization*. Springer, New York, 1999.

[104] Neal Parikh and Stephen Boyd. Proximal algorithms. *Found. Trends Optim.*, 1(3):127–239, January 2014.

[105] Xinjun Peng. A nu-twin support vector machine (nu-tsvm) classifier and its geometric algorithms. *Inf. Sci.*, 180(20):3863–3875, October 2010.

[106] J Platt. Sequential minimal optimization: A fast algorithm for training support vector machines. *Microsoft Research*, pages MSR–TR–98–14, 1998.

[107] John C. Platt, Nello Cristianini, and John Shawe-Taylor. Large margin dags for multiclass classification. In *Advances in Neural Information Processing Systems 12*, pages 547–553, 2000.

[108] Danil Prokhorov. Ijcnn 2001 neural network competition, 2013.

[109] Fernando Pérez-Cruz, Jason Weston, DJL Herrmann, and B Schölkopf. Extension of the nu-SVM range for classification. *NATO SCIENCE SERIES SUB SERIES III COMPUTER AND SYSTEMS SCIENCES*, 190:179–196, 2003.

[110] Alexander Rakhlin, Ohad Shamir, and Karthik Sridharan. Making gradient descent optimal for strongly convex stochastic optimization. In *Proceedings of the 29th International Coference on International Conference on Machine Learning*, ICML'12, pages 1571–1578, 2012.

[111] Sashank J Reddi. *New Optimization Methods for Modern Machine Learning*. PhD thesis, 2016.

[112] Peter Richtárik and Martin Takáč. Iteration complexity of randomized block-coordinate descent methods for minimizing a composite function. *Math. Program.*, 144(1-2):1–38, 2014.

[113] Herber Robbins and Sutton Monro. A stochastic approximation method. vol-22:pp. 400–407, 1951.

[114] Mark Schmidt. Convergence rate of stochastic gradient with constant step size. Technical report, 2014.

[115] Mark Schmidt, Nicolas Le Roux, and Francis Bach. Minimizing finite sums with the stochastic average gradient. *Math. Program.*, pages 1–30, 2016.

[116] Bernhard Schölkopf, Alex J. Smola, Robert C. Williamson, and Peter L. Bartlett. New Support Vector Algorithms. *Neural Computation*, 12(5):1207–1245, 2000.

[117] Nicol N. Schraudolph, Jin Yu, and Simon Günter. A stochastic quasi-newton method for online convex optimization. In Marina Meila and Xiaotong Shen, editors, *Proceedings of the Eleventh International Conference on Artificial Intelligence and Statistics*, volume 2 of *Proceedings of Machine Learning Research*, pages 436–443. PMLR, 2007.

[118] Shai Shalev-Shwartz, Yoram Singer, and Nathan Srebro. Pegasos: Primal estimated sub-gradient solver for svm. In *Proceedings of the 24th International Conference on Machine Learning*, ICML '07, pages 807–814, New York, NY, USA, 2007. ACM.

[119] Shai Shalev-Shwartz and Tong Zhang. Accelerated Mini-Batch Stochastic Dual Coordinate Ascent. *Nips*, 1(3), 2013.

[120] Shai Shalev-Shwartz and Tong Zhang. Stochastic dual coordinate ascent methods for regularized loss. *J. Mach. Learn. Res.*, 14(1):567–599, 2013.

[121] John Shawe-Taylor and Shiliang Sun. A review of optimization methodologies in support vector machines. *Neurocomputing*, 74(17):3609–3618, 2011.

[122] Ziqiang Shi and Rujie Liu. A better convergence analysis of the block coordinate descent method for large scale machine learning. Aug 2016.

[123] Melacci Stefano and Belkin Mikhail. Laplacian Support Vector Machines Trained in the Primal. *JMLR*, 12:1149–1184, 2011.

[124] Trond Steihaug. The conjugate gradient method and trust regions in large scale optimization. *SIAM Journal on Numerical Analysis*, 20(3):626–637, 1983.

[125] Ingo Steinwart. Sparseness of Support Vector Machines—Some Asymptotically Sharp Bounds. *Advances in Neural Information Processing Systems 16*, pages 1069–1076, 2004.

[126] Guillaume Stempfel and Liva Ralaivola. Learning svms from sloppily labeled data. In *Proceedings of the 19th International Conference on Artificial Neural Networks: Part I*, ICANN '09, pages 884–893, Berlin, Heidelberg, 2009. Springer-Verlag.

[127] J. Suykens, J.A.K.; Vandewalle. Least squares support vector machine classifiers. pages 293–300, 1999.

[128] Martin Takáč, Avleen Bijral, Peter Richtárik, and Nathan Srebro. Mini-batch primal and dual methods for svms. In *In 30th International Conference on Machine Learning*, pages 537–552. Springer, 2013.

[129] Choon Hui Teo, Alex Smola, S. V.N. Vishwanathan, and Quoc Viet Le. A scalable modular convex solver for regularized risk minimization. In *Proceedings of the 13th ACM SIGKDD International Conference on Knowledge Discovery and Data Mining*, KDD '07, pages 727–736, New York, NY, USA, 2007. ACM.

[130] P. Tseng. Convergence of a block coordinate descent method for nondifferentiable minimization. *J. Optim. Theory Appl.*, 109(3):475–494, June 2001.

[131] Ioannis Tsochantaridis, Thomas Hofmann, Thorsten Joachims, and Yasemin Altun. Support vector machine learning for interdependent and structured output spaces. In *Proceedings of the Twenty-first International Conference on Machine Learning*, ICML '04, pages 104–, New York, NY, USA, 2004. ACM.

[132] Vladimir N. Vapnik. *Statistical learning theory*. Wiley, New York, 1 edition, Sep 1998.

[133] Huahua Wang and Arindam Banerjee. Randomized Block Coordinate Descent for Online and Stochastic Optimization. *arXiv preprint*, (1):1–19, 2014.

[134] Steve Webb, James Caverlee, and Calton Pu. Introducing the webb spam corpus: Using email spam to identify web spam automatically. In *CEAS*, 2006.

[135] J. Weston and C. Watkins. Support vector machines for multi-class pattern recognition, 1999.

[136] Kristian Woodsend and Jacek Gondzio. Hybrid MPI/OpenMP Parallel Linear Support Vector Machine Training. *JMLR*, 10:1937–1953, 2009.

[137] Stephen J. Wright. Coordinate descent algorithms. *Math. Program.*, 151(1):3–34, June 2015.

[138] Lin Xiao and Tong Zhang. A proximal stochastic gradient method with progressive variance reduction. *SIAM Journal on Optimization*, 24(4):2057–2075, 2014.

[139] X. Xie and S. Sun. Multi-view twin support vector machines. *Intelligent Data Analysis*, 19(4):701–712, 2015.

[140] Yangyang Xu and Wotao Yin. Block stochastic gradient iteration for convex and nonconvex optimization. *SIAM Journal on Optimization*, 25(3):1686–1716, 2015.

[141] Yuan Yang, Jianfei Chen, and Jun Zhu. Distributing the stochastic gradient sampler for large-scale lda. In *Proceedings of the 22Nd ACM SIGKDD International Conference on Knowledge Discovery and Data Mining*, KDD '16, pages 1975–1984, New York, NY, USA, 2016. ACM.

[142] Zhuang Yang, Cheng Wang, Zhemin Zhang, and Jonathan Li. Random barzilai–borwein step size for mini-batch algorithms. *Eng. Appl. Artif. Intell.*, 72:124 – 135, 2018.

[143] Jieping Ye and Tao Xiong. Svm versus least squares svm. In *JMLR W&P*, pages 644–651, 2007.

[144] Hsiang-Fu Yu, Cho-Jui Hsieh, Kai-Wei Chang, and Chih-Jen Lin. Large linear classification when data cannot fit in memory. In *Proceedings of the 16th ACM SIGKDD International Conference on Knowledge Discovery and Data Mining*, KDD '10, pages 833–842, New York, NY, USA, 2010. ACM.

[145] Guo Xun Yuan, Chia Hua Ho, and Chih Jen Lin. Recent advances of large-scale linear classification. *Proceedings of the IEEE*, 100(9):2584–2603, 2012.

[146] Tongzhou Mu, Chao Zhang, Zebang Shen, and Hui Qian. Accelerated doubly stochastic gradient algorithm for large-scale empirical risk minimization. In *IJCAI*, 2017.

[147] Aston Zhang and Quanquan Gu. Accelerated stochastic block coordinate descent with optimal sampling. In *Proceedings of the 22Nd ACM SIGKDD International Conference on Knowledge Discovery and Data Mining*, KDD '16, pages 2035–2044, New York, NY, USA, 2016. ACM.

[148] Tong Zhang. Solving large scale linear prediction problems using stochastic gradient descent algorithms. In *Proceedings of the Twenty-first International Conference on Machine Learning*, ICML '04, pages 919–926, New York, NY, USA, 2004. ACM.

[149] Yuchen Zhang and Lin Xiao. Stochastic primal-dual coordinate method for regularized empirical risk minimization. In *Proceedings of the 32Nd International Conference on International Conference on Machine Learning - Volume 37*, ICML'15, pages 353–361, 2015.

[150] Peilin Zhao and Tong Zhang. Accelerating Minibatch Stochastic Gradient Descent using Stratified Sampling. *arXiv Prepr. arXiv1405.3080*, pages 1–13, 2014.

[151] Peilin Zhao and Tong Zhang. Stochastic Optimization with Importance Sampling for Regularized Loss Minimization. *ICML*, 37, 2015.

[152] Tuo Zhao, Mo Yu, Yiming Wang, Raman Arora, and Han Liu. Accelerated Mini-batch Randomized Block Coordinate Descent Method. *Advances in Neural Information Processing Systems*, pages 3329–3337, 2014.

[153] Ji Zhu, Saharon Rosset, Trevor Hastie, and Rob Tibshirani. 1-norm support vector machines. In *Neural Information Processing Systems*, page 16. MIT Press, 2003.

Index

Printed in the United States
by Baker & Taylor Publisher Services